The Villa as Hegemonic Architecture

The Villa as Hegemonic Architecture

*Reinhard Bentmann and
Michael Müller*

Foreword by Otto Karl Werckmeister

*Translated by
Tim Spence and David Craven*

HUMANITIES PRESS
New Jersey ▾ London

Originally published as *Die Villa als Herrschaftsarchitektur* 1970 by Suhrkamp Verlag Frankfurt am Main

English translation first published 1992 by Humanities Press International, Inc., Atlantic Highlands, New Jersey 07716, and 3 Henrietta Street, Covent Garden, London WC2E 8LU

Library of Congress Cataloging-in-Publication Data

Bentmann, Reinhard, 1939–
    [Villa als Herrschaftsarchitektur. English]
    The villa as hegemonic architecture / Reinhard Bentmann and Michael Müller ; foreword by Otto Karl Werckmeister ; translated by Tim Spence and David Craven.
      p.   cm.
    Translation of: Die Villa als Herrschaftsarchitektur.
    Includes bibliographical references (p.   ) and index.
    ISBN 0-391-03757-9 (cloth)
    1. Upper classes—Italy—Dwellings. 2. Architecture and state—Italy. 3. Architecture, Domestic—Political aspects—Italy.
    I. Müller, Michael, 1946–
    NA7594.B4413   1992
    728.8'01'03—dc20   91-46746
                            CIP

A catalog record for this book is available from the British Library

Printed in the United States of America

Contents

List of Illustrations

Foreword

OTTO KARL WERCKMEISTER

THIS BOOK IS a testimony from the time when two graduate students in art history, aged thirty-one and twenty-four, were able to put forth the first confident challenge to the established norms of their discipline in the Federal Republic of Germany after the Second World War. They did it by connecting art-historical scholarship to the Marxist tradition of thought, without the political backing of a socialist government and its scholarly institutions, buoyed only by the revalidation of Marxism in the aftermath of the student rebellion of 1968. It was this tradition that informed their argument with the strength of a philosophy demanding coherence in the understanding of art-historical monuments as part of the economic, social, and political history of their time. Looking back from today's art history, with its technical oversophistication, conceptual introspection, and political disarray, we appreciate the undeterred assurance whereby those two young authors deployed the Marxist key notions of base and superstructure, class and ideology, to the elucidation of their theme. In their book, the Italian sixteenth-century villa stands exposed as an ideological transfiguration whereby a group of landholders from the urban bourgeoisie vindicated their control of newly constituted *latifundia* in the countryside as a God-given benefit to the land and its peasant workers.

The authorities of German Marxist art history around 1970 are invoked throughout the text: Arnold Hauser's 1958 *Philosophy of Art History*; Max Horkheimer's essays from the time of the Great Depression; Herbert Marcuse's transfers of psychoanalytic suppression theory from Freud to ideology critique; and Ernst Bloch's *Principle of Hope*, with its speculations about a socialist utopia. In the afterword to the second edition of 1971 (Chapter 20 in this translation), the authors add Theodor W. Adorno's writings on aesthetics to their references, in an attempt to integrate the issue of artistic quality into their sociological argument.

Those were the theoretical parameters of Marxist art history in the Federal Republic during the years 1970–1974, and its political concerns are stated no less openly. The villa, "de facto a reactionary phenomenon," is related to Krupp's paternalistic workers' housing programs, to the blood-and-soil ideology of National Socialism, to Martin Heidegger's withdrawal into his Black Forest blockhouse, to the conservative agrarian policy of

Konrad Adenauer's Christian Democrats, and, finally, to the penthouses and suburbs of the rich in the rebuilt West German cities. The authors' ultimate confidence in the connection between a social history of past architecture and a definition of socialist policies for an architecture of the future sustains the force of their inquiry.

Today, in 1992, twenty-two years after the book first appeared, both its authors and its readers are faced with some fundamental questions. What has remained valid of the book's historical conclusions? How have its political concepts stood the test of time? Most important, has the premise that Marxist politics can inform scholarship, not as a bias but as a critical concept, been compromised by contemporary history? These questions have not yet been decided, neither by the inconclusive pluralism of postmodern methodologies, nor by the demise of socialism as a form of government in the Soviet Union and its former client states in Eastern Europe. They remain open, and it will take the political nerve and the scholarly acumen demonstrated by the authors of this book to press for their resolution.

Introduction

DAVID CRAVEN

SINCE IT FIRST appeared in a Suhrkamp edition of 1970, *Die Villa als Herrschaftsarchitektur* by Reinhard Bentmann and Michael Müller has become almost legendary among European intellectuals. This standing has been gained both because of the severe attacks that this study has weathered and because of the considerable admiration that the book continues to elicit.[1] Yet, in spite of the fact that this now classic application of critical theory and new-left concerns to a critique of Venetian Renaissance villas has sold over 25,000 copies, generated intense debate, gone through several editions in a number of different languages, and been praised by internationally recognized thinkers like Jürgen Habermas,[2] it had yet to appear in its entirety in English until the present edition by Humanities Press, which is entitled *The Villa as Hegemonic Architecture*.

Many factors no doubt explain this delay of over two decades between the book's first appearance in 1970 and its first full publication in English in 1992, but two reasons in particular should be noted. First, there has been weighty opposition on the part of the mainstream artworld establishment in the United States—which until recently was one of the most conservative of any country in the world—to the publication of any sustained ideological critique of the great monuments in Western art, however brilliant such a critique might be. Conversely, the second reason is a result of the lamentable lack of familiarity on the part of most art historians from the United States (and also Great Britain as well) with contemporary German art historical scholarship of the post-1968 generation. Nonetheless, few if any other Western countries can lay claim to having many art historians to rival either the scholarly breadth or theoretical sophistication of the group in Germany that includes Martin Warnke, Klaus Herding, Horst Bredekamp, Monika Wagner, Jutta Held, Berthold Hinz, Franz Verspohl, and Hubertus Gassner, as well as Michael Müller and Reinhard Bentmann.[3] Furthermore, to these names should be added those of Karl Werckmeister, Peter Bürger, and Andreas Huyssen (who like Werckmeister teaches in the United States). Although the two latter figures are professors of literature, they have each authored a book about the avant-garde that is of fundamental importance to art historians.[4] It is of note here that Bürger, who is a professor of French at the University of Bremen (where Michael Müller is a professor of cultural studies and architectural history), was responding in his book to a 1972 debate on the nature of art's "autonomy" that contained insightful discussions by Müller, Bredekamp, Verspohl, and others.[5]

The state of neglect often confronting contemporary German art historians in general and Müller and Bentmann in particular is all the more ironic, since among mainstream art historians in the United States and in the United Kingdom there is a clear consensus that the most notable texts of early Western art history were largely produced by German-trained scholars. Erwin Panofsky, who was a celebrated professor of art history at the University of Hamburg before he fled the Nazis in 1933, could rightly state in 1953 that in the beginning Western art history's "native tongue is German."[6]

If the unjustifiable lack of attention in the United States to *Die Villa als Herrschaftsarchitektur* is obvious enough, the justifications for ending this neglect are far more compelling. The first reason for making the book by Bentmann and Müller much more accessible to a U.S. audience was provided by James Ackerman in his recent study entitled *The Villa: Form and Ideology of Country Houses* (which is based on his 1985 Mellon Lectures at the National Gallery of Art in Washington, D.C.). Easily the best book in English on the subject and by an eminent scholar, this book contains the following acknowledgment by Ackerman (who is exceptionally well informed about the literature in this field):

> I am much indebted for the articulation of villa ideology to the innovative treatments of R. Bentmann and M. Müller, *Die Villa als Herrschaftsarchitektur: Versuch einer kunst-und sozialgeschichtlichen Analyse*, Frankfurt a. M., 1970 and of Grazia Gobbi, *La villa fiorentina*, Florence, 1980.[7]

Quite aside from the way that his indebtedness to the study by Bentmann and Müller helps to account both for the title of Ackerman's book and also for his notable discussion of the class-based formations underlying the villa typology, there is also an elective affinity between the conclusions of these respective critiques. As Ackerman notes in his postscript, "What distinguishes a villa from a farmhouse or a country cottage in their buildings . . . is the intense, programmatic investment of ideological goals."[8] And, of course, the *first* and still the most sustained analysis of the ideological values advanced by the Venetian villa is the one in *The Villa as Hegemonic Architecture*.

The second reason for presenting the study by Bentmann and Müller in English translation is that the book has made a significant (if not always recognized) contribution to the rise of what has been variously termed "critical art history," the "social history of art" or, in a certain sense, the "new art history."[9] While their new-left critique draws on a Marxist analysis to disclose the class-based considerations and economic concerns related to the formal construction of Venetian villas, this analysis features a supple, indeed creative, use of historical materialism that goes much beyond the economic reductionism, unself-conscious scientism, and crude "reflectionism" of the Stalinist "dialectical materialism" that all too often marked the work of earlier efforts in art history within the Marxist tradition.

Unimpressed by the mechanical conclusions of "unreflectively materialist" approaches, Bentmann and Müller have addressed instead a "parallelogram of forces" that are unevenly formative (not just reproductive) and densely mediated, so that there can be no such thing as a villa that merely replicates some putatively monolithic (hence *internally* noncontradictory) class ideology. Rather, the sixteenth-century villas of the Veneto were the concrete *and* varied manifestations of various historical forces (economic, aesthetic, political, and social) in relation to individual family strategies whereby a certain class fraction defined itself as both a paradoxical part and a representative element of the system being produced in Venetian territories during this period. Hence, Bentmann and Müller not only disallow the view that these villas simply "reflected" ruling-class ideology, as if the villas themselves were neither material means whereby these ideologies were *created* nor *sites of contestation* wherein issues of class were "resolved." Accordingly, their critique evokes recollections of how Antonio Gramsci distinguished the complex set of relationships, both ideological and coercive, sustaining "hegemony" from the more monodimensional concept of "domination" (which makes ideology into a passive "reflection," or contingent afterthought, of mere ruling-class coercion). Indeed, it is this Gramscian tenor via the Frankfurt School (though Gramsci is never directly cited in their text) that reminds us that the book is a product of the new left and also necessitates the translation of *Herrschaft* as "hegemonic" rather than as simply "domination." Hence, the most appropriate English title for the book is *The Villa as Hegemonic Architecture*, rather than *The Villa as Architecture of Domination*.[10]

Precisely because they advanced beyond the old-time economic determination of 1930s Marxism to a more broadranging conceptual framework, the book by Bentmann and Müller featured some important analytical stress points that were new to art history (with the exception of some essays by Meyer Schapiro): an understanding of ideology as operating on an unconscious as well as a conscious level (thus being more than a matter of "false consciousness"); an approach to the villa as an embodiment of resolutely patriarchal familial values (the structural connection is well made, following Max Horkheimer, between the etymology of *padrone*, the head of the villa estate, and *padre*, the head of the family); the framing of religious values in instrumentalist terms (thus there is the implication that religious values are not *necessarily* always "reactionary"); the location of the emergence of the

villa not only in relation to the economic logic of incipient Venetian capitalism but also in the context of the larger "city versus country" conflict about
which Marx and others have written; and a look at "villa ideology" in terms
of the Western concept of nature that it represents (thus of the ecological as
well as class consequences that follow from it).

In a brilliant and highly original formulation, Müller and Bentmann demonstrate how the convergence of all these factors—certainly including irre-
ducible aesthetic concerns of undeniable refinement and sophistication—all
led to the actual function of the Venetian Renaissance villa as a "negative
utopia," that is, as the ruling-class rejoinder to the utopian promise of the
good life for *everyone* to an equal degree. By constituting an inequitable and
exploitative "utopia" for the fortunate few, this *asymmetrical* social configuration (however symmetrical the Villa Rotonda itself is) served to cancel
out the more egalitarian, hence also more socially symmetrical and humanly
harmonious "positive utopias" envisioned by Thomas More and Tommaso
Campanella.

As such, the Palladian villa presented a formally "perfect" and classically
balanced architecture as if it were accurately representative of a politically
unstable and economically imbalanced (because highly unjust) social structure. Accordingly, the villa signified the claim of an ascendant class that
such a manifestly imperfect social formation was "natural" and thus was the
only "perfection" attainable, the maximum "progress" realizable.

Their exemplary discussion of the villa as a "negative utopia" in turn
leads Bentmann and Müller to address an overarching problem of Western
society in general, namely, the uneven development between modern urban
society and the "timeless" arcadia of the countryside. By being a material
embodiment of an imagined rustic past, over and against the future-
oriented vision of utopia for urban development, the villa served as a
counter to the general logic of Western postfeudal society toward ever
greater urban concentration. This was the case even though the primary
groups orchestrating this return to the past were members of a class of
urban bourgeois/patricians whose wealth had come at the expense of the
traditional agrarian social structure of feudalism. The analysis of "ideal"
country life as a somehow more "natural" mode of existence surfaces quite
tellingly when Bentmann and Müller rightly remind us of how Fascist
ideology was later predicated on the appeal to a "natural order" with its
attendant rural associations, and never more so than when Fascists were
using modern Western technology to implement their "rural" and "earthy"
fantasies. Here it is important to note that a number of excellent critiques
along these lines have been written subsequently by several British culture
critics and art historians, specifically, Raymond Williams, Alex Potts, Neil
McWilliam, and John Barrell.[11]

The third reason that *The Villa as Hegemonic Architecture* deserves a much larger audience among U.S. scholars is related to its precocious historiographic place in the history of post-1968 art history. In many regards, the 1970 book by Bentmann and Müller (along with the works of Warnke and Werckmeister) can claim a position in the methodological life of the discipline on the continent that is analogous to the position enjoyed in the English-speaking artworld by Linda Nochlin's 1971 essay—"Why Have There Been No Great Women Artists?"—and by T. J. Clark's two books of 1973—*The Absolute Bourgeois* and *Image of the People*. Many of the progressive theoretical shifts within the Marxist practice of art history so incisively made in Clark's essay "On the Social History of Art" (Chapter 1 of *Image of the People*) still serve as significant analogues for what was also notably new in the book by Bentmann and Müller. Clark, who like Raymond Williams and Terry Eagleton studied at Cambridge University, wrote about these issues in a way that would have provided an appropriate introduction for the earlier *Die Villa als Herrschaftsarchitektur*. He advocated approaching art as a material force with active political and ideological agency in its own right as opposed to "the notion of works of art 'reflecting' ideologies, social relations, or history."[12] Clark pointed out as well that the analysis of patronage cannot be done comprehensively "without some general theory—admitted or repressed—of the structure of a capitalist economy."[13] Consequently, Clark declared:

> What I want to explain are the connecting links between artistic form, the available systems of visual representation, the current theories of art, other ideologies, social classes, and more general historical structures and processes. . . . [Thus] I have been arguing for a history of mediations.[14]

Just as Clark wrote of understanding artworks as conjunctural phenomena that operate on numerous levels, so he wrote of approaching an artistic category with "a sense that the category itself is fundamentally unstable."[15] Interestingly, one of the earliest critiques of such a category as the villa as "fundamentally unstable" was *Die Villa als Herrschaftsarchitektur* by Bentmann and Müller. Similarly, the reason that this book remains highly important up to the present is because *Die Villa als Herrschaftsarchitektur* is, above all, an extended history of mediations handled with admirable sensitivity.

That the scholarly and political projects of T. J. Clark, Michael Müller, Reinhard Bentmann, Martin Warnke, and Karl Werckmeister would have shared some noteworthy points of intersection in the early 1970s is not surprising. All five art historians were indebted to the Frankfurt School (Walter Benjamin in the case of Clark; Adorno, Horkheimer, and Benjamin in the case of Müller and Bentmann). In fact, Müller and Bentmann were students of Adorno and Horkheimer at Frankfurt University, which is no doubt one reason that *Die Villa als Herrschaftsarchitektur* is such a subtle and nonreductive exercise in critical analysis. Furthermore, Clark, Müller, and others also drew, in new-left fashion, upon other traditions of critical theory as well—those represented by Ernst Bloch, Henri Lefebvre, and Arnold Hauser influenced Müller and Bentmann, while those advanced by Pierre Macherey, Guy Debord, and Meyer Schapiro had a salutary impact on Clark—so that their respective uses of Marxism were distinctively flexible and yet equally rigorous in a way that those of earlier art historians generally were not.

Aside from John Berger's striking use of Walter Benjamin's ideas in the widely debated BBC series of 1972 entitled "Ways of Seeing" and Karl Werckmeister's early use of the Frankfurt School in his own work, the assimilation of "critical theory" (the term coined by the Frankfurt School members, although it has since come to be applied to other theoretical tendencies on the left as well) proceeded very slowly in the United States during the 1970s. The most impressive art history department in a North American university during this decade concerning itself with the incorporation of critical theory into the discipline was the one at U.C.L.A., where both T. J. Clark and Karl Werckmeister taught during the late 1970s. And, in fact, the current vitality of the "social history of art" or "critical art history" is unquestionably related to the group of scholars who emerged from U.C.L.A. during this period—Thomas Crow, Barbara Abou-El-Haj, Serge Guilbaut, and Leonard Folgarait, among others.[16] Along with Clark and Werckmeister, there were several other scholars on the left who taught at U.C.L.A. during this period, including Albert Boime, David Kunzle, and Cecilia Klein, as well as Alan Wallach, Carol Duncan, and Nicos Hadjinicolaou (the last three of whom were visiting professors). Previously, T. J. Clark held a professorship at Leeds University in England, which established the first M.A. degree anywhere in the Social History of Art. Leeds, which is where Arnold Hauser had earlier taught, remains one of the strongest departments in the West, with such scholars as Griselda Pollock, Fred Orton, and Anthony Hughes teaching there at present.

Among other deparments of art and art history in the United States, only the University of North Carolina at Chapel Hill, where Donald Kuspit was a professor in the mid-1970s (and where Edgar Wind had earlier taught in the 1920s), was producing any noticeable amount of art history based on critical theory. Kuspit, who pursued his Ph.D. under Adorno in Frankfurt, had several students, such as Annette Cox, Patricia Mathews, and myself, who in the 1970s drew on critical theory and new left politics and who have since continued to work with this orientation.[17] Just as the University of Marburg, and later the universities of Hamburg and Bremen, were centers for post-1968 art history in Germany, so in all these above-mentioned countries there were important leftist journals that were conceived in the 1970s. In 1972, the radical Ulmer Verein in Germany started *Kritische Berichte*, while around the same time a group of Althusserian art historians in Paris, most notably Nicos Hadjinicolaou and Michel Melot, started publishing *Histoire et Critique des Arts*. In 1976, a group of art historians in the United States, led by T. J. Clark and O. K. Werckmeister, started the Caucus for Marxism and Art, which published an annual collection of articles, and in 1979 the British journal *Block* was created at Middlesex Polytechnic in the United Kingdom.[18] The considerable impact of all these institutions and journals on the discipline of art history was such that by 1978 when the British Art Historians Association first published an official journal, this "mainstream" publication immediately served as a major forum for the social history of art. Thus, when Bentmann and Müller's book is seen in light of these recent developments, it is clear that *Die Villa als Herrschaftsarchitektur*, or *The Villa as Hegemonic Architecture*, deserves a prominent place in any serious history of critical art history. The publication of our English translation, then, should make clear to scholars in the United States and in the United Kingdom what has long been known on the European continent about the historical import of this book.

Cortland, New York

1

The Dream of the Countryside: The Flight from Venice in the Sixteenth Century

T HE DREAM OF the countryside (with its flight of city-weary people from their supposed confinement by palaces, town halls, churches, and marketplaces to the imagined freedom of the countryside) has paradoxically accompanied Western urban existence as a constant ideal since antiquity. From architects, painters, and poets to philosophers, politicians, and economists, notable figures have been much involved with mediating between this dream and actual social practices. The dream of the countryside originated in Italy, where it has endured the longest. During antiquity, this concept took artistic form as the *villa rustica* and an idealized social form as the *vita rustica*, just as during the Renaissance this idea was a precondition for the *habitazione del padrone* (manorial estate) or *casa di villa* (manor house) along with the *villeggiatura*, or the rural lifestyle of the landlord.

In his important essay of 1910 on the villa, Rudolf Borchardt used Tuscany as an example to illustrate the opposition between the city and the countryside, which was manifested socially in the Latin-based form of the villa. By using a broad historical perspective, he pointed out how, from antiquity to modern times, the Italian *vita rustica* has persisted as a cultural and social leitmotiv. Borchardt already recognized that despite the villa's glittering, even luminous, appearance, villa architecture was a testimony to gentrified character, a claim to power, and concrete economic interests. Thus, he noted: "As an ancient Latin habitat [the villa] is completely tied to money and power; it must be forcefully maintained in order to increase, to certify, to capitalize, and to inherit money and power" (Reprint, Frankfurt, 1952, p. 19).

It is no coincidence that the villa was one of the cultural institutions whereby the Italian Renaissance was most clearly realized. Above all, there were three areas of the Italian countryside in which the villa came to play a

1

FIGURE 1.   *Portrait of Daniele Barbaro, Patriarch of Aguileja and Padrone of the Villa Maser*, 1513–1570, Circle of Paolo Veronese, Rijksmuseum, Amsterdam

dominant role both as a representation of lifestyle and as an architectural project: Tuscany, Veneto, and Rome. In each of these regions, the climax of the villa culture coincided with the respective stylistic epoch in which each type of artistic landscape was realized most successfully. The typical Tuscan villa is associated with the concept of the Early Renaissance; the classical Veneto villa with the Venetian Late Renaissance; and the classic designs for villas of the Proto- and High Baroque were developed in the areas outlying

Rome, for example, in Tivoli and Frascati. The Venetian *villeggiatura* not only signified the historical center of this sequence but also its climax both qualitatively and quantitatively. With the villas they built during the two generations between 1540 and 1600, Sansovino, Sanmicheli, Falconetto, Palladio, and Scamozzi established obligatory models for the architectural development of the whole of Europe. In Tuscany and in Rome, the villa culture failed to assume a social and artistic character as total and as complex as it had in Veneto. Even today there are over two thousand monuments that testify to the villa in Veneto as a cultural institution, the history of which can be traced back to its origins in the fifteenth century and followed through to the eighteenth and nineteenth centuries. More than any other example, the Venetian *villeggiatura* exemplified how changes in the conditions of production, which determined the social substructure within the limits of politics and economics, were mirrored in the cultural superstructure—whether in distorted, retarded, or disguised form.

Two prerequisites made the Venetian villa culture possible, thus characterizing it to a greater extent than in Rome or in Tuscany. First, there was the *renovatio* (revival) of the architectural styles of antiquity, which in art historical terms has been primarily linked with Andrea Palladio. Second, there was the reform of the *beni inculti* (uncultivated estates) in the Terraferma (the Venetian hinterland), at the center of which stood Alvise Cornaro as a symbolic figure. Thus, the Venetian villa appears at the vanishing point of two perspectives that were dialectically interrelated: on the one hand, the cultural ideal of the revival of antiquity as a classical superstructural phenomenon and, on the other hand, the total revolution in the Venetian economic structure around 1500 as a classical substructural phenomenon.

The Italian villa in general and the Venetian villa in particular were until recently still discussed with recourse to the purely aesthetic criteria of early art history, as, for example, in the work by Fritz Burger and Patzak. In their research, Mazzotti,[1] Muraro,[2] Fiocco,[3] and Ackerman[4] attempted, however, to do justice to the villa's social dimension beyond the confines of art history and art criticism. In other words, these scholars attempted a cultural critique of the villa. The economic conditions for this villa-mania, although misinterpreted as a spontaneous phenomenon, were attributed to the noticeable changes in the economic foundations of Venetian urban society between the late fifteenth and early sixteenth centuries. For, between 1530 and 1540 a villa-mania seized the Venetian nobility and continued until the eighteenth century, when Goldoni gave one of his three famous villa comedies the title *Le smanie per la villeggiatura* (roughly translated as Villa Mania). This recent socioeconomic interpretation, by means of a one-sided analysis of economic historical facts, seems adequate for explaining the cultural form assumed by the *villeggiatura* yet not for grasping the complexity of the developments that led to the villa.

In 1453, Constantinople was lost to the Turks and a powerful confrontation arose from the economic competition between the Venetians and Turks in the eastern Mediterranean. Gradually the Venetians were forced to give up their forts and trade monopolies on the islands of the Aegean and the Adriatic and along the coasts of the Levant. Toward the end of the Quattrocento, the discovery (by Vasco da Gama) of direct sea routes to India and the Far East around the southern tip of Africa rendered increasingly insignificant the old caravan trails through Arabia, North Africa, and the Turkish Empire—whose flow of goods had been linked to Europe by the Venetian commercial fleet. In 1559, Sansovino described this situation as follows:

> Gli uomini allhora attendevano per la maggior parte alle cose del mare, ch'erano in grandissimo pretio; e i cittadini della prima infanzia si mandavano in Levante, là dove fatti ricchi, vivevano la vecchiezza loro in santissima pace. Ma hogi, prima C. Colombo e poi i Portoghesi hanno trovato le nuove navigationi per le quale le mercature son venute a meno in Venezia.

> [In the past people directed their attention mainly to exotic overseas goods, which were priced extremely high. Thus from early youth, citizens devoted themselves to the trade with the Levant. Having made a fortune, they were able to pass their old age in spiritual peace. Nowadays, however, first Columbus and then the Portuguese have discovered new sea routes that have caused the commerce in Venice to diminish quite noticeably.][5]

Finally, at the beginning of the Cinquecento, the League of Cambrai and the Peace Treaty of Bologna also brought to an end Venice's hegemonic designs on the mainland of North Italy. The whole situation served as a compelling motivation for the city of Venice to turn to its own continental territory—the Terraferma—in light of the new economic interest in agriculture, in native manufacture, and in capital investment in real estate.

The self-consciousness and self-understanding of a society, however, are not determined only by the economic substructure, that is to say, by its being (*Sein*). A decisive raison d'être is found in the cultural superstructure, in the ideology or network of ideologies there, that is, in the social appearance (*Schein*) that must legitimate society's being in the historical context of necessity and under pressure from the reality principle, the consequences of which are not yet recognized and have been ideologically repressed. With respect to the northern Italian *villeggiatura*, one ought to ask whether the restructuring of the economy (which only superficially explains the Venetian nobility's migration from the city, its interest in agriculture as a new form of income, and its concern with living in the countryside as a new lifestyle and cultural practice) was not first of all made possible by social tendencies that could only be explained in sociopolitical or sociopsychological terms. To what extent did the philosophical commentaries in the theoretical treatises on architecture help prepare for the development of "agricultural humanism" in the books on villas? Likewise, to what extent did the ascendancy of the rural form of income to the level of "Santa Agricoltura" (Saint Agriculture) prepare for the withdrawal from the city? What systemic social significance did the return to the countryside have in this context? To what extent did the dream of the countryside determine the architectural representations of the Renaissance villa, as well as those of the modern villas of the nineteenth and early twentieth centuries? Is it possible to use the dialectical interplay of ideology and economics to explain the dynamic of city flight as an art historical problem (the new task of designing the *casa di villa*), as a sociohistorical phenomenon (*villeggiatura, via rustica*), as a practice-derived theorem (books on villas and villa-like forms in lyrics, drama, and novels), and as a theory-derived social practice (agricultural humanism)?

Thus, the point is not just to construct yet another sociopolitical interpretation of the villa as a hermeneutic addition to the previously mentioned works on economics by Mazzotti, Muraro, Fiocco, and Ackerman. Rather we need to demonstrate a direct correlation between the two approaches. Obviously, the two driving forces, the ideological and the economic, form an indivisible dialectic unity. The dialectic of the villa is thus one that occurs in several dimensions. Hence, further questions to be addressed are as follows: To what extent is the villa as an aesthetic phenomenon enshrouded in economics and as an economic phenomenon enshrouded in aesthetics? To what extent are both the former phenomena, the concept of the beautiful villa and the concept of the economic villa, enshrouded in politics? From this *parallelogram of forces*—aesthetic, economic, political, and philosophical—converging in the villa, there emerges the main question this research addresses: the overriding question of the "villa as ideology."

2

The Economic Background of Migration from the City

T HE POLITICAL AND economic history of the city of Venice provides ample material for explaining in socioeconomic and sociopolitical terms the sixteenth-century conquest of land in the Terraferma and its settlement in accordance with the *villeggiatura*. In 1422, the city of Venice had a population of 190,000.[6] With the help of figures handed down from the Quattrocento, we can well imagine the extent of the economic importance of the city's harbor, the so-called Arsenal, which was built in 1104 and enlarged in the early sixteenth century. The political records compiled in 1423 by Doge Mocenigo recount that the 3,000 smaller boats (*navigli*), 300 large ships (*navi*), and 45 galleons employed 36,000 men in the service of Venice and furthermore that 16,000 ships' carpenters earned their living in the Venetian boatyards.[7]

In addition to these workers were those in various occupations who indirectly lived from seafaring and mercantile trade. These included sailmakers, ropemakers, cartwrights, ship's saddlers, coopers, longshoremen, packers, warehousemen, officials in the ports and customs authorities, along with clerks, banking staff, and correspondents. The city was also the location for sections of the manufacturing industry. It can be assumed, taking present-day relations as a guideline, that the number of people so employed would hardly have been less than that of the seamen and shipbuilders. In other words, virtually the entire population of Venice at that time was either directly or indirectly dependent on shipping and mercantile trade.[8] Thus, any fluctuation, however slight, in the economic and political conditions of mercantile trade must have affected this monopolistic, highly structured, and thus particularly vulnerable state organism to its core in social, political, and psychological terms.

The prosperity of the city was founded, just as in late capitalist economies, on the most insecure of all "means of production," namely, money and its independent circulation. In the year 1423 (again according to the

6

FIGURE 2. Jacopo de Barbari, *View of Venice*, 1500, woodcut

Mocenigo document), Venice's trading volume totaled ten million ducats, with a profit margin of four million ducats. The estimated value of real property in the same year was seven million ducats, which in turn produced rental income of 500,000 ducats. As could be expected, the social differences not only between the propertied and the propertyless classes but also within the upper class were very marked: The incomes of the thousand or so members of the nobility were on a scale from 70 ducats to 4,000 ducats. Figures from the end of the fifteenth century put the value of Venetian assets between 100,000,000 and 200,000,000 ducats. This was a colossal sum at that time and was nearly matched by the fortune of the Florentine bankers, which itself was greatly exceeded only by the banking empire of Agostino Chigi (800,000,000 ducats in 1520).[9]

In the first half of the fifteenth century, economic crises were isolated occurrences that the capitalist state system was able to navigate rather effortlessly. In the second half of the century and in the early sixteenth century, however, the intervals between such crises became shorter and shorter, until around 1530–1540 a state of "permanent crisis" was reached and had to be responded to with effective measures in an almost classical reaction of the ideological superstructure to changes in the economic sub-structure. This reaction involved a rechanneling of large-scale capital assets into landed property and agriculture, new appropriations of land in the Terraferma, and, lastly, the cultural establishment of the *villeggiatura*. In 1423, state revenues were still at a level of 1.1 million ducats. By 1450, they had already dropped by 25 percent to 800,000 ducats as a result of the Turkish conquest of Constantinople, and by 1522 Venice had finally lost its renowned place as the richest city in Italy to Genoa and Rome.[10] For the period that interests us here, namely, the Quattrocento and Cinquecento (1400–1580), Francesco Sansovino calculated in his *Venezia Città nobilissima e singolare* a 50 percent fall in the value of money.[11]

It is true that Venice did not cease to trade with foreign countries, and the nobility continued to invest considerable sums in the *cosa del mare* (maritime affairs). New trading routes were opened up to northern Europe, to Russia, and to Germany (specifically, to Prague, Danzig, Swedish ports, and Moscow) where the oriental goods traded by Venice—fabrics, wax, copper, and silver—were still avidly sought after. Toward the end of the sixteenth century, attempts were made to expand the Venetian production of luxury goods (silks, brocades, woolen materials, and fine glass) as well as to increase the local manufacture of leather, wood, and metal, all at the expense of the Terraferma. The printing trade also flourished in Venice at that time. But trade with the Levant remained as always an extremely risky enterprise, even though the Priuli trading house was still able to carry on a very good trade in oriental jewelry and pearls in the 1560s.

With the conquest of Egypt by the Turks in 1516, the route to Alexandria remained open only until the 1530s. In 1536, however, the links to Syria were disrupted and they were not to be reestablished until 1541; after 1555 they disappeared altogether. The old overland trade route to the Far East via the Red Sea, Cairo, and Alexandria was revived around 1550; pepper, exotic spices, dyes, and Arabic medicines came to the city via this route. But at the beginning of the 1580s, the Persian-Turkish War blocked the last routes to India. Between 1577 and 1580, the well-known trading houses of Sanudo, Priuli, and Contarini withdrew totally from business. After a series of bankruptcies, the last private bank, Pisani-Tiepolo, had to close its doors. Venice was soon overtaken in oriental trade, first by the Iberian and French trading centers of Seville, Lisbon, Barcelona, and Marseilles, then by Genoa and Pisa, which were more favorably located, and, finally, by the cities of Antwerp and Amsterdam, which enjoyed close links with Portuguese and Spanish traders. At the turn of the seventeenth century, the Dutch began to make inroads with their oriental wares into the established Italian domains of the Mediterranean.

In order to supply the raw materials from overseas that were so vital for the local luxury-goods industry, the Venetian Senate had to increase constantly the risk premiums for each galley during the 1530s—from 500 to 1,000 to 2,000 and finally to 3,000 ducats. But in spite of these high costs, there was no shortage of people interested in the "suicide missions" to the Orient, during which one was threatened at sea not only by the Turkish blockade but also by buccaneers. The loss of lives was reflected by the changing size of the Venetian population. While it had increased from 100,000 to 175,000 in the period between 1500 and 1575 through the formation of an urban proletariat, the population dropped to 140,000 by 1600.

The collapse of the economic basis for mercantile shipping owing to the events recounted above resulted in increased labor resources in the city of Venice. Due to the specialization of occupations, however, it was not possible for the unemployed to be easily integrated into the rigidly structured guild system of artisanal production. These productive forces had to be restructured and "diverted" to counteract the risk of pauperization and thus prevent this group from becoming politicized and mobilized against the ruling class. The material base became very narrowly defined since the one-sided orientation of the state toward shipping and commerce had led to the decline of numerous previously arable Terraferma estates back into wasteland or marshland. In the central areas of the Terraferma between Padua, Treviso, and Verona, 25 percent of the agrarian infrastructure had deteriorated in relation to its use during the Middle Ages. According to contemporary records of the Senate, 200,000 of the 800,000 fields could no longer be used for agricultural purposes.[12]

In the late fifteenth and early sixteenth centuries, Venice obtained its sustenance largely from its maritime activities. When the flow of goods from overseas grain stores dried up—Venice, no longer an autarchic state like Rome, depended on them heavily—the city was forced to fall back on its hinterland. The decline of mercantile shipping caused devaluations of money that alternated with periods of capital shortage. Public authorities no longer possessed liquid capital sufficient to buy grain abroad.[13] Instead, grain had to be grown within their own territories, that is, in the Terraferma. The Venetian state archives contain a letter to the doge in which Senator Cornaro imploringly describes Venice's precarious situation:

> Our city is justified in its fear of famine among the population for the following reasons: The number of inhabitants has grown to such an extent that 45,000 measures of grain are not enough, whereas 30,000 per month used to suffice, and one must assume that our city's grain requirements will continue to increase in the future. We need forty ships (carrying provisions) to guarantee the supply of grain. At present there are but eighteen. To change this, our city would have to own Cervia and Ravenna and numerous cities in Apulia, which are all exploiting the shortage of supplies we are currently facing and are acting like cutthroats with their increases in customs duties and freight rates. Cyprus could supply as much grain as we require. But at present nothing, or only very little, comes from there, because they . . . have let the grain estates go to rack and ruin. Furthermore, the population in the hinterland has increased, and floods have turned numerous fields into marshy land where crops can no longer be grown.[14]

A visible sign of this situation was the establishment of the special *magistrato dei beni inculti* (magistrate for fallow or idle farmland). It commenced its work in 1545, frequently supplying voluminous reports of expert opinion, as for example in 1563.[15] The *dei beni inculti* commission was charged with the task of investigating the situation in agriculture in order to produce a long-term plan for land amelioration.[16] The Terraferma was completely reorganized in agrarian and in industrial terms. The additional laborers needed were obviously recruited from the ranks of the unemployed in urban areas.[17]

3

The Political Basis for the *Villeggiatura* and the Settlement of Land in the Terraferma

T HE *VILLEGGIATURA* SHOULD not, however, be seen in the sense of emancipation from urban life as an ad hoc reaction to the development of the city. While villa building boomed and became a task of immense importance involving the highest artistic quality (especially the work of Sansovino, Falconetto, Sanmicheli, and Palladio), it occurred at a breakneck pace within narrow, historically circumscribed boundaries between 1540 and 1560. This could only be explained by the apparently very sudden thinning out of Venetian trade opportunities from 1530 onward. This sudden decrease in trade opportunities was not a spontaneous process but was the result of a long-term one. The production of the "classical" Venetian villa and the economic crisis around 1530–1540 are nothing if not the final consequences of a previous social crisis that had been latent in the late fifteenth century and then had intensified rapidly on into the sixteenth century. It was not only outside political events that shook the Venetian state and economy to its foundations but also the contradictions within the Venetian state itself during the transition from the Middle Ages to the New Age.

The history of the Venetian conquest of land and settlement of it is proof of this process, extending as it did far back into the fifteenth century.[18] The historical facts define this settlement of land as a *conquista* by a genuine *comprador* class. The Venetian nobility had been effectively preparing their "second" conquest and settlement of land around 1530–1540, ever since Tommaso Mocenigo. Their "first" *conquista* in the Quattrocento was primarily motivated by political and strategic, instead of economic, considerations and clearly reflected colonizing and imperialist ambitions.[19] The old feudal class was pushed aside by a new bourgeois class of landowners. This political situation was clearly colonialist in character; the city of Venice and the Terraferma were not political partners with equal rights.[20] To

11

FIGURE 3.   Petrus de Creszentius, Frontispiece to *De Agricultura Vulgare*, Venice, 1495

compensate for its external dependency, the Terraferma was granted significant internal municipal liberties. The motto on the Terraferma's coat of
arms, *Pro summa fide summus amor* (greatest love for the greatest loyalty),
reveals the real motives for this apparently quite liberal system: The liberal
legislation effectively robbed the established feudal lords in Padania of the
privileges they had so vigorously defended. A power vacuum developed,
which the haute bourgeoisie in the city of Venice were able to exploit
during the late fifteenth and early sixteenth centuries. The conflict in the
rural towns of the Terraferma, which were pushing for emancipation from
the old feudal *padroni*, was deliberately aggravated by skillful tactical moves
on a political and constitutional level. In this way, the Venetian bourgeoisie
were able to establish themselves in the lordships of the country.[21] It is

indicative of the nature of the liberal mentality of the urban bourgeois elite that they abstained from any brutal demonstrations of power during the first *conquista*. Legal and economic manipulation were found to be more effective means of gaining hegemony.

During the fifteenth century, the conquest and settlement of land had continued without any system or precise definition of aims. In the sixteenth century, however, during the Barbaro and Cornaro era, this dominance obtained a certain inner logic as a consequence of increased political and economic pressure. The removal of the old feudal lordships by the elite of the Venetian haute bourgeoisie was obviously complete by around 1540, and the first "classical" Venetian facades can be dated to the same period— the Villa Garzoni in Pintecasale; the Villa Priuli and, somewhat later, the Villa Soranza in Treville near Castelfranco; the Villa Giustinian in Roncade; and the Villa Godi in Lonedo. The congruence between the economic and the art historical developments exposes the social "content" of the Venetian villa, which could be termed, in exaggerated fashion, as the "fortress of urban capital."

4

The Settlement of the Countryside and the Idealization of Agriculture as the Economic and Ideological Foundation of the *Villeggiatura*

THE NOTIONS PRESENTED here could constitute a sociological explanation for the ennobling of the peasantry in the literature, art theory, and philosophy of sixteenth-century Venice, all of which proceeded with an updating of the position of Alberti, Petrarch, and Piero de Crescenzi. Ruzante's "villanesque" peasant plays and dialect comedies provided the foundation for a whole dramaturgical genre that extended to Goldoni's rural comedies. The colloquial language of Paduan was employed by the Cornaro, Bembo, and Speroni circle as a literary instrument. The literary form of the *rei rusticae scriptores* (agrarian theoreticians) of antiquity and the Middle Ages—Cato, Varro, Columella, Palladius, Crescenzi (Figure 3)—was given a new humanistic content. A characteristic literary form that trod a perfect middle way between academic writing, moralist tracts, a bourgeois philosophy of life, and belles lettres—namely, the sixteenth-century "villa book"—emanated from the blending of agronomy and *studia humanitatis* in the works of Giuseppe Falcone, Alberto Lollio, and Agostino Gallo in northern Italy or in the works of Giovanno Vittorio Soderini and Giovanni di Vincenzo Saminiato in central Italy. That these books were designed for a broadly based readership is evidenced by the unusually large number of books published of each edition right into the seventeenth century.

A humanist and philosophical superstructural apologia for the new villa culture was finally supplied with the publication in the mid-sixteenth century of Alvise Cornaro's famous work entitled *Discorsi intorno alla Vita*

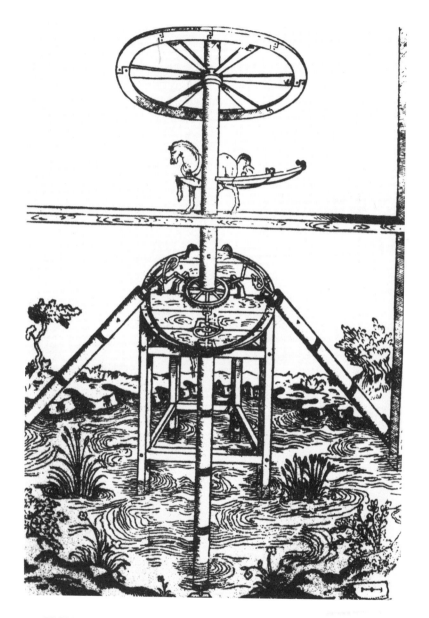

FIGURE 4. Giuseppe Ceredi, *Waterlifting Device*, Parma, 1567

Sobria. This broadly theoretical contribution to consolidating the super-structure was aimed without a doubt not only at the haute bourgeois class in the Venetian capital and in the rural townships of the Terraferma but also at the urban proletariat. One can well imagine that the attempt was thus being made to avert a social disaster by convincing the seamen, port laborers, and clerical workers (who were then sitting around unemployed in their cramped city dwellings without any specific function to perform) of their new social role, thus rendering it acceptable by means of a social trans-figuration that was necessarily intended to function as propaganda. The tendency was an obvious one: The "fourth estate," robbed of its links to commerce and to the financial markets, was to be relocated, or better, rooted in the safety and security of rural life with its stable occupations and fixed abodes, thus providing the urban employed with a new social exis-tence. It seems quite certain that the glorification of the peasant that was so loudly indulged in was not directed at the inhabitants of the countryside, who had been farmers for generations. The domiciled farmer had no need for any elevation of his standing. He knew his world and the conditions of his existence and had reconciled himself to them.

This observation is confirmed by the historical facts: The reclamation of land introduced by the *magistrato dei beni inculti* was not the achievement of the established peasant families but of new settlers from the cities. These immigrants received aid from the Senate in the form of expert advice and technical equipment for draining and irrigating the land, some of which was specially developed by scientists for land cultivation (Figure 4). Nowhere in Cinquecento Italy did hydraulic engineering and the art of engineering reach such a high state of development as in Venice.[22] The Senate supported the reclamation of land and its subsequent settlement by means of credits, subsidies, and tax benefits. Ownership of a part of the land that was made arable was transferred to the settlers themselves.[23] Admittedly, this should not be interpreted as a protosocialist program; the state supplied equipment and financing for the settlers, but this did nothing to alter the fact that the ruling class continued to hold a monopoly over the means of production or the fact that the dependent settlers (mostly tenant farmers) remained in the debt of the state or private financiers for years or even decades to come.

The ameliorization of the land was predominantly in the hands of the urban nobility, as the new villas built in the sixteenth century in the Terraferma show. Many of Falconetto's, Sansovino's, Sanmicheli's, and Palladio's creations were erected on newly reclaimed lands whose bound-aries followed the new courses of the rivers and recently dug canals. Whenever land was made arable, this occurred within the framework of capitalist property relations: The *padrone* organized and financed the land ameliorization and then placed his villa at the center of the newly won *podere*, or manorial estate, as a sign of his hegemony. The social benefits—private plots of land and tax remissions—were soon revealed as alibis, since as "bonuses" they hardly changed anything with respect to actual property relations. *Padroni* of the new *beni* remained or became the urban Venetian *nobili*. They idealized their altered economic interests, their new interest in agriculture, by making of agriculture itself an aesthetic doctrine of salvation cloaked with ethical aspects that served to cover their solid economic goals. This is particularly evident in the case of Falcone, the agrarian theorist who "[released] the *rusticitas* from its peasant imbecility and [turned it into] a virtue of the *padrone* in the countryside," as Rupprecht observed.[24]

Cultural practices and natural philosophy followed the gangs of dam builders and canal workers into the countryside after they had endured there years of heavy laboring; this situation was symptomatic of the standard of living for those responsible for this "second conquest of the land" in the Terraferma. Here we can note that an upper class that is obviously too self-reflective to resort still to the mechanisms of oppression "naively" creates a legitimation for its action by means of a cultural and ideological superstructure that exists not only for itself but also for its dependents, who can no longer accept their dependency uncritically. The firm foundation for this ideological presentation of new agriculture formations were the *auctoritas historiae* (historic authorities)—the *rei rusticae scriptores* of ancient Rome (Varro, Columella, Cato, Palladius), whose works were constantly being republished[25] so as to bring the ideal picture of the ancient farm estate up-to-date.[26]

5

Alvise Cornaro
as Symbolic Figure

THE SYMPTOMATIC FIGURE of this generation, and the most eloquent propagandist on behalf of the *villeggiatura*, was Alvise Cornaro, who amassed his own *latifundium* (large estate) within a few years. In his programmatic work on the *vita sobria* and in his epistolary writings, he provides a classic example of what must be called the "manipulation of consciousness" in favor of the ideological legitimation of the economic interests of a capitalist ruling class.

In his 1542 letter to Sperone Speroni, a declaration about his business career, he masks the real motivation for his efforts with ethical, pacifist, and religious pretexts. It was not the League of Cambrai, the Peace of Bologna, and the decline in the city of Venice's maritime power that led him back to the still intact and ideal realm of *agricoltura*, all of which he ennobles with the title Santa Rusticitas, but his peace-loving nature: "non con mezzo do arme e sforzi e danni altrui, nè con il mezzo di passare i mari con infiniti pericoli di vita [not with the force of weapons or with brutality, and not with overseas trade with its great danger for life and limb]."[27] In the same letter, however, he discloses himself to be a man who built a private empire in the Terraferma with hard and effective methods. As adroit politician, villa ideologist, and organizer of land ameliorization, he had helped to create the preconditions for this very same accumulation of capital. It therefore comes as no surprise that this same protagonist for the *villeggiatura* and for Venetian agrarian ideology rose to become the most powerful *padrone* in the Padua region.

In the *vita sobria*, Cornaro elevates the aesthetically translated conception of agrarian capitalism to the ethical plane to the point of religious excess. In the *Parti prese dall'eccellentissimo Senato in materia de'Beni Inculti* (The Role of the Most Excellent Senate in Matters of Fallow Land), the Venetian settlement and improvement of land in the Terraferma was already compared to the story of divine creation in Genesis: First, there was the separation of

18

Heaven and earth, then the separation of land and sea, and finally there was the settlement of the newly won land with animals, trees, and corn.[28] Cornaro fancies himself to be in the role of an omnipotent demiurge who not only creates new land with good climatic conditions for God but who also presents him with new souls by building new villages, farmsteads, and churches. The agrarian capitalist disguised as an agrarian humanist sees himself in the role of the fulfiller of a divine plan for salvation. He draws his legitimation from the mission of salvation in the first and last instance: "io posso dire con verità che ho dato in questo luogo à Dio altare e templio, ed anime per adorarlo [I can say in truth that here I have given God the present of an altar and a temple, and souls to worship him]."[29] Cornaro's train of thought reminds one of the religiously based model of legitimation for early capitalism in Calvinist Holland, which culminated in the doctrine of predestination: wealth as the visible sign of divine grace and poverty as a moral stain (for which the individual concerned is personally responsible) symbolizing a lack of grace.

Cornaro transfigures agrarian capitalism, turning it into Santa Agricoltura. Not only in his works but also in all the villa books right up to the relevant chapters in Vincenzo Scamozzi's *Idea dell'Architettura Universale* (1615), there is a presentation of the biblical and classical *sapientia veterum* (ancient wisdom) as the principal witness for this ideology. Besides Xenophon, Plato, Servius Tullius Cicero, Attalus, Pliny, Ovid, and Cincinnatus, Hiob and Noah also figure as examples for Sancta Rusticitas.[30] By raising the cultivation of the fields to the status of an ethically supreme lifestyle—"il miglior mezzo e più laudevole di ogni altro [the best means of acquiring capital, which is more praiseworthy than all others]," as Cornaro wrote—the profits from agrarian capitalism were transfigured to become "justly won property," for "whoever cultivates the land derives an ethical benefit from it."[31]

In his letter to Daniele Barbaro (Figure 1), which was written shortly before his own death in 1566, Alvise Cornaro reveals the conflict between the town and the country as involving the urban drive for emancipation versus the old rural order embodied in the villa (evidently more pleasing to God in terms of real "class struggle"). Yet at the same time, he simply presumes to be dealing with the generational conflict between youth (which signifies folly and distance from God) and old age (which signifies reason and proximity to God). Using set phrases and a narrow vision, he counterposes a distorted picture of the urban "vita senza ordine e senza ragione [life without order and without reason]" practiced by a critical and liberal young generation with the rural "vita con ordine e ragionevole [a life with order and reason]" practiced by the wise old villa *padroni*, who in their old-fashionedness, piousness, and upright erudition have become rich.[32] In this way, he addresses the salient problem of the first timid stirrings of enlightenment in the city. What appeared to be an ascendant liberal consciousness did not, however, prevent Paolo Veronese from being brought before the Inquisition in 1573 for what was purported to be a blasphemous portrayal of the Last Supper. Significantly, Veronese based his defense on the artist's role as "court jester."[33]

6

The Relationship between the City and the Country as a Conflict of Authority: The Social and Psychological Background of the *Villeggiatura*

T HE PROBLEM THAT the ideological facade of agricultural humanism concealed is easily uncovered. In disclosing it, however, we must
assume that neither the villa ideologues nor those being proselytized were as
conscious of the sociopolitical problem as would be apparent from a
sociological analysis of the *villeggiatura* today. As has been noted: "Just as
the individual remains unaware of the mechanism of rationalization (in
psychoanalysis), its motives and purposes, so the members of a social group
remain similarly unaware of the fact that their thinking is determined by
the material conditions of existence, since otherwise 'it would be all over
with ideology.'"[34]

Parallel to the growth of the urban population, the number of groups
"isolating" themselves increased. They became more independent of
archaic class structuring for "lords and serfs." The range of information in
the city is greater, which also means, however, that the dependent find
better opportunities to arrive at a critique founded on a mass basis, hence to
form a "critical consciousness." The dependent find their identity in groups
that stand in an oppositional relationship to the patriarch, be he an authoritarian city regent "father figure," a doge, a master craftsman, or a patrician
in the commercial world. The competence of the patriarch is questioned
more frequently in the metropolis on the threshold of the modern age. But
in the countryside this authority remains effortlessly guaranteed by facts
that in themselves imply an "irrational order."

The aesthetic manipulations of villa philosophy, which in the case of

21

Alvise Cornaro are raised to the point of pseudoreligious excess—agriculture as divine worship, the agrarian lifestyle as the expression of a God-given and "eternal" order—are a reflection and a cause of the "irrational order" in the countryside. This order strengthens the fixation on authority because its structural precondition is the authority principle, the "living out" of authority or the translation of it into a practical form of social behavior. Accordingly, "the father establishes his domination in his own interest but is justified in doing so by his age, his biological function and, above all, by his success: He creates that 'order' without which the group would immediately disintegrate."[35] The visible facts, and the "order" that is based on them, ensure that the competence of authority is not questioned in the countryside. The *padrone's* property and omnipotence legalize his patriarchal authority. The Italian concept of the lord of the villa—*padrone*—is derived from *padre*, or father, since the father "embodies in his person and function the inner logic and unavoidability of the reality principle. He has 'historic rights.'"[36]

Vita rustica as an ideal form of existence is raised to metaphysical heights in Cornaro's villa philosophy. For the legitimation of the relationship between lord and serf as well, reference to the transcendental is made. We are all children, "children of God" before the divine father figure; before God the Father we are all serfs, that is, "servants of God." Santa Agricoltura becomes transfigured as a divine service, a divine servants' service. In this way, the authority exercised by the worldly lord of the villa toward his earthly servants is ostensibly minimized and made bearable by this supernatural criterion. The authority of the *padrone* is supposedly "God given" and therefore "unchangeable." The *padrone* as an autocrat placed by God in his *podere* can claim the most effective of all thinkable legitimations for his domination: belief that is rooted, as Horkheimer has stated, "in the idea of God as the father, as the wisest and oldest, and as that being whose age alone suffices for him to be respected and feared."[37]

The ideological use of religion here veils the conflict between the lord and the serf. The latter, childlike, approaches the villa *padrone*, the *padre di famiglia*, who with virtue and *masserizia* (economy) "ciascuna sua cosa bene governa e conserva [regulates all his affairs well and preserves what has been achieved]," as Leone Battista Alberti wrote in his *Liber tertius Familie*.[38] This book by Alberti was modeled after Xenophon's tract on agriculture and was dedicated to Xenophon's *Economicus*. Thus the serf never even becomes critically aware of his socially constructed but "religiously" defended role.

In his study, Alberti names the two key concepts of villa ideology: *governo*, by which was meant autocratic, undisputed hegemony, and *conservazione*, by which was meant the stabilization and maintenance of the existing order through the recourse to archaic societal models. The only social framework in the villa was that of the patriarchally governed family, since

> the forms of community interest are not preordained, nor are those of the nation, state, or clan; community only exists by virtue of the lifestyle peculiar to the villa. . . . The community includes . . . the *familia* in its Latin sense, namely, the other inhabitants of the house, the friends as well as the domestic servants and farmhands—especially the villa farmers. As befits the character of villa culture, these common interests can [only] be but small.[39]

Virtually every villa tract, from that of Alberti to Falcone, contains long, obligatory sections dealing with the relationship of the villa lordships to the serfs. Citing biblical patriarchs, the archfather figures of the Old Covenant/Testament (Henoch, Noah, Abraham, Isaac, and Jacob), and including revealing references to Jesus Sirach (from *Ecclesiasticus*) served an obvious purpose in this regard. Passages on the farmer's worldly wisdom, expressed in the figure of Jesus Sirach, were quoted almost word for word by Giuseppe Falcone[40] or Alberti:[41]

23. Remain the first on your estate and let no one deprive you of your honor. . . .
25. To the donkey belongs his feed, [the scourge of] the whip and his burden; to the serf his bread, his punishment, and his labor.
26. Keep the serf at his work, and you will have your peace with him; let him walk at his leisure, and he will want to be a nobleman.
27. The yoke and the ropes bow the neck; the stick and the club bow the bad servant!
28. Drive him to his work so that he may not walk idly.
29. Idleness teaches much evil.
30. Give him work fitting for a serf; if he does not obey, put him in the stocks. . . . But give none too much and observe moderation in all things.
31. If you have a serf, then show respect for him as you do for yourself, for you need his body as you need your own.
32. But if you keep him so badly that he rises up and runs away, where will you find him again?

Jesus Sirach's biblical and fatherly image provided the *auctoritas sacra* (sacred authority) for the ideal of the villa patriarch. In view of this, Falcone's directions for contracts and for the skillful leadership of men on the country estate—significantly, warnings creep in about the lack of respect shown toward property by the *villano* (serf)[42]—hardly appear as simply a sign of "a genuine, warm understanding for the country people" and of "clever humanitarianism," as is claimed in Rupprecht's interpretation.[43] Nor can Alvise Cornaro be seen as a mere selfless friend of the "proletariat" or as a protosocialist reformer and the first champion/advocate of *populismo*, this being a position to which Fiocco implausibly elevated him.[44] Such thinking is, rather, evidence for the psychological shrewdness of the new dominant class in the countryside, which did not repeat any of the old mistakes and whose methods of exploiting others had become sublimated by a long merchant tradition with its roots in the city. While the practice of expropriation was refined by the "philanthropist" in the garb of the humanist, the human consequences were in no way eliminated.

All of this is not to suggest that Falcone, Alberti, Daniele Barbaro (Figure 1), and Cornaro did not themselves believe in the integrity of the role of a philanthropist in the guise of a humanist or in the truthfulness of humanitarian objectives based on agricultural humanism. The apologist was not, of course, subjectively aware of his role as a philanthropic advocate for the peasant and serf estates in the sense of having a studied attitude. Instead, this role was internalized as "second nature." Objectively speaking, however, this demonstrates nothing but a "strategem for class struggle." This is the case "because people do not always think, feel, and act according to principles that could be characterized in the psychological sense as their interests. But they mostly think and act in accordance with their class consciousness, for which the preservation of the class in question is the decisive goal, even if it is not always the one that is admitted."[45]

7

The Social and Religious Authority Principle

A CLOSE CAUSAL interrelationship exists between the principle of religious authority and the social principle of authority. Besides the socioeconomic and political explanation, an explanation could also be put forward that is based on church history for the fact that the *villeggiatura* ideal was realized on such a broad basis, especially between 1540 and 1560 and particularly in northern Italy. The Counter-Reformation Council was held between 1545 and 1563 in Trento, in the immediate vicinity of the center for the Venetian *villeggiatura*. The council fathers and the laymen who participated indirectly in the council were in numerous cases those same ideologists of the *villeggiatura* as well as the prominent builder-owners of villas. Such was the case with Alvise Cornaro, the aforementioned *padrone* of the Villa dal Bene north of Verona, or with Marc-Antonio and Daniele Barbaro.[46]

The *tertium comparationis* (comparative medium) of the religious ideology of the Counter-Reformation Council, and of the political ideology of the *villeggiatura*, consisted of the reactionary tendency to "save" or to reestablish "past good" relations so as to stifle emancipatory strivings within the Church or in the social field and thus also to conceal the mechanisms of social and ideological tutelage. The villa ideologists modernized the *vita rustica* of ancient times with its apparently still intact relations of authority, turning it all into an illusory arcadian utopia. The Tridentine ideologists of the Counter-Reformation brought forth the existing religious weltanschauung of Christianity during the Middle Ages, turning it into an ecclesiastical "arcadia." Scholasticism achieved renewed eminence as a superstructural formation of concepts.

The villa ideal, then, embodied religious ideals. The biblical and medieval concepts of "divine servanthood" and the unchallenged authority relations between lord and serf in the country villa were conjoined as retarding principles in their fundamental antipathy to any form of enlightenment.

25

The unwritten motto of the Council of Trent was *Vestigia terrent* (retention of the old ways). The council fathers were all too well aware of the consequences of the religious enlightenment championed by Martin Luther on the other side of the Alps, where the dissolution of the seemingly natural "God-given" relations between lord and serf led to the Peasant Wars, the first modern revolutionary movement, which was suppressed only because the time was not yet ripe for overthrowing the status quo and because the resources of the feudal opposition proved to be too powerful.

8

Andrea Palladio: The Aesthetic Rationalization of "Irrational Order" in the Countryside

T HE SOCIAL RELATIONS described previously are, in aesthetic terms, accurately reflected in the *Gesamtkunstwerk* known as the Venetian villa, which found its ultimate realization in the buildings of Andrea Palladio. The ideal geometry of his villa plans and their mathematical proportions, which were derived from contemporary music theory and the Pythagorean cosmology of *rationes* (ideal arithmetical proportions) and which in turn pervaded all the spatial dimensions as well as the structural organization of his buildings, guaranteed that this architecture represented a divine order. In this way, the villa became a social, ethical, economic, and artistic phenomenon all at once. Even in the programmatic themes of the frescoes that decorated the interiors of such villas as Palladio's Villa Maser (Figures 5 and 6), there was an astrological and Christian framework in the *salotto* (or small hall)[47] that elevated the building to a cosmological center around which the surrounding *podere* (estate) was arranged autocratically, or rather hegemonically. All of this referred directly to the claim of the *villa padrone* (landlord) as the earthly guarantor of God's divine ordering of the "irrational" countryside.

By aesthetically ennobling his residence as a cosmological center, the client thus exalted himself as a vassal of the demiurgic Lord who rightfully ruled the entire world. Here one can recall Cornaro's comparison of the soil-enrichment program of the *beni inculti* with the creation of the earth as part of the divine genesis. Through this symbolism, Barbaro and Cornaro not only allowed themselves to be recognized as extraordinary powers in the divine and astrological scheme of things but also to be seen as disciples of order. The charge to instill order, which the very highest authorities supposedly imposed on the aristocracy, was then directly transposed by these lords to their worldly domain: to the villa and its retinue of servants.

FIGURE 5.   Andrea Palladio, Villa Barbaro in Maser, begun 1557–58

This state of affairs was made clear when the well-ordered and well-cultivated villa—an image of the divine *Weltordnung*—was celebrated as the *locus amoenus* (ideal place) in humanist terms and as the *paradiso terrestre* in Christian terms, or when Scamozzi put forth its enhanced *maestà* (majesty), as the reason behind the domineering presence of the villa (*altezza*).[48]

The rigorous rule-endowing spirit of Palladio's villa architecture, based as it was on Palladio's adherence to the classical concept of order, provided an aesthetic rationalization for the "irrational" social order in the countryside.[49] This authoritative principle was also expressed in the villa's *compartimento*, that is, in the individual hierarchical composition of its building elements, even though different functional categories were materially united in the villa *sotto un tetto* (under one roof). Thus the villa as *casa grande* served as the residence for the entire authority-obsessed extended family in the countryside, which included the landlord's wife, children, and relatives, his personal guests, the domestics, the steward and tenants, and the farmworkers and grooms. Nevertheless, the diverse tasks within the Palladian villa remained ideal, strongly segregated domains and were distinguished from each other in a clearly ranked hierarchy that went as follows: (1) those who represented the demands of a city palace, (2) those who served in the residence and in the landlord's household, and (3) those who worked in the rural economy.[50]

The dualistic relationship between *habitazione* (living quarters) and *fattoria* (farmhouse), which was regulated according to a strictly ranked order, emerged unequivocally from contemporary architectural theory. Through aesthetic and economic arguments, Scamozzi substantiated the "unione di queste fabriche," that is, the material unity of *cour d'honneur* and farmyard buildings, of "habitazione degli huomini [living quarters]" and "case per i loro stromenti, e animali [toolsheds and stables]."[51] Palladio also emphasized the formal separation of the two domains, which were not to compete against each other in their aesthetic claims despite their mutual unity.[52] The contradictions of this order lay in the combination of its intrusive authoritarian surveillance by the extended family as part of agricultural activity and the contrary principle of segregating the detached ideal sphere of the *casa del padrone* as the seat of the Muses, of the *litterae*, and of the fine arts, all of which supposedly transcended the lower material sphere of the *fattoria* with its stable smells and servants' clatter, along with the noise of flails and the rattle of milkbuckets.[53]

This concept of order distinguished the Palladian villa from both the ordinary farmyard with farmhouse and the loose addition of individual elements in the archaic conglomerate villa. If in the case of the traditional *casa colonica*, the rustic country house—with which Palladio's *usanza nuova* (new architectural style) broke—the economic interest was projected more strongly than in Palladio's villas, so in the case of the ancient country villa the agricultural presence was totally alienated from the main habitat. Hence, the Palladian villa mediated between these two other traditions of rural building by applying the decorum of the city palace to the countryside without casting aside the *economia* of the rural form of livelihood. The Roman villa of antiquity and of even more recent times was financed by

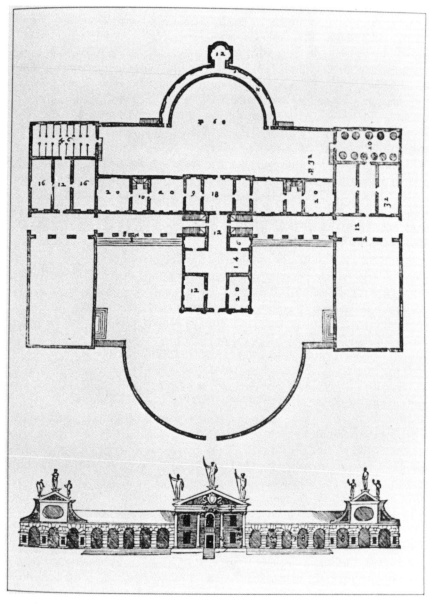

FIGURE 6.   Andrea Palladio, *Plan of the Villa Barbaro*, from *I Quattro Libri dell'Architettura*, Venice, 1570

capital accumulated in the city through commerce and banking (Maecenas, Lucullus, Agostini Chigi, Ippolito d'Este).

As early as in Alberti's writings,[54] however, and later in those of Scamozzi,[55] it was demanded that the northern Italian villas be supported by the *podere*, that is, by the profit from the surrounding agricultural estate. *Palladio found a formula for the synthesis of agricultural capitalism with agricultural humanism*, of urban cultural demands with rural economic planning, all of which were expressed in the style of his various villa designs: "L'industria, et arte dell'agricoltura [The art and craft of agriculture]."[56] In Palladio's view, agriculture belonged simultaneously to the realm of fine arts and to the domain of sober economic concerns. At the turn of the seventeenth century, agriculture as the economic basis of the villa ideal was finally elevated to a fine art. Scamozzi rationalized the elegant villa *padrone*'s occupation in agriculture by referring to the *sacre lettere* both from the Bible and from antiquity so as to *incorporate agriculture into the domain of the artes liberales*.[57]

The hierarchical order of the Palladian villa prevented the decorum of the *habitazione del padrone* from sinking to the trivial level of the rustic farm. The difference of rank between the *casa del padrone* and the *fattoria* was maintained through the more or less complicated vaults along with the relative heights of the rooms, the painted and sculpted decoration, the extravagant door and window frames, the festive enhancement of interior architecture through illusionistic painting, the feigned wall openings looking onto fake landscapes, and the distance of respective rooms or wings from the heart and womb of the house, namely, the *sala*. Similarly, there was a hierarchical articulation of the whole organism of the villa through long symmetrical axes of a higher or lower order; the canonical application of Doric, Tuscan, Ionic, Corinthian, and composite styles in accordance with the building's degree of dignity; and the compliance with esoteric principles of proportion, Pythagorean ratios, and mathematical-musical relations to set the dimensions of the rooms, all of which subordinated the entire building as a whole to an overriding order of cosmological and hierarchical principles.

The ancient theory of proportion—as conveyed by Vitruvius, Euclid, and Nicomachos—was combined with the concepts of consonance and harmony from contemporary music theory, later summarized by Gioseffo Zarlino in his Venetian *Supplementi Musicali* of 1588. Thus, a link was established between the architectural notion of truth and musical proportion—whether it was in thirds, fourths, fifths, or octaves. This connection was unequivocally defined by Daniele Barbaro in his 1556 commentary on Vitruvius:

FIGURE 7. Interior of the Villa Maser, wall paintings by Paolo Veronese, 1560–62

Divina forza de'numeri tra se con ragione comparati—Questa bella man-
iera si nella Musica, come nell'Architettura è detta Eurithmia, madre della
gratia e del diletto.

[The divine power of rationally correlated numbers in music as well as in
architecture is a beautiful mode of composition that is called *eurithmia*, the
source of grace and aesthetic satisfaction.][58]

Within either the Pythagorean or the Ptolemaic cosmological framework,
order meant hierarchy—that is, a model of the world in which there were those
who dominated and those who were dominated, with a concomitant perspective on society that included one top and one bottom. It thus becomes clear
why in the sixteenth-century villas, the astrological, astronomical, and
cosmological subjects were applied with particular preference as ceiling
decoration, as in Chigi's Villa Farnesina or Barbaro's Villa Maser (see Figures 1
and 5). Here, an abstract social model was illustrated in painting, and the villa as
a cultural phenomenon already took on (as in the astrological theme of the Sala
dello Zodiaco in the Villa Maser) the character of an undisguised tendency that
quite exceeded the character of any unconscious acknowledgment, not to
mention ideology.[59] In the iconographic program for the Villa Maser, which
was conceived by Barbaro, himself the prelate and the head of the council, not
only did Pythagorean cosmology live on but so also did the cosmographic
social theory of Claudius Ptolemy, whose *Cosmographia* appeared in Bologna
and Vicenza in numerous editions between 1462 and 1477 and was continuously reedited in northern Italy throughout the sixteenth century. As has been
noted only recently by scholars:

The ptolemaic global conception of the universe . . . established the earth
with humanity at the center of everything. It ordered the planets in
regular orbits and systems around the earth, while relating each planet to
a specific social layer. This idea found particular resonance in the Church,
which viewed the world as a large hierarchical system, from God through
humans down to the lowest forms of animal life. Society was similarly
subdivided into political classes—the aristocracy, the clergy, and the
commoners—each of whom was assigned a particular task.[60]

Standing at the center of the *podere*, the villa ordered the landscape and
compartmentalized it. As a whole organism, however, it not only framed
its overall natural environment autocratically but also expressed hierarchical
structures through its internal articulation, thus signifying the claim to
hegemony. The full range of functions necessitated by agricultural estate
management converged in the *casa di villa*, which was the heart and the main
locus for the *podere*, that is to say, for the *latifundium*'s various arteries: the
country roads, the canal system, and the irrigation ditches of the agriculturally utilized *possessioni* (country estate), that in turn articulated the artistic

prospects, avenues, gardens, fruit orchards, and plantations. From this point of view, the representative *sala* likewise stood similarly at the heart of the house. As is the case with the blood vessels in the bodies of humans or animals, all the functions of the house emanated outward from the *sala*, including access to the rest of the living or utility areas along with the ventilation and lighting of them (Figure 7).[61]

According to Alberti's and Palladio's guiding principle that defined the house as a small city and the city as a large house,[62] the forum or the piazza, which was the center of the city, became comparable to the *sala*, which was the center of the villa. Consequently, the latter space was the center for the haute bourgeois representation and presence in the countryside, along with being a center for the rural *governo* and for the holy temple-precinct of the rural *arte della pace e della conservazione* (virtues of peace and values of tradition). These above-mentioned functions support the interpretation that *the villa was a substitute for the civic symbols of hegemony*, the structure of which was beginning to disintegrate in the city. The extended rural family that found shelter and a guarantee for its social health in the *casa grande* of the villa became the representation of and the model for a social order that was still intact. The feudal family that dominated the surrounding rural communities and farmhouses was the embodiment of civic rule in the countryside and in the provinces.

The *casa di villa* reproduced the architectural structures of domination in the city. The Palazzo di Ufficiatura (the Office of the Estates) and the Quartiere della Fantoria (the Seat of the Bodyguard) on the other edge of the fortifications of the Barco della Regina (see Figure 22)—where the Venetian villa's history began—corresponded to the city's administrative authorities, as did Scamozzi's *Luoghi per la Castaldia, o fattore di villa* (The Site of the Steward of the Estate or the Land Agent of the Villa). As the sanctuary and ceremonial room of the *padrone* family, however, the *sala* of the Palladian villa took on the function of the great representational rooms of the medieval municipal palaces. To quote Alberti, "Civitas philosophorum sententia maxima quaedam est domus [In the philosopher's opinion, the city is nothing more than a large house]."[63] To cite Palladio on *la città picciola*, "The city is no more than a large house and conversely the house is a small city."[64]

Accordingly, one could interpret Palladio's and Scamozzi's ideas as involving the projection of the loggias out from the villa like arms, *come braccia*, and extending into open space, which was a critical form of almost all Venetian villa buildings of the Renaissance and of the Baroque, so that "paiono raccoglier quelli, che alla casa si approssimano [they are intended to gather all those who approach the villa],"[65] In this way, all functions were directed so that all lines of power emanated from the *possessioni*, while at the same time all aesthetic interests moved toward the dominating *habitazione del padrone*. These complexes thus embraced the central axes by which the claim to domination of the *casa del padrone* was transposed from the actual building to the *podere* and even beyond that so as to extend into the uncultivated landscape as far as the eye could reach.

The *sala* was the throne of both Santa Agricoltura and of Christian Divina Sapientia. These two "patron saints" were the ones who—figuratively speaking—placed the *padrone* at their side since he was the knightly trustee of both their plans for salvation and their principles for ordering the countryside. As such, these "patrons" awarded the villa and the surrounding *podere* to him as his knightly fiefdom. For this reason, it was absolutely essential that the particular dignity of the *sala* be obtrusively manifested even on the exterior, both in practice, as in Palladio's and Scamozzi's buildings, and in architectural theory, as in the above postulates. On the main side of the *sala* were the principal entrances, or *porte principali*, of the villa, while extending in front of the *sala* was the forecourt, where in midsummer the approach of the well-laden harvest carts took place as a mythic reenactment in honor of Ceres and Bacchus, the patrons of the villa (see Cartari, Marsiglio, Ficino). The forecourt was also where, in autumn, the pompous procession of coaches and the arrival of hunting parties on horseback were staged as bourgeois substitutes for the knights' tournaments during rural festivities (especially as Doni described them in his book on villas and as they are illustrated in the wall paintings of the Venetian manor houses). Owing to its elevation, the classically dressed frontispiece towered in front of the *sala* either as a scenographically pleasing wall illustrated with models of ancient columns, Roman beams, and classical pediments or as a freestanding portico.

The whole structure was equipped with a wide staircase or ramp and Latin inscriptions, in the lettering of antiquity, that boasted of their proprietor's genius and victories, which were also conveyed by masks, trophies, festoons, Hellenistic putties, Augustan acanthus leaves, and a coat of arms, all of which carried the claim of the haute bourgeois landlords across the central avenue and into the *podere* which, as the real economic base for the feudal lifestyle of this privileged class, was then superceding the offices, the arsenal, and the Mediterranean commercial fleet of *La Serenissima*. In his section on the *casa di villa degli antichi*, Palladio openly acknowledged the architectural claim to hegemony of the *habitazione del padrone*, both in the structure of the villa and in the ancient origin of the forms expressing this concern. In writing on the ceremonious frontispiece of his villas, he declared: "Servono alla Grandezza, e Magnificenza dell' opera [They serve the grandeur and magnificence of the building]."[66]

This principle is illustrated most clearly in the Villa Maser (Figure 5), which was the chronological centerpoint and the artistic zenith of Palladio's villa designs. It hardly seems a coincidence that it was precisely the study of Palladio's villas and palaces that provoked a precocious and prescient critical conscience in the case of Goethe in 1786 and later in the case of Fritz Burger, who in 1909 was the first to present Palladio's villas monographically.[67] In his remarks on "truth and falsehood" in Palladio's works, Goethe pointed out the simultaneous coexistence of the highest artistic quality, on the one hand, with art as the representative of reactionary social norms, on the other hand. In noting that these two contrary characteristics do not necessarily exclude one another in every case but often even coincide, Hauser wrote: "Die Voraussetzungen der künstlerischen Qualität [liegen] jenseits der Alternative von politischer Freiheit und Unfreiheit [The prerequisites of artistic quality are beyond the alternatives of political freedom and nonfreedom]."[68]

When architecture illustrates so clearly the structures of authority and the relative rank of those by whom and for whom it was constructed, even the dovecotes embody power symbols through their transformation into corner projections. As was the case with the Villa Emo (Figure 23) or the Villa Maser, there was an undisguised symbolism of domination even in preceding villa designs that had already modified the crenelated corner towers of the Barco della Regina or of the Castello da Porto Colleoni (Figure 20).[69] It was not just the frontispiece, the portico, the staircase, the main entrance relief ornament, the size, and the height of the whole that made the *sala* (Figure 10) the "parte più eminente, più maestosa, e più magnifica [most important, most dominating, and most magnificent room]" of the villa, however, but rather these elements in conjunction with the painted decoration of the interior. The most noble themes of the design plan were reserved for the ceilings of the *sala* and the smaller *salotto* that accompanied it. The presently white-washed *soffitto* (ceiling) of the salon in the Villa Maser might well have been completed with Apollo's image, and on the walls one can still see the Muses with their musical instruments. They not only referred to the villa as the sober residence of conventional *agricoltura* and rural morality but also as the *nuovo parnasso*, the Academy of Fine Arts, which had found its way from the context of urban *civiltà* to the empire of rustic *virtù*. Nonetheless, broad illusionistic passages through ideal classical landscapes unfolded between the Muses. The central protagonists in the heroic landscape themes, then, were not people but rather classical Roman ruins—all of which attested to the significance of Roman architecture and to the diligence of Roman engineering.[70]

9

"Roma qvanta fvit ipsa rvina docet." The Ideal Ruins: Landscape as a Decoration for the Villa

IN SPITE OF the seemingly spontaneous, sketchlike technique used in executing them, the arrangements of ruins in the frescoes were more than a decorative idea aimed at creating fleeting effects. In 1966, two sets of engravings—one by Hieronymus Cock in 1551 and the other by Battista Pittoni in 1561—were definitively identified as the prototypes of the Villa Maser's landscape frescoes.[71] Published in Antwerp and Venice respectively, the two series, which appeared in over sixty pages, were closely related to each other both topographically and archaeologically and included accurate views of ancient Roman monuments under the title *Praecipua Aliquot Romanae Antiquitatis Ruinarum Monumenta* (On Certain Outstanding Examples of Monuments of Roman Antiquity). In their ideal landscapes for the Villa Maser, Veronese and his colleagues quoted literally from the most important passages of Cock's and Pittoni's views of Roman antiquity, which were considered totally authentic in an era prior to photographic reproduction.

Previous research, however, even that of Pallucchini in 1960,[72] was mistakenly premised on the illusionary view that the wall painting was the dominant issue. Thus, these scholars sought to disclose affinities with actual Venetian locations that the view from any Veneto villa could theoretically have presented—locations such as Lake Garda, Sirmione, the Piave valley, the Brenta valley, the Asolan mountains, Colli Euganei, or Valpolicella. According to this unreflectively materialist interpretation, the role ascribed to the classical ruins was one that was used only in a very general and ideal sense so as to elevate the real Venetian landscape through proximity to an ideal of classical antiquity that was comparable to the backdrop scenery of an open-air theater.

FIGURE 8.   Paolo Veronese, *Landscape with Ruins*, wall painting, Stanza della
Lucerna, Villa Maser, 1560–62

Yet the discovery of the Cock and Pittoni series actually reversed the assumed relationship between the real and the ideal. If measured now against the real Venetian landscape, the factual content of the Maser frescoes is very limited. These views were anything but faithful copies of the surrounding landscape; the paintings did not reproduce exact views or general panoramas of real situations. In terms of factual honesty and truthfulness to life, the character of the painted views would have meant an immediately controllable claim on reality that hardly suited the ruins' scenery, all of which demonstrated that underlying the presentation of these ruins was more a social and literary program than an aesthetic one.

The morphology of the landscapes imitated the real Venetian scenery only to the extent that the trompe l'oeil remained convincing, in other words, only up to the point where the contradiction between actual window views and painted wall openings did not appear too crude. A methodical geographical study of the picture presented of the Veneto did show[73] that the essential characteristics of the Terraferma's industrial and agrarian structure—its geomorphology, tectonics, settlement structure, hydrography, and vegetation—were incorporated into Veronese's frescoes. Nonetheless, it was not Veronese's intention to paint the individual physiognomy of particular parts of the Terraferma but rather to summarize in broad encyclopedic fashion all the above traits, thereby characterizing the Venetian landscape type only in this way. The rural appearance was generalized, not singled out; Veronese sought the general, not the particular. Through the exaggeration and the enhancement of this general concept of a rural ideal, he satisfied the demands that art theory since Alberti had presented for the justification of landscape, namely, as wall decoration in the villa.

The simulated window openings were supposed to represent the view of a rural ambience that corresponded to the theoretical postulates for the villa's ideal site, even though these aesthetic postulates were hardly satisfied by the *casa del padrone* even in the best of circumstances. This was due to the fact that the villa's economically motivated location was at the center of the agriculturally utilized *possessioni*, on a site chosen to afford the best surveillance of the rural processes of production and with easy access to all the regions of the farm. It was these considerations more than aesthetic criteria that situated the villa. *Thus the programmatic themes of the paintings, by idealizing the actual rural relationships, were meant to eliminate the contradiction between the beautiful villa and the economic villa. Here, idealization implied displacement in a very tangible sense.* Since the landscape paintings of the Venetian villas were generally enclosed in an illusionistic architectural frame, they had as much a claim to reality as did the real window views. As counterparts of the actual views, these illusory views were meant to displace the impression of the sober agrarian landscape that was marked more by a sense of economy and industry than by a sense of beauty and leisure, all of which in real life extended right up to the front gates of the villa.

Certain villa theoreticians such as Gallo and Falcone attempted to eliminate this contradiction between the beautiful villa and the economic villa by means of an inverted realization. Consequently, they advanced from the aesthetization of *agricoltura* to an aesthetization of the agricultural landscape per se. In the catalogs of scenic splendors that supplemented the elevated location of the villa, Gallo and Falcone also introduced the *campi* (the intensely well-cultivated fields) as having an aesthetic value in and of themselves that existed alongside the canonical setting of the *locus amoenus*, not to mention the views of distant mountains and sea, and of nearby hills, forests, and brushlands. By means of this aesthetic mobilization of the *campi*—within the framework of an Aristotelian aesthetic that was derived from ethics—the circle of relationships involving *utilità*, *virtù*, and *bellezza* was closed. In simplified terms, *the rationale was constructed as follows*: Profits from *agricoltura*, when elevated to a morally high-standing art, constituted wealth that was acquired virtuously by means of good and beautiful money. In the practical Aristotelian philosophy of action, virtue was a function of utility and vice versa, that is, *utilità* was a function of *virtù*. Simultaneously, then, beauty was a function both of appropriateness and of utility. *Accordingly, lands that were well cultivated in terms of* virtùs *and* utilitàs, *which were here seen as the visible manifestation of* bella agricoltura, *thus attained the dimension of beauty.*

Clearly this contrived means of rationalization remained an obscure theory derived from the refined vantage point of the urban villa *padroni* of the Cinquecento. With urban *civiltà*, the refined aesthetic demands of the city were also imparted to the countryside and to the villa. The modest villa landlord of the Quattrocento was still able to gain satisfaction from the proud panorama of his property, which encompassed well-fed herds, along with well-organized fruit orchards, vegetable beds, and cornfields. Yet, in the sixteenth century, the *padrone* sought through the villa to combine urban *civiltà* and rural *utilità*. Although the view of the *tronchi e zolle* (or the tree trunks and clods of earth, as Alberti [1966] observed in his passage on the villa, p. 194ff.) around the villa that was still enveloped by rusticity could hardly be reduced to a common factor, the envisioned ideal landscapes on the walls certainly could. The rapid diffusion of this genre amongst the northern Italian villas from the mid-sixteenth century onward demonstrated the effectiveness of this means of painted illusion for making invisible the dry economic reality of the villa, at least within the confines of the *casa del padrone*. Furthermore, these paintings also secured at the same time for the *habitazione* as *luogo privilegiato* (privileged site) a rank that rose above the lowliness of common economic interests. As with all acts of repression, the *repression of the real environment* of the villa through the ideal landscape paintings on the walls was *a largely unconscious process*. It was certainly not achieved as intentionally, for example, as analysis might otherwise lead us to believe.

The northern Italian, or Paduan, lowlands, which were bordered on the east by the Terraferma with its strong northern European and continental character, differed distinctly from the Mediterranean peninsular and insular hinterland of Italy that was south of the Apennine barrier. The nature of the northern countryside was totally "non-Italian." In the painted landscapes of the Villa Maser, formal idealization was used, and Veronese's method was a prime example of the overall development of this decorative art in the Venetian villas. Without diluting the character of the Terraferma, Veronese exaggerated the *Italianità* in his views of the countryside. He approximated them to the most typical of all Italian landscapes, namely, the campagna *Romana*. This "Italianization" of the Paduan countryside was achieved by the notable conflation of landmark elements within a limited space. In his ideal image of the Terraferma, Veronese included the multiform tectonic spectacle, the narrow juxtaposition of the changeable, interlocking, petrographic phenomena, which were characteristic of Italy south of the Apennines, particularly below Rome. The mountains—specifically the Alps to the north, the Apennines to the south—were drawn closer to each other as boundaries of the Paduan plain. Their profiles were dramatized, the dynamic of the hydrography was exaggerated, and even the relief of the inner plain was expressed more tectonically, so that in the end, the *pianura* (lowlands) appeared more like a turbulent hillscape.

The Maser landscapes attained their ideal character through an exaggeration of Mediterranean characteristics. The openness of the Paduan plain, its endless width, its often melancholic and scant horizons were sacrificed in favor of a greater richness of forms. The antagonism between continental Italy and insular Italy was eliminated in the Maser frescoes in order to reduce these two heterodox geographical terms to a common factor, that is, mainland and insular Italy. For the Italian connoisseur, the viewing of these paintings would evoke in his imagination the *convergence of two landscape experiences*: the cultivated countryside around Venice and the classical countryside around Rome. There emerged a synthesis of the Terraferma with Latium, the homeland that Veronese sought to describe in a transfigured way and the classical ideal against which he measured the altered image of the homeland.

As the figurative means of Italianization, the ruins were not just any ancient fragments, but, as it was later established, the actual views of identifiable buildings from the ancient Roman urban setting. Palladio's conception of the villa thus aimed at the reconstruction of the ancient house, and the landscapes of ruins on the walls completed this concept. The scenographic ruins defined the settings as ideal images of the ancient landscape (Figure 8). These images were not, however, considered in a general antiquarian sense but in an archaeologically accented one, since it was clearly the Roman landscape in which the magnificent villas of people like Augustus, Caesar, Hadrian, Maecenas, or Lucullus once stood, the brilliance of which the Palladian epoch sought to reawaken. In his architecture, Palladio reconstructed the building mentality of Roman antiquity.

Along the same lines as his friend Alvise Cornaro and others who wrote books on the villa, Daniele Barbaro, who was Palladio's client, reconstructed in his commentary on Vitruvius as well as in his philosophical essays the social ideals of Roman antiquity in conjunction with its artistic ones. Veronese, who was Barbaro's protégé, then added to that process the reconstruction of the ancient landscape and thus concluded the *Gesamtkunstwerk* known as the Palladian villa through the dialectical interplay of art, economics, and politics. In the villa as a total work of art, aesthetics acquired a sociopolitical dimension, while the social and the political conversely attained an aesthetic dimension. In a way similar to Giovanni da Udine, to Polidoro da Caravaggio, or to Perin del Vaga, Veronese carried the approach to antiquity as far as possible through his technique of using nervous Pompeian-like brushstrokes with background figures and comparable devices of composition and coloring.

The Palladian epoch did not yet have a precise conception of the character of villa decoration in antiquity, nor did it have a conception of the favored theme cycles of antiquity, that is, the illusionistic representation of monumental works of architecture in addition to the rendering of ideal landscapes. Only with later discoveries in the seventeenth, eighteenth, and nineteenth centuries in Rome itself as well as in the villa and spa regions around the gulf of Naples (Pompeii, Herculaneum, Baiae, Pozzuoli) was it possible to inspect directly such devices. Consequently, it was with an attitude toward imitating the painting of antiquity by using the greatest possible imitatio and in light of literary reconstructions of villa architecture in antiquity that Veronese thoroughly exhausted the two well-known passages on Roman landscape illustration in Vitruvius's *De Architectura* (VII, 5) and in Pliny's *Naturalis Historia* (XXXV).

In his Maser frescoes, Veronese did not render merely a free interpretation of the two texts on art theory, but rather a true illustration of them in which he combined Vitruvius and Pliny. Therein he elaborated to the same extent upon the theme cycle and the topology of his landscapes and differentiated them in the same manner, and with the same detail, as did the two Roman authors. A scenography that was composed of the same elements as the decorative villa landscapes in Vitruvius's and Pliny's descriptions was animated by Vitruvius's pastoral background characters, *pecora, pastores* (herds and shepherds), and was combined with Pliny's genre figures, who performed various activities. Some of these figures were entangled in comic situations—from traveling by sea or by land in boats, on donkeys, and in coaches to laboring in the *villeggiatura* alongside Pliny's fishermen, hunters, vine-dressers or near cavaliers carrying their ladies over swampy moats into the countryhouse, swaying under their sweet burden.[74]

In the Villa Maser, one could see seaside towns and ports, land reaching far into the sea as peninsulas or capes, far-stretching beaches, rivers, streams and canals, along with mountain springs, groves, deep forests, and high mountains. In addition, one could see pleasant gardens and parks, villa colonies, and loose arrangements of rural architecture in the Naples spa region. In other words, one could inspect the "portus, promunturia, litora, flumina, fontes, euripi, fana, luci, montes" of Vitruvius and the "villas et porticus et topiaria opera, lucos, nemora, colles, piscinas, euripos, amnes, litora . . . maritimas urbes" of Pliny. The Palladian villa became an almost identical reproduction of the ancient countryside through its imitative decor, namely, the wall paintings (Figure 9). In this way, the Veronese frescoes contributed to the notion of the Palladian villa what ancient frescoes had already signified for the villa of antiquity.

The Villa Maser's mock windows with their fake views apparently looked out upon the same world as did the real and painted openings of any earlier Roman villa. Through the illusionistic images in the Palladian villa, the contradiction between truth and falsehood that was later established by Goethe was partly eliminated. The ancient world that was feigned behind the gates of the villa *was false; but this was in fact the truth of the Palladian villa,* just as the anachronistic ornaments of antiquity that masked it did not present an insurmountable contradiction to its actual economic and social function. On the contrary, it was precisely the dialectical interplay within the architecture—between *historical mask* and *social reality*—that asserted the villa's aesthetic and social truth. As a continuation of the idea of *renovatio,* the villa represented an attempt to approximate the ancient villa by means of a pictorial illusion consistent with the villa's topographical ambience. In attempting to be like the ancient villa, the Palladian villa began by resembling itself.

In the frescoes of the Villa Maser, two categories of Plinian landscape theory were treated with particular conspicuity and were thereby updated. The categories involved were (1) the presentation of generic villa landscapes, that is to say, nature with views of humanity's artificial intervention in it, for example, actual villas and gardens (*villas et porticus et topiaria opera*); and (2) the staging within the landscape of everyday, unpretentious genre

FIGURE 9.   Paolo Veronese and Assistants, wall paintings with ruins and
illusionistic architecture, 1560–62, in the Villa Maser

scenes. With these decorative motifs, Veronese did not emerge as a historian, but he did interpret Pliny systems immanently. He transposed no ideal views of ancient villas into his paintings; contemporary country houses appeared in the Stanza di Bacco and in the Salotto dello Zodiaco. In one case, there is a slightly old-fashioned building, still equipped with the rudimentary forms of the Quattrocento Castello villa, such as corner towers, decorated embattlements, and a two-storied center piece that is perforated by a series of arcades so as to be an ideal *concetto* (conception) of a villa that might have been used to illustrate any contemporary villa book. In another case, one sees a country house that, according to type and composition, evidently represents a variation on the Villa Maser itself. These two villa prospects do not have the character of isolated, picturesque views, but they are integrated within the illusionary system of the landscape so that they have the same claim to reality as do the other views that are framed by *aperture finite* (simulated openings).

In addition, there appear in the landscapes contemporary decorative figures next to wholly Pompeian ones that have been idealized according to a classical standard. These figures have stepped into the role of Pliny's itinerants at sea and on land, joining his retinues of horsemen and sailing parties on excursions without having exchanged the period costumes and the everyday clothing of the sixteenth century for the heroic ancient dress. A similar updating ensued with the remaining decorative motifs. Thus, idealized reconstructions of ancient monuments in full splendor and without any apparent signs of decay also kept company with the representations of ancient debris. However, contemporary architecture such as monumental civic edifices and rural accommodations of modest dimensions, along with that of the recent past, existed harmoniously with this collection of ancient buildings. All these contradictory motifs were sheltered by the identical Roman-Venetian landscape and determined according to an ideal topography as well as in relation to an ideal temporality. This close proximity of contradictory facts, in which the principle of casuality appears to have been invalidated as in an encyclopedic diagram, determined the particular character of the realism and the claim to actuality of the scenes.

Here, there was not only the combining of two landscape manifestations that were spatially separated—Terraferma and Latium—but also a fusion of two temporarily separated epochs: the past in the form of classical antiquity and the present (the sixteenth century) as a classicist epoch. In other words, the paintings functioned both as the historical original and as its contemporary reproduction. By the manner in which the present was constantly made visible in the landscape beneath the transparent cover of history and also by the illusionistic way that placing the classical representational concept within a majestic space distanced the image from the viewer, the scenes

FIGURE 10. Andrea Palladio, Interior of Villa Rotonda, Vicenza, 1566–70

attained an extraordinary presence in comparison with the actual views through the windows. In other words, the former could lay the same claim to actuality as the latter.

In the Palladian epoch, the once-upon-a-time of antiquity was exalted as the *hic et nunc* of the modern villa. The reconstruction of the ancient rustic villa was the raison d'être for the modern *casa del padrone*, and it could be compared to a role in a classical play. The villa behaving as if it were ancient was confronted with illusionistic paintings as an incidental stage in the *villeggiatura*'s spectacle, which had been composed in classical hexameters. In this composition, the past and present, ideal time and real time, image and ideal image, were woven into an inextricable texture in which the present gained the dimension of transience and, in a quite concrete sense, the transient acquired the dimension of actuality. Thus, the decorative villa landscapes reflected two things: (1) the ideal ambience—specifically as it was demanded by contemporary theoreticians from Alberti to Scamozzi—for the existential space of the *casa di villa* and (2) the ideal conception of the historical landscape into which the humanist imagination of the sixteenth century could project the villas of Roman antiquity.

Even in its formal detail, the Palladian villa followed the literary physiognomy of Plinian country houses as envisioned by Palladio and the contemporary dealers in antiquities on the basis of residual elements of ancient villas that were then graphically recorded, excavated, and surveyed. Internally, the Palladian villa was decorated with the ancient country house ornamentation that Veronese and Palladio had extracted from literary sources. As ideally reconstructed in the Villa Maser, the ancient villa diverged quite notably from the building that was confronted by modern archaeology much later, as in Boscoreale. Nevertheless, the Renaissance villa was closely related to the latter in its essential form.

The Maser frescoes represented the ancient landscape in two dimensions. On the one hand, there was the ambience in which the ancient villas were joined together to become magnificent colonies that structured and dominated the landscape. On the other hand, there was the decorative ambience that created the ideal painted landscapes in the interiors of the same villas. The landscapes dreamed in the Palladian villas, however, were noticeably different from the ancient landscape, both as it actually existed and as it was then painted, particularly in the use of their main leitmotiv, namely, the ruin. In the ideal image of the ancient world that the Palladian landscapes conveyed, history was not affirmed as an unproblematic factor, but historicity was represented as a constantly enacted process. In other words, the dimension of time was turned into a problem of fate. The ancient world did not appear as it formerly was but as it subsequently became. Perhaps it existed in the sense once described by Heidegger: "The oldest of the ancient follows us in our thoughts, and yet it also comes toward us."

Furthermore, this narration of history with its acknowledgment of the fall of the ancient world also unmistakably features pastoral and melancholic characteristics that signify the bucolic lament over the loss of innocence, over the decline of the *aetes aurea* (golden age), and over the impossibility of reestablishing it. To a large extent, then, the ancient relics appeared in a condition of picturesque decay with the proud orders collapsed, the columns broken, the pediments and capitals smashed, the brick cores of the walls robbed of their splendid marble mask and widely covered with vegetation. In this state, with the forums, arenas, and avenues overgrown so as to serve as a pasture for sheep and goats, *the ruin became half nature once again absorbed by the vivacious green countryside* (Figure 8).

Basically, the same idea was concealed behind the depiction of ruins as testimonies to the Roman past as was lurking behind Pirro Ligorio's quite unusual desire to transform a fountain in the garden of the Cardinal's Villa d'Este in Tivoli (begun by Ippolito II d'Este shortly before the Villa Maser was begun and completed only decades later) into a seemingly scenographic miniature reproduction of ancient Rome. This so-called *Rometta* was a compressed compendium of classical Roman ruins, which included the Pantheon, *Dea Roma*, Capitoline Lupus, Navicella, the Obelisk, and an allegorical figure representing the Tiber River. The decorative painting of ruins in the Roman facsimile embodied an idea that was already determined by the planners for the villas of the imperial era of Roman antiquity. It was here that the phenomenon of simulated historicism emerged; the Palladian and Ligorian villas were not Renaissance imitations of ancient originals but rather *sixteenth-century imitations of ancient imitations*.

The Roman imperial villa itself already represented a lost ideal that was projected back into a historical period that had long since passed. For, the Roman villa was inspired by an idealized view of Greece as the basis for all the arcadian dreams of flight from the city, of escape from the world, and of weariness with civilization. Thus, it was already Roman antiquity that combined the art of the villa with historical self-consciousness. The *tertium comparationis* (comparative medium) for the Villa Maser as well as for the Villa d'Este was the ancient Villa Hadriana.[75] In its iconographic program, the latter anticipated in exemplary manner the melancholic and arcadian traits that were later to determine the social dimension of the Renaissance villa. As another author has already observed:

> [The villas] in Italy will form an ideal Greece, as every distinguished person will want to live like a Hellenistic prince and will want to possess at least the images of the shrines around which the Greeks lived. In

horticulture, the appropriate composition of Greek motifs was called *ars topiaria*. The best pictorial representation is in the bedroom of Boscoreale. . . . The *ars topiaria* is demonstrated in monumental dimensions by Hadrian's villa in Tivoli with its hallowed valleys of Tempe and Canopus, with holy islands, Lykeion, an academy and the colored hall, all of which were named after respective buildings and groves in Greece, even though they were not exact copies.[76]

In the sixteenth century, the ideal was displaced from Greece to Rome by taking a historical leap. Now Rome became the "promised land" and Roman antiquity the arcadian period that was simultaneously celebrated within and elevated above history as an ideal form of existence. The adjuration of the Latin monuments guaranteed to the Renaissance villa its engagement with the spirit and the form of the ancient villa, as well as with the ancient mode of life. By means of garden decoration and frescoes, the Villa d'Este and the Villa Maser each became an ideal Rome in miniature. Alongside, or even prior to, literature, the ruin was the sole authentic proof of an ancient "essence." Hence, the ruin functioned both as a melancholic symbol for the decline of all historical monuments and as a powerful call to restore that historical moment. The path back to a Roman past bore the Latin road signs of ancient literature and was bordered by the crumbling remnants of antiquity.

A revealing title appeared on a large sheet featuring an illustration of Roman palatial ruins from Marten van Heemskerck's Roman sketchbook of around 1535: "Roma Qvanta Fvit Ipsa Rvina Docet" ("Even the Ruins Still Give Evidence of Rome's Former Stature").[77] A few years later the same programmatic statement was chosen as a motto for the frontispiece of *Terzo Libro*, Sebastiano Serlio's architectural treatise, first published in 1540 in Venice. Heemskerck's Palatine view offered an entry into one of the landscape ruins in the Villa Maser via the detour of a 1550 etching from the series on Roman antiquities by Hieronymus Cock entitled "Rvinarivm Palatii Maioris Cvm Parte Septizoni Prospectvs" ("View of the Ruins of the Large Palace on the Palatine with a Part of the Septizonium"). The Latin motto about the ruin as proof of Rome's former historical stature could also have stood atop the narrative about the fate and honor of Roman architecture that Veronese wrote on the walls of the Villa Barbaro. As transmitted in three stages (by Heemskerck in 1535, by Cock in 1550, and by Veronese in 1560), the Palatine view can be literally traced to the landscape paintings in the *salone* of the Villa di Rovero in Caerano, where frescoes were executed during the 1570s in direct succession to the Villa Maser.

10

Architectural and Social Ideal: The Ideal State, the Ideal City, the Ideal Villa, the Villa as Social Model

In THE PALLADIAN epoch, Roman ruins were neither dry historical facts nor merely an academic organizing thread for a doctrinaire aesthetic system. Palladio saw in the residual components of classical architecture an indication of the moral and social qualities of Roman antiquity. A study of the ruins paved the way for an understanding of the *virtus Romana*, and this recognition apparently struck him deeply. The *virtus Romana* was, however, a political and social ideal as well as a moral and utopian one. If architecture were to be endowed with an ethical dimension in the classicist art of construction during the sixteenth century, then the ancient ruin was an exemplary way to mediate the gap between architecture and social demands, between architecture and ideology, so that architecture indeed emanated from ideology. In his preface to the first and second books of his *Quattro Libri* of 1570, Palladio wrote the following along these lines:

> . . . rendono anco nelle grandissime ruine loro chiaro, & illustre testimonio della virtù, e della grandezza Romana: in modo che ritro vandomi io grandemente esercitato, & infiammato ne gli ottimi studij di questa qualità di virtù, & havendo con gran speranza messo in lei tutti i miei pensieri.

> [. . . as grandiose ruins, the ancient buildings still give a clear and fine indication of the virtue and grandeur of the Roman nation, to such an extent that the study of these qualities of virtue have repeatedly fascinated and enthused me; I directed all my thoughts to them with the greatest of expectations.][78]

The core of the Palladian theory of architecture was formed by the integration of *art and science* as expressed in dialectical terms: the aesthetization of

50

FIGURE 11. Benedetto Caliari, *Garden of a Villa near Bergamo*, late sixteenth century, Academia in Carrara

science and the scientification of aesthetics. The union of *ars* and *doctrina* brought to the fore the concept of the moral (or, more specifically, the social) virtue within art. This central maxim of the humanist Giangiorgio Trissino's Vicentine Academy, which impressed the young Palladio, ultimately determined the direction of the Vicentine Accademia Olimpica as well, which Palladio cofounded in his maturity in 1555. The study of mathematics as a fundamental science stood at the center of the Olympian Academy by setting the standards not only for all the other sciences but also for the arts, especially architecture. One sought the ultimate and eternal values in the art of construction, while the other sought the *verità delle cose* (the truth of things) by translating mathematical theories, ideal arithmetical proportions (*rationes*), symmetry, and spherical trigonometry into architectural practice. In the Palladian era, the concepts of *verità*, *bellezza*, and *virtù* spread as a coherent system through the prevailing conceptions of art as well as those of science. *With an exact adherence to the laws of the true, the beautiful, and the good in mathematics, architecture also became an emanation of the true, the beautiful, and the morally good.*

When considered as absolute arts, music, mathematics, and architecture form a triad of reciprocal dependence and determination. The sixteenth-century interrelationships between musical and architectural theory were in turn based on the system of proportions previously mentioned. Similarly, there was a connection that had already found a place during antiquity and in the Middle Ages and it was reestablished in the sixteenth century, as has already been mentioned. This was the linkage between the *harmonic concept of order in the cosmology* of Pythagoras and the *cosmographic social theory* of Claudius Ptolemy, in which social harmony and social interdependencies became synonyms for and representations of astronomic relationships and their corollary of a strictly hierarchical notion of society. The same hierarchically and harmonically orientated laws of composition seemed to determine the construction of the universe, of a piece of music, of a mathematical deduction, of a political system, of a political group, of the family as the smallest social unit and root of all larger ones, and finally also the structure of a palace, of a church, of a villa, or even of an entire city.

Through their illumination, the good and the evil heavenly stars supposedly reflected the social habitat of man on earth. In this way, *the social microcosm appeared as the reflection of the heavenly macrocosm.* The social constraints of the system were projected into the extraterrestrial sphere and were thus simultaneously rationalized and legitimized. Only the sage or the magician were privy to the eternal paths of the constellations, which seemingly regulated the unending path of society and its history—yet only as a *circulus vitiosus* (vicious circle), not as *progressio*. Parallel to the awakening of knowledge in the natural sciences, the chimerical hallucinations of superstition through astrology nonetheless continued to mark the path from the earthly here and now to the heavenly everywhere and always, and these tendencies had to bear the blame when enlightenment was condemned as heresy.

During the Renaissance, astronomy and astrology remained almost identical facets of the same coin, which suited the Church quite well. If it had to choose between the plague and cholera, the Church preferred to choose the heathen nuisance of astrology, which was annoying only as competition, not because of the qualities that it held in common with the Church. The nature of religious faith and its related virtue of blind subordination to the constraints of a religious order were not appreciated as such but were received almost voluntarily. There were also constraints of divine providence, which, ideally, conditioned humans to accept their own uncritical subjugation to the strictures of an authoritarian social order. Architecture stood at the intersection of the cosmological, the astrological, and the social perspectives. The social utopias of the sixteenth and seventeenth centuries were advanced by the architectural and urban utopias of the fifteenth century. The treatises by Filarete and Francesco di Giorgio Martini from the fifteenth century were dedicated to architecture and town planning, but at the same time they also delineated a social dream. Sforzinda was not only the utopia of an architectural formation but also of a social order. Conversely, Tommaso Campanella's famous *Città del Sole* (City of the Sun) was not merely a utopian social construction but also an architectural one as well. The ideal state and the ideal city were two faces of Janus's head, both of which looked in the same direction. Architecture always had a social foundation, while society always had an architectural foundation. Criticism of the one was always mediated by criticism of the other. Theoretical demands in architecture would be incomplete without a carefully considered social utopia, just as a social postulate would only be a theoretical half measure without an architectural ideal. In the Renaissance and after, a new architecture always implied a new society and a new society always implied a new architecture.

Yet whenever social utopia led in antiquity to the most liberal of all liberties—that is, anarchy—there was always a social dream without architecture. Diogenes inhabited a barrel; cynics such as Aristipp had no other shelter than the continually changing and coincidental hostels of the itinerant; and in his biting satire entitled *The Birds*, Aristophanes even banished the cynics Euelpides and Peisthetairos to a cuckoo's nest. When utopia became framed, however, either by a reactionary conceptual order, as with Plato, or by an anticipatory one, as with Filarete and Campanella, then the proximity to architecture was more than a metaphoric one. It was expressed in literal images so that the social organism became the

construction of state or humanist architecture, while individual members of
the built architecture served as images of the many-membered social organism. As Ernst Bloch has pointed out, there is in Plato's *Politeia* and in his
Nomoi a conservative tripartite class society that is stratified according to the
schema of Spartan helots (peasants), *spartiates* (soldiers), and the Council of
the Old *Geruisa* (regents). All of this is done in architectural terms, as Bloch
notes, so that "humans are plinths, walls, and windows, in which everyone
is only at liberty to be supporting, protecting, or illuminating in the
construction of the members."[79]

Leone Battista Alberti dealt with these issues in a comparable manner in
his architectural treatise, which is of equal historical value for architecture
and for society; the architectural utopia was merely the other side of a social
utopia. Alberti did not simply call for a civil architecture that was differentiated according to the rank of the inhabitants concerned or, as the case may
be, of the clients involved. This entailed a precise hierarchy of architectural
forms corresponding to the social status of the prince, the royalty, the haute
bourgeois, the merchant, the craftsman, the peasant, and the day laborer.
Furthermore, his architectural understanding also ordered the world in a
greater interrelationship with respect to the measures of the contractor and
the plumb line of the master builder. As such, humanity, the family, the
house, the city, and the state were all reciprocal reflections of each other.
Just as *civitas* was the image of the family and the societal was the image of
the *domus*—*domus pusilla urbs* (the house as a small city)—so the architectural
appearances were the images of social ones: "Civitas maxima domus,
domus minima civitas [Civilization on the grandest scale is a home, while
the home is the minimal starting point for civilization]." Palladio adopted
this same position in his *Quattro Libri* of 1570: "La città una casa grande, la
casa una città piccola" (Book 2, p. 12). Yet he was unable to realize his
conception of the ideal city anywhere in a new establishment. This achievement was granted only to his student Scamozzi in Palmanova.

The villa, however, provided a surrogate for the ideal city. Close relationships existed between the ideal city and the ideal villa, and the relationships stretched from the location of the Palladian country house to its
pictorial decor. The interrelation between the villa as a scaled-down city and
the ideal city as a large villa became visible in the ornamentation program
for the Villa Maser (Figure 6). What Campanella was to formulate later in
his *Civitas Solis* as a utopia was here made concrete in a series of paintings.
In Campanella's treatise, the urban organism was the image of the world's
body, of the cosmic organism. This was symbolized in the planetarian
circular streets of the city. Just as the stars revolved around the sun, so the
streets circulated around a Mons Virtutis, a Mons Olympus, or a Mons

Musarum—depending on the given interpretation. The hill bore the solar shrine on its peak. Seven holy lamps were suspended inside the temple of the sun, however, dedicated as they were to the seven astrological planets. *Locus amoenus, paradiso terrestre, sito delle Muse*—the contemporary metaphors for the villa all converged at Parnassus, the site of the Muses. The Muses were indeed the guardians of the harmonic order of the cosmic spheres and they escorted the heavenly bodies on their orbits. As has been suggested already, the Muses, the music of the spheres, the canonic keys, and the planets themselves constituted the exchangeable parts of a closed system that extended from the thought of Pythagoras to that of Boethius. The seven lamps at the center of Campanella's solar state were thus merely a different expression of what the seven painted planetarian deities represented on the ceiling of the Salotto del Zodiaco at the Villa Maser. Paintings of the Muses as well also had a secure place in Campanella's cosmographic ideal city. At the time of its classical formulation in theory during the fifteenth and sixteenth centuries, the ideal city remained an unrealizable utopia (particularly if one disregards the few examples of Palmanova, Sabbioneta, or Granmicheli in southern Italy, the latter of which was a late echo of Campanella's *Città del Sole*). It was, then, in the villa of the sixteenth century that the concept of the ideal city found realization, even if it was only partial. One of the two patrons of the Villa Maser, Daniele Barbaro's younger brother, Marcantonio, personally embodied the connection between the villa and the ideal city. Around 1560, he was in charge of the construction of the Villa Maser. Together with Palladio's student Vincenzo Scamozzi, Marcantonio Barbaro was decisively involved in a dual capacity as architectural dilettante and Venetian civil servant with the conception and layout of the ideal radial city of Palmanova toward the end of the sixteenth century.

The vision of an ideal city considered in relation to the planets, which had already been obscurely indicated in Plato's *Nomoi* (779), found complete conceptual clarity in the iconology of the villa and that of the ideal city of the sixteenth century. The painting on the ceiling of the *salotto* was of Divina Sapientia (Santa Ragione), which towered above the center of the Villa Maser and was synonymous with divine providence, the fundamental root of all existence and the axis around which the planetary gods rotated. In Campanella's *Città del Sole*, which was inspired by Plato, the spiral orbits had the names of the planets and led to the temple of the highest being, namely, of superordinate reason, which, after Copernicus's scientific insights, now fused with the image of the sun itself. The seven planets that embellished the dome of Campanella's temple of the sun were, however, identified with *virtù magica* (celestial virtue). For Campanella, it was the same social *qualità di virtù* that Palladio associated with *vera architettura* along with the study of the ancient, ideally proportioned ruins that were referred to at the beginning of the *Quattro Libri*.

Concomitantly, this transfer of mathematical, cosmological laws of proportion to the architecture of the Palladian epoch by no means occurred as a separate aesthetic development. Mathematical, architectural, and social proportions were seen as a unified entity that was covered by the notion of mathematical, architectural, and social truths or norms. These scholarly, artistic, and social norms in turn were determined by a divinely established and therefore unchangeable hierarchical order in pursuit of perpetuity. This order became increasingly deformed in political terms through the "domination by too few over too many" right up to the age of the bourgeois revolutions in France and in the United States (which, after all, rang the death knell for the Baroque as a social entity and as an extension of the Renaissance). *Vera architettura* became the image of the true and just society. Consequently, a just society could only produce architectural forms that were adequate to its scholarly and artistic notions of the truth. This was where the hermeneutic role of the ruin was situated, where the social justification for the committed study of the remnants of ancient buildings were founded, and finally where was located the "mania for ruins" to which Palladio had subscribed on behalf of his epoch (with the remarks "grandemente esercitato, e infiammato [grandly forceful and impassioned]." The reconstruction of the ancient house was synonymous with the reconstruction of the ancient social order. Conversely, the reconstruction of the ancient familial structure as a necessary social norm that had created the ancient house as its shelter and its image was itself formed and determined by the ancient house.

In the preface to the third book of his *Vitruvian Commentary* of 1556, Daniele Barbaro justified his exposition of the theory of proportions as "a ritrovar la verità delle cose [in order to find absolute truth]" and "divina è la forza de'numeri tra se con ragione comparati" [divine force of numbers with comparative rules]." As such, he did not merely have architecture in mind, he also advocated a deified notion of order and truth for society in general. The ruin thus provided the opportunity to trace this concept of proportion and order in a way that was independent of the frequently fragmentary or corrupt transmission of ancient texts. This way was also independent of Vitruvius's architectural system, which merely confined itself to aesthetics and was consequently increasingly devalued as well as relativized in writings from Alberti to Cornaro through Barbaro and Palladio up to Scamozzi. In this regard, the ongoing criticism of Vitruvius was also apparently based on the lack of a sustained formation leading to a social theory. In the Palladian epoch, the study of ruins was a key to understanding the social

FIGURE 12. Petrarch's country residence in Argua, near Padua in the Euganeic hills, fourteenth-century structure with sixteenth-century villa loggia added

constitution of the ancient world. The paintings of ruins on the walls of Palladio's villas did not just demonstrate to the contemporary viewer the artistic truth of antiquity but also the social truth of antiquity that served as the basis for all that the Palladian villa represented.

Already in the fourteenth century during the period immediately preceding the ascendancy of classical humanism and the Italian Renaissance, ruins signified an essential part of the dream landscape in literature. For sensitive spirits such as Boccaccio or Petrarch, ruins awoke more than a mere diffused nostalgia along with elegiac feelings, which were bound up with the irretrievable loss both of innocence and of happiness because of the demise of the "organic" and coherent world in an imagined, earlier paradisiac age "free" of conflict. This presumed happiness transfigured melancholic memories and made of the past a "golden age." As such, this nostalgic frame of mind endured into the nineteenth century, when the young Goethe visited the Museo Maffeinano in Verona and, deeply moved by his first direct encounter with works from antiquity in their original surroundings, wrote in his *Italienische Reise* on 16 September 1786: "Der Wind, der von der Gräbern der Alten herweht, kommt mit Wohlgerüchen wie über einen Rosenhügel [The wind that blows from the graves of the ancients bears a fragrance as if it came over a rose-hill]."[80]

Ruins stimulated a well-directed historical consciousness in Petrarch and Boccaccio and formed the beginning stage for an invocation of the great spirits of ancient culture. As has been observed elsewhere:

> Petrarch informs us of a frame of mind that was divided between the classical and the Christian. He tells us how he and Giovanni Colonna often climbed up the colossal vaults of Diocletian's hot springs. There in the pure air, in deep silence, in the center of the panorama, they talked together where, with a view of historical ruins surrounding them, Petrarch pleaded for antiquity while Giovanni argued for the Christian era. They then spoke about philosophy and the discoverers of the arts.[81]

Poggio provided the impulse in his *Ruinarum urbis Romae descripto* (Description of the Ruins of the City of Rome) for an academic critique of the ancient remains, which took into consideration the written sources based on ancient literature and Latin inscriptions. He chose the Venus and Roma Temple as his favorite place for meditating and in his daydreams the old walls evoked encounters with some of the greatest Roman orators, such as Cicero, Crassus, and Hortensius.

11

The Villa as "Negative Utopia": History as Ideology in the Works of Francesco Colonna, Niccoló Machiavelli, and Tommaso Campanella

IN THE EIGHTEENTH chapter of Colonna's *Hypnerotomachia Polifili I* (The Dream of Polifilo), which was first published in 1499 in Venice, the contemplation of the ruin was widened from being a one-dimensional antiquarian interest to being a complete historical concept with numerous dimensions. The view of the Roman world extended far beyond the backdrop of historicism, which terminated with a list of "great" men, chronologically fixed facts, and an inventory of cultural remnants. Colonna understood history within a hierarchical, metaphysical framework and perceived the ruin as an "antichità generale quasi metafisica." Passage into the historic world of the Romans did not stop with a lamentation over its decline but rather led to the promise that the Golden Age would rise again and ended with an appeal to commence its reconstruction at once.

Yet this particular reconstruction of antiquity simultaneously proceeded with a transcendence of history altogether. The historical and philosophical stance aims at extracting the quintessence of history, to grasp the higher meaning "beyond" history, thus legitimating the activity of the historian in the present. Great men and deeds of the past were not extolled but instead brought up-to-date in light of current social interests. The cause and simultaneous effect of this generalized and *metaphysical* notion of history was a social ideal. The architecture of this ideal appeared to rise from the same pedestal as did the social utopias that the Renaissance and the early Baroque had brought forth with Thomas More in 1516 and Tommaso Campanella in 1623. Appearances are deceptive, however. Colonna's ideal ultimately

59

recoiled into resignation. For Colonna it was not so much a matter of constructing a new world but rather a case of reconstructing an old one. Colonna's social imagination attempted to square the circle and for this reason he had to fail. The problem of this apparently utopian notion of history and of a notion of utopia that seemed to focus on history was that the utopia and history stood in the way of each other.

The protrusion of this "desired period" into the past, instead of the projection of it into the future, left utopia's goal behind. Concerning utopian thought, the alteration of what exists is initially focused on what might be possible, not on what was once possible. After all, what used to be has caused the hopelessness of what is. Hence, in Colonna's thought *there was no dialectical relation between history and utopia.* Both canceled each other without forming a third entity or something new, something that might have stood above both. On the contrary, this line of thought led to an incomplete, fragile, and unstable architecture, since decayed ruins cannot be reconstructed. And if complete demolition had been decided on and if, thereupon, a conservative consciousness had forced the faithful reproduction of the old forms within a newly reconstructed framework, then the result could only be an imitation of what was not the original itself. The social "architecture" of the villa is actually of the latter kind. The sisterly union of social ideal and political historicism produced only a "negative utopia." The parallel to the villa as a historical idea and as an embodiment of ideology was the "villa as sham utopia." *In its emancipatory stance this bogus utopia ultimately had to fail, as it did not seek support for new freedoms by superceding old constraints but rather imagined salvation as a return to the "empire of order," in which order is so overpowering and self-evident that the alternative social liberation specified by utopian thought is not even contemplated—indeed cannot be contemplated.*

In the above-noted section of Colonna's book *Polia,* the allegorical incorporation of antiquity, the hero Polifilo is on his way through the gardens and through the countryside of his dreamworld, a gigantic field of ruins. In the Venetian first edition, this scene was illustrated by a woodcut that anticipated the style and mood of the scenes of ruins on the walls of Palladian villas. In this woodcut were the debris of peristyles and basilicas, of fragments from architraves, of shafts and other architectural elements, all of which were overgrown by bushes and by the Mediterranean heraldic trees, as well as by laurels, cypresses, and plane trees. The only remaining thing was an obelisk (which also later reoccurred in numerous frescoes of the Villa Maser) that was united with the figure of a tree to form an expressive group. Polifilo and Polia were engulfed in the contemplation of this image, with Polifilo listening and looking and Polia looking and explaining, while both were caught up in "the magnificence, like children in a fairy tale."[82]

The social ideal that the walk through the ruins evoked in Polifilo was not sustained, however, by the social hopes of approaching fortunes but was rather fed by the reminiscences of past fortunes. The inhabitant of *this idealized image was neither a contemporary individual nor a "new" person.* Instead, he was the exemplary figure of antiquity, that is, *he was the "old" human.* Hope was not focused on the near future but on that which had long passed, on that which had already been betrayed. What nourished this embittered hope was the sourness of reaction. Without being tempered by the salts of utopia, this historical empire of shadows was enlivened only by the shadow genii of history, who are as transient as their home in the papery graves of historiography. It was thus that Polifilo's social imagination had passed by just like the history with which it had identified itself, and with just as little "substance" as the latter. For, as Max Horkheimer has observed in a noteworthy critique:

> History considered per se has no reason; it is not a "substance" however it might be constituted. Neither is it a "spirit" to whom we should bow down, nor a "power" in itself. . . . No one is either called to life or killed by "history"; neither does history pose tasks or solve them. Only real people act to overcome obstacles and they alone are able to reduce individual or general suffering. . . . History's pantheistic act of independence from a homogeneously substantial being is nothing but dogmatic metaphysics.[83]

In Hegel's idealistic system, for which Horkheimer's criticism was intended, this dogmatic concept of history as "absolute" and as "metaphysical" remains the same as it was in the case of Colonna, for whom antiquity was seen as an ideal, thus becoming an idealist concept of history with a meaningful "entity" fossilized into the dogma of "antichità generale quasi metafisica." For this reason, Hermann Bauer was only partially justified in writing the following about the scenes of the ruins in the *Hypnerotomachia*:

> Here the meaning of the ruin was concerned less with transcience and its supercession and more with the chance of the hermeneutic and the possibility to advance to the ahistorical domain of the golden era by means of this hermeneutic. . . . The ruin [is a] timeless symbol that promises and indicates a larger state of affairs. There is no principal difference between this antiquity as an ideal and as a utopia.[84]

Nevertheless, Bauer did recognize the fact that behind the Renaissance mania for ruins was always the flash of a social fantasy, a social "ideal." This ideal, however, did not "surmount transcience" but sought instead to immortalize the past by actualizing it. Indeed, the ideal of antiquity that was documented by the paintings of ruins, by contemporary archaeology, and ultimately even by the villa itself, was a parallel to the Renaissance ideal of utopia, yet both social ideas moved in quite opposite directions. The arcadian dream of the ruin and of the villa, for which an idealized antiquity supplied the basis of its meaning, was the reverse side of the utopian dream in this period.

The countryside of "Arcadia," in which the villa was situated, and the countryside of "Utopia," in which the Città del Sole was located, were further from each other than the "Old World" was from the "New World." The latter's so-called discovery in the epoch of Columbus, Vasco da Gama, Cão, Díaz, Cabrilho, Magalhães, and Vespucci stood in more than a superficial relation to the development of the grand social utopias of the Renaissance.

Underlying the social fantasy of Colonna and that of the villa culture was evidently the "theory of the unchanging nature of man," which had determined Machiavelli's system. As such, the antithesis of Machiavelli's system on the one side and Bacon's, More's, and Campanella's on the other was reflected in the antithesis of arcadia and utopia. It hardly seems coincidental that we are indebted to Machiavelli, who was a firm proponent of the *villeggiatura*, for an unequivocal definition of the "negative utopia" program that simultaneously acted as a cause and an effect of the villa. In his *Discorsi* of 1531, Machiavelli wrote the following:

> Wise men tend not to say without thought or reason that whoever intends to see into the future should look into the past, for all things on earth have always had a similarity with the past. It is because these things have been accomplished by humans who continually possess and have always had the same passions; consequently the result must ever be the same.[85]

In order to counter those who had refused to toe the line of this reactionary concept of the past's projection into the future, Machiavelli based his argumentation on the seemingly incontestable scientific observation that those who opposed his view may as well act "as if the sky, the sun, the elements, and human beings were now different in motion, form, and strength from what they had been in former times."[86]

One would even suspect an anticipation of the genial thought of the "archetype" underlying Machiavelli's considerations were it not for the actual presence of Claudius Ptolemy's cosmographic social ideal. In his *Politeia* and in his *Nomoi*, Plato oriented his concept of a three-caste society to the stars and based it on a historical model from Sparta. Subsequently, Machiavelli legitimated his conservative concept of the state by means of the eternal path of the heavenly bodies and by means of the "eternal," therefore inescapable, path of history as an "essence" that moves in cyclical terms. To Ptolemy, the world had appeared as a hierarchically structured system's motion, which occurred within a tightly ranged "freedom" and was determined astrologically by the movement of the stars. Consequently, the Church could define the content of all political activity as a conservation of the ever invariable division of people into three castes. Thus, *the conservative social ideal of the villa shared this major factor with Machiavelli's social ideal, namely, a view of the past as simultaneously the basis and the already anticipated aim of future changes.*

It is not surprising that the Renaissance utopians spoke out unequivocally against Machiavelli and Machiavellianism. Campanella accused Machiavelli of seeing only the evil motives of human deeds, only the dark side of human nature. To More and to Campanella, people did not appear to be fundamentally evil by nature. On the contrary, they were of the opinion that man only became evil "by involvement in earthly institutions, above all with property."[87] The utopian movement bore the motto *Property is at fault*[88] on its banner, since the perversion of religion into a mere instrumental means of political and ideological influence in the Machiavellian sense was deeply repugnant to this movement. Campanella, who like More was a Catholic of idealist, arch-Christian observance, complained about how the Machiavellian politicians used religion "merely as the art of domination."[89]

Taken in a narrower sense, this reproach also applied to Alvise Cornaro's efforts and to those of the other villa ideologists to raise agriculture to the level of Santa Agricoltura, thus establishing themselves as omnipotent demiurges who not only donated newly cultivated land to the "Lord God" superior but also provided devout souls as well. This very manipulation of faith struck the utopians as an abuse of religion in the service of political power. For, if transfiguration toward the religious is rooted in the memory of archaic acts of compulsion, then this move belongs to the most important prerequisites for the socialization of humans. This is precisely where Horkheimer recognized a "social aptitude" that goes back to the archmemory of such cultic acts of compulsion as the sacrifice of the firstborn, rituals of castration, and other religious acts by which humans were made "sociable" at the beginning of history.[90]

That which was transformed into the cynical via Machiavelli—the theory of power and its preservation as the theory of the state and its preservation—and that which took on the traits of pathos and moralizing with utopians such as More and Campanella became located exactly at the center between both of them in villa ideology, which represented, so to speak, the line of conformist reason. Cornaro's and Barbaro's concept of society was neither as insidious as that of Machiavelli nor as good and admirable as that of Campanella or More. These ideas were neither forced completely into the iron mold of Machiavelli's "power politics" as simply politics of the state nor completely liberated on behalf of the golden formations of More's and Campanella's social ideal. *The villa's social domain was not reduced to a conscious and therefore cynical idolatrization of the "empire of utility," but neither did the villa's gate open onto the "domain of freedom" as had been envisioned by utopians.* The villa's "empire of order," like the irrational order of the countryside that was rationalized by the villa, was the geometric means between the empire of the *Principe* and the empires of Utopia, Città del Sole, or Nova Atlantis.

Both contemporary fantasies, the progressive one of utopia and the regressive one of *negative utopia*, took the city (with its changed modes of income, its accommodation of wealth, its resulting development of large-scale manufacturing and other new means of production that were free of guilds within the city) as the point of departure for their considerations. The utopians complained that power was becoming less and less based on sovereign titles and inherited rights, that positions of power depended less and less on the previous standards that regulated who became a governor or a master artisan. Accordingly, it was exactly here that the conception of villa ideology started. Utopia, however, left this lamentable state of affairs behind as a historical one and therefore as one capable of being surmounted. Rather than conserving the old order, utopians attempted to construct a transformed "new world" and a "new" society founded on this knowledge. Wherever "the disposal of humans and their labor" had become "more and more identical with wealth as the ownership of labor"[91] was precisely where the utopians wanted to begin the transformations.

However, villa ideology transferred the archimage of the patriarchal figure, with all his historical "rights," to the countryside and to the villa. Moreover, the very disposal of human labor power, which was increasingly guaranteed by the monopolistic ownership of the means of labor, played a decisive role. Contrary to this development, the utopians' avowed aim was a radical upheaval within the conditions of ownership, in which (to quote Horkheimer) "they were conceptually designing a Communist society whose realization in a fantastic way appeared possible to them by contemporary means."[92] They did not project the contemporary world onto a past and unreal one but onto a sphere of existence that was already tenable even though it had not yet been experienced. Thomas More displaced his Utopia to a distant island in the vast ocean; Campanella located his Città del Sole at the center of Ceylon. Here, one could almost speak of a concrete utopia.

If, as in Palladio's villas, the same landscape of ruins removed reality as it had in Polifilo's dreamworld, then the same intention underlay Colonna's novel, namely, the transcendence of the real and present world by means of the unreal and past countryside of a *negative utopia*. Submergence within the supposed salvation of ancient history, which was misunderstood as the emanation of all hopes for a golden age, was to help people forget a hopeless present. But to the degree that it was oriented "backward," the social ideal was the opposite of utopia, even as it attempted to resemble the historical negation of utopia.

Within the ideology of the villa, the strict and frequently rationalized method for making connections to history amounted to the perfection of history. Social models that had a "former life" and that had been legitimated by their historical claims provided the support for the authority-directed social order of the Renaissance villa. One has to ask oneself whether this urge to "internalize" and to perfect the historical totality cannot in the end be explained as a transposition of the archimage of the father (with his "historical rights") into the social totality of the villa. History, seen in this light, becomes the history of the "alter ego" in much the same way that the archetype of the father was coupled with the ideal dream of the *aetes aurea* that was projected back onto Roman antiquity. This largely uncritical relation to history that was consistently turned into its glorification formed the philosophical and historical raison d'être of the villa ideology.

One therefore also has to ask oneself whether or not it is the case that social practice in the countryside was reflected in social theory, a social practice based on a pious, subconsciously traditionalized orientation toward a hierarchical urban class structure that became an image of the "wholesome" authority-fixated and extended family of the countryside. Here, an uncritical philosophy of history, negative social theory, and reactionary social practices all appear to be arranged together in a fatal manner. The *padrone* of the villa, in the role of the ancient Roman *pater familias*, thus resembled himself. Conversely the haute bourgeois family patriarch of the Renaissance found his identity in the role of the villa magnate of antiquity, who in turn was seen as the legitimate successor of the "archfather," who was described in the Old Testament and who thus possessed the *auctoritas sacra*. The realization of an apparently new social order thus represented itself within the Renaissance villa as a social order that, via rational speculation, could be approached only by means of a "discovered" old order, one that had been found in history.

In Colonna's novel, as well as in the paintings of ruins in the Palladian villas, the fixation with antiquity, the incantation of the ruin, the passage through history into dreams of fortune and of existence in a social paradise (all of which assumed legitimation through the *auctoritas historiae* and the *sapientia veterum*) was nothing but self-deception, indeed an extraordinarily resilient form of it. In the case of those who decorated the villas, for example, Veronese and his work in the Villa Maser, this self-deception showed itself very directly in the trompe l'oeil, a style of painting meant to deceive the eye. In the case of Colonna, this social self-deception found adequate literary form in the dream journey, in the fiction of a fiction. As such, A. R. Turner has noted that

> the Renaissance landscape is a place for contemplation, not only because of its amenity and quietude, but because frequently it suggests thoughts of the past. At times this evocation was gained through ruins, as with . . . Veronese at "Maser". Or again the pastoral landscape is but another variation on this feeling for history, the dream that a simpler age once offered a more direct and sincere mode of life.[93] [Figure 8]

The core of the Renaissance utopia was based on sustained social criticism. This socially critical stance was necessarily missing from the villa's *negative utopia*. According to Horkheimer, Thomas More's *Utopia* did not present an abstract model but rather characterized the condition of the underprivileged masses in sixteenth-century England and formulated their concrete social desires. More projected the suffering of humans into his utopia, and the utopia was to serve as the means for surmounting suffering. More and Campanella started with practical, social problems. They sought change at the places where they thought they found the cause of the suffering, where the oppression of humans by humans and where social hopelessness were manifested most clearly. These sites were in the city that stood on the threshold of capitalism with its manufacturing precursors of industrialization; that is to say, the city was on the threshold of the proletarianization and pauperization of broad masses who had been disengaged from the social ties of cooperation, fraternity, and production in familial units.

As has been shown for the *villeggiatura*, the criticism of the *vita urbana* was also the stimulus for social dreams. While villa ideology repressed the social conflicts in the city, however, by focusing on a flight to the countryside rather than on solving these problems, utopians grasped the evil by its roots. The utopians' aim was the conquering and surmounting of urban suffering, but not by relocating from the city to arcadia, as if it were an empire devoid of conflicts. On the contrary, they sought historical change through the city, or rather in the "new city"—Utopia, Città del Sole, or Nova Atlantis. Utopia always remained an ideal urban image. Conversely, Cornaro, Barbaro, Machiavelli, and other villa theorists had only the fortunes of the privileged in mind, that is to say, the fortunes of their own class. Meanwhile, More, Campanella, and Bacon moved beyond their own class to concern themselves with the fortunes of the masses. The answer of the privileged sector on behalf of the "old city" was through the ideal villa, More's and Campanella's answer to the old city was the ideal city. As a concrete utopia, the ideal villa was only a utopia for the rulers. In other words, for this elite, the past became the utopia of the upper class. The *positive utopia* of Campanella and More was an unrealized (and unrealizable) dream of the dominated.

It is thus no longer surprising that none of the utopian treatises wasted words on the villa as an architectural, social, and cultural form. *There was no place in utopia for the villa.* The outskirts of Utopia and Nova Atlantis were not embellished by a garland of gleaming country houses. Just as the villa is "something that is thoroughly converted to money and power" (to quote Borchardt), so it presupposes the dominance of some people over others. There is only one power in Utopia, namely, that of the just God, and there is only one belief, that is, in the "good nature" of human beings. Accordingly, there is no anonymous money as a disinterested means of power but rather the shared ownership of everything by everyone. There is no longer the dominance of a few over the majority but, if anything, the power of all on behalf of all and the power of none over no one. In the case of More, Bacon, and Campanella, an implicit criticism of the villa as a social phenomenon was expressed by the very exclusion of it. For all three of these utopian thinkers were constantly confronted with the villa and its specific culture, since the *villeggiatura* as a negative and simultaneously concrete utopia found its most complete expression in the age of the first utopians in Italy and England during the epoch of Bacon, More, and Campanella.

More's and Campanella's utopias necessarily remained "utopian" because the prevailing social forces were still too powerful for utopian theory to be able to translate itself into utopian practice. There was a further reason for the fact that Chancellor More could not act in the manner he, as political theorist, was thinking. As Horkheimer has shown in his critique *Utopie*: "[More] did not recognize the (utopian) desire itself as a reaction to the social situation in which the masses were living and suffering, and instead he naively projected the contingents of this desire into a spatial and temporal kingdom to come. The utopia of the Renaissance was the secularized heaven of the middle ages."[94]

This is the point at which the *negative utopia* of the villa and the positive utopia of More and Campanella met, since the villa also represented a projection. The philosophical as well as the social "enlightenment" of the Renaissance, in the wake of the *studia humanitatis* and protocapitalist economic forms, allowed religion's function as consolation to become brittle both for the rich and for the poor from the Quattrocento onward. The poor and the rich alike no longer allowed themselves to be diverted by the medieval solace that one "could only enter utopias with death."[95] The vindication of all social privations during life on earth by the religious hope of ensuing good fortune in the next world through the good graces of a "just God" became increasingly untenable as a social stabilizer. The "autumn of the Middle Ages" faded into the "winter of belief."[96] However, the reaction of the genteel to this situation was different; it was above all less naive than that of the utopians. Their secularized heaven was not transferred through space and time into a distant utopia of this world but rather was transposed into the nearby reality of the villa. *For the affluent, the villa became a secularized heaven on earth, but it was a heaven that was reserved for themselves alone.*

Utopia and ideology were intimately interwoven in the *negative utopia* of the villa. If the *negative utopia* of the villa has been identified above all with its history of perfection, then the result can be inferred from its dualistic use of history as ideology. The transcendence of history as ideology led to the nucleus of what the villa was to represent in the *negative utopia*, namely, the *paradiso terrestre*. In all agricultural and villa treatises of the Renaissance (and even in the belles lettres of the period), the terms *paradiso terrestre*, or "earthly paradise," and *sito delle Muse*, or "the seat of the Muses," were the most frequently used metaphors for the villa and its pleasure gardens. These metaphors disclose how the villa and those who made the villa, along with the theme of the *paradiso terrestre*, acquired the basis for their existence and their philosophy. The image of the *paradiso terrestre* represents the contribution of the Christian Middle Ages to the formulation of the villa. The same image also emerged in utopian thought of the period, though in a different way than it did with the villa. The attempt to equate a *sham utopia* with reality in order to make *negative utopia* concrete seems to have succeeded in the case of the Palladian villas.

12

The Villa as "Earthly Paradise" in the Writings of Francesco Petrarch and Antonio Francesco Doni

T HE VILLA IDEOLOGISTS and the utopians were good historians who had recognized the following: "In various places in Europe during the Middle Ages (as was true with certain primitive tribes and collective farming), the 'organic' relationship between the individual and society was such that the well-being of one was inseparable from that of the other."[97]

The psychological security provided by an unquestioned Christian belief that was not yet entirely perverted by the ideology of power enabled the sporadic existence of such islands of "social paradise" during the Middle Ages. For Campanella and More or for Cornaro, Barbaro, Falcone, Gallo, and Lollio, the reconstruction of medieval belief was a prerequisite for the creation of an "earthly paradise" in the villa and in Utopia. While the religious bond meant for the utopians a strengthening of ethical standards in general as a precondition for the happiness of all in the *paradiso terrestre* of Utopia, for the ideologists of the villa religion meant something different, since they redefined the awakening of "religious enthusiasm as phraseology."[98] As such, the religious bond in the *paradiso terrestre* of the villa was for them merely a prerequisite for the happiness of a few, owing to their class-specific form of happiness.

The utopians sought instead to create an "organic" relationship between the individual and society, that is, a happy one in the *paradiso terrestre* through the return to medieval piety as a reconstruction of original Christian brotherhood and sisterhood. Similarly, they desired a return to medieval social forms as a reconstruction of the collectivist economy, thus linking both eras along the lines of a "primitive Christian communism" that was practiced by the first Christian communities. Conversely, the villa

69

ideologists, who were of the same mind as the Tridentine Council taking place at that time, had a different vision of the return to medieval piety. They grasped what Machiavelli had pointed out, namely, that "religion has always been an instrument for keeping the classes being ruled under control."[99]

For the ideologists of the villa, religion was simply a means of attaining happiness for a few without consideration of the consequences for the rest of humanity. Anything but naive, the *padrones* saw in religion an instrument of psychological and political domination. They reconceived the "organic" relationship between individual and society as a "wholesome" seemingly natural social order of "lords and peasants" that demanded preservation. By presuming that the perpetuation of this seemingly organic relationship between lord and serf was actually the teleology of the Christian religion, they reduced religion to ideology by correlating power, domination, and repression. The villa thus became the earthly "heaven of the rich," even as Utopia remained nonetheless the otherworldly and therefore unattainable "heaven of the poor."

If Horkheimer's concept of "utopian projection" is applied to the villa and to the Venetian society of the Late Renaissance, it becomes difficult to relate the formation of the villa ideal to the social yearnings of the "common" Venetian people. The voices of those who saw their claim to domination threatened by the new urban form of existence were the ones who were most distinctly heard. The *villeggiatura* was a condemnation of the city as the location of "misfortune" for the privileged rather than as the site of misery for the masses. The difference between "positive" utopia and "negative" utopia crystallizes at this point as one that emerges with the differing origins of utopia and the villa.

The extent to which the villa represented a perfect corollary in the form of a social and aesthetic "work of art" to the system of ideological safeguards is illustrated by the history of the term *paradiso terrestre*. Here we can return to the starting point of our considerations, namely, to the painted ideal landscapes on the villa walls. In fact, these paintings provided the *padrone* with the capacity to dream not only of the ancient world as an *aetas aurea* but also of the medieval *paradiso terrestre* as a negative utopia. The concept of *paradiso terrestre* finds its clearest expression in the villa book of 1550 by Agostino Gallo, a Brescian author. His *Dieci (Vinti) giornate della vera agricoltura piaceri della villa* (Ten [Twenty] Day's Work on True Agriculture and the Delights of Villa Life) begins and ends by extolling the blissfulness of the "earthly paradise" that is the villa. Such praise of the villa became indistinguishable from the description of the villa as *paradiso terrestre* per se. The dream of an existence in *paradiso terrestre* thus found its realization in the following formulation: "vivere sempre in villa elatassi come terrestre paradiso [permanently living in the villa, which has been made into an earthly paradise]."[100]

The northern Italian villa, in a manner analogous to the Roman villas and the sixteenth-century gardens dedicated to the Muses where humanists gathered, was totally absorbed by the concept of "earthly paradise." Adam and Eve were driven out of the Garden of Eden, from a condition of innocence in which the world and paradise were still synonymous. Yet to cite Gallo: "Through divine mercy Adam [was] left the *agricoltura*, not only for his benefit but also for refreshment and for pleasure in times of distress."[101] (As such, Gallo legitimized the "age and dignity of *agricoltura*," that is, the dignity and manners of the villa and the *vita rustica*.) In the course of history, virtue, art, and inventiveness have supposedly recreated the Garden of Eden and have found—via the villa—paradise lost. The religious ideal of paradise and the societal ideal of utopia thus congeal into the "apparent utopia" of the villa.

In the epic literature of the Middle Ages and in the humanistic poetics of the Renaissance, the notion of *paradiso terrestre* as the correlate of all poetic ideas about a dream landscape embraced a broad range of meaning. Like that of the villa, the medieval concept of *paradiso terrestre* can be traced in numerous directions. The latter concept has the head of Janus and looks backward to pagan antiquity as well as forward to the humanism of the modern age. As early as the twelfth century, the topos of *paradiso terrestre* replaced *locus amoenus* as the legitimate successor to the ideal landscape of ancient literature. The location of the ancient pastoral idyll, Theocratus's and Virgil's arcadian dreamland (which was the favorite place of shepherds whose viewpoints they used, with its canonical decoration of laurels, plane trees, cypress and pine groves, shady trees, meadows, floral motifs, cool springs, murmuring brooks, the chirping of birds, and refreshingly gentle breezes) was integrated into the Christian notion of paradise by Alanus of Lille. In this way, the Christian Divina Sapientia moved into the realm of the heathen Dea Natura. The arcadian *locus amoenus*, the center of which was the residence of heavenly reason, remained unchanged. It merely assumed the name *paradiso terrestre*.[102]

The castle that Alanus assigned to Divina Sapientia, however, was nothing other than the anticipation of the "dream of the country," the dream of the villa. In the sixteenth century, when Dea Natura and Divina Sapientia found their conjugal home in the realm of Santa Agricoltura and the Pia Rusticitas, namely, in the villa, there was an obvious temptation to interpolate the ancient and Christian ideas of paradise with the notion of the modern villa. *Locus amoenus, paradiso terrestre, locus locorum, sito delle Muse, frigida Tempe* (that is, the cool vale of Tempe, a special form of *locus amoenus*), the hill of Bacchus, and the pastures of Ceres (Marsiglio Ficino) were all inextricably interwoven in the villa. At the vanishing point of both the heathen and the Christian perspective, the villa shined forth as the "*locus religiosus*."

The link between the "heathen paradise" of *locus amoenus* and the villa was already forged in the Middle Ages, when Galfrid von Vinsauf and Johannes von Hanville adopted the ideal appearance of the paradisiac "place of lust" in their poetry, based as it was on Pliny's villa descriptions. The *paradiso terrestre* is the wider framework within which the various lines that form the outline of the villa image come together. These included the rustic virtues of Cato's Rome, the idea of Roman lyric poetry in the Golden Age (Horace and Virgil), the realm of Santa Agricoltura, and the Christian-humanist concept of the *santa e pia rusticità*.

When Agostino Gallo compared the villa to an earthly paradise, he was continuing a tradition that had begun at the same time as had that of the modern villa. As early as 1450, the villa is proclaimed in Alberti's fragment as "Dio, uno proprio paradiso [by God, a true paradise]." Doni and Lollio also identified the villa with *paradiso terrestre* in their villa books, wherein the latter (like Gallo) viewed the villa as a synthesis of an "apparent utopia" and a religious ideal. As Rupprecht has observed of this process: "Lollio's evocation of paradise in his discussion of the villa . . . derived its depth of meaning from the religious sphere, as was also the case with Gallo." The association with the "biblical paradise was established in the statement that the life God prescribed for Adam was the *vita rustica*, and its location was in the *paradiso terrestre*."[103]

In Renaissance art theory commentaries on the ideal landscape surrounding the villa, the *sito commodo*, and on the idealized rural landscape paintings inside the villa or the ideal landscape as a painting motif in general, the literary *locus amoenus* and *paradiso terrestre* were immanently present. Lomazzo's *luogo privilegiato* and his *sito dilettevole*, Palladio's *luoghi sollazzevoli*, Paolo Giovio's *parerga amoena*, Paolo Pino's *dilettevole giardin del mondo*, and Giovanni Battista Armenino's *paesi dilettevoli* all entailed nothing more than the evocation of "earthly paradise" by using the techniques of painting, architecture, or landscape design.

In the High and Late Middle Ages, the adoption of the ancient *locus amoenus* mostly led to a somewhat bloodless, largely abstract and generally stereotypical version of the literary dream of the "earthly paradise" landscape. In the epoch of Petrarch, however, the literary conception of *locus amoenus* was linked to the concrete experience of nature through an identification with the *vita solitaria*, the paradisiac form of life in the country. The world of Theocratus, Horace, and Virgil was sought and found in the country, while the essence of Roman bucolic and pastoral poetry compared with one's own experience of nature and landscape. This enriched considerably the *locus amoenus* of antiquity. Those sumptuous, strangely modern-sounding descriptions of landscapes came into being and provided the basis within the development of the classical northern Italian villa after 1500 for the "paradisiac" landscape that the landscape architect and mural painter conjured up in the interior of the villa and in front of its gates.

In all of the following—in Petrarch's description in the *Epistolae Metricae* of the *campagna Romana,* or in relating his experiences on the Genoese Riviera and Monte Capranica in the *Epistolae Familiares,* in his letters describing the *villeggiatura* of Garegnano near Milan and in Selvapiana or the view from Mont Ventoux and San Colombano, the otherworldly literary dream of Arcadia was transformed into the worldly and concrete experience of "earthly paradise." The raison d'être of this experience of paradise was, even for Petrarch, the *vita rustica,* yet not in the ideology of the "villa" as defined in the social form of the fifteenth and sixteenth centuries.

The combination of ancient *locus amoenus* with the Christian idea of paradise and the new social ideal of *vita rustica* found clear literary expression in Antonio Francesco Doni's description of the Villa Priuli (which is no longer standing) in Treville, near Castelfranco Veneto. The villa used to be situated just a few kilometers away from the Villa Maser. Doni wrote his description of it only a few years before the Barbaro family established their country residence in Maser. He gives the reader a simulated view from the windows of the villa. The lucky one who finds himself inside has that enhanced enjoyment of life and nature that allows the *luogo privilegiato* of the villa to become *paradiso terrestre.* As Walter Benjamin noted: "The landscape hangs like a painting in the window frame, but the signature is God's." In this regard, Antonio Francesco Doni's description is very revealing:

E dalle finestre tu vedi venire carrette di gentili e belle donne, uomini onorati a cavallo, e da diverse parti, solamente a veder il tuo luogo e visitarti; onde in una occhiata tu vedi bellisime donne, paesi, giardini, conviti, balli e molti piaceri uniti, infin' dell'armonia de'fonti e degli uccelli, con l'odorato de'fiori degli orti, e de'profumi di casa artifiziati. E se io fossi stato padrone, mi sarei voluto cavare un capriccio di fare un bagno sopra quella montagna colonata.

[And out of the windows you see coaches carrying high-ranking and beautiful women and horses bearing noblemen, all streaming together from every possible direction just to see your villa and to visit you. At one glance you catch sight of the most beautiful women, the open landscape, the gardens, the guests outdoors, the dancing, and numerous amusements simultaneously; to this is added the harmonious sound of a bubbling spring and the chirping of birds, the fragrance of the garden flowers, and exquisite perfume. Were I the master of the house, I would allow myself the capriciousness to have a bath surrounded by columns built on the hill.][104] [See Figure 13.]

Even then, around the middle of the sixteenth century, the basic design of the ancient *locus amoenus* provided the scaffold for the literary description of the villa "paradise" via the following elements: a beautiful garden (*giardini*), murmuring springs (*armonia de'fonti*), the chirping of birds (*armonia degli uccelli*), perfume and floral work in the decorative garden (*odorato de'fiori degli orti*). By then the ancient *locus amoenus* had achieved its realization in the villa and the rural paradise had decidedly changed in relation to Petrarch's view of nature. In his description of the Selvapiana as a "sheltered" *locus amoenus* surrounded by forest, Petrarch lay down in his favorite spot with "a green lawn for a bed" and in proud misanthropic loneliness. It is the "bucolic camp theme"(Curtius) of shepherd poetry; the poet has a special preference for the loneliness of the place. Nothing distracts him from the exquisiteness of natural phenomena in hidden recesses, such as a thick beech grove on a green hill, a green meadow adorned with brightly colored flora, the murmuring of a brook and a spring, a mild breath of wind, the song of birds, precious fragrances, and cool shades. The enjoyment of nature was more direct here than in ancient poetry.

No longer was a pastoral rococo scene—the shepherd, tired from pursuing the forest nymph, lies down in his favorite spot, and so on—the occasion and "opportunity of form" for the portrayal of nature. The shepherd was no longer the obligatory figure through whose eyes the poet saw nature, through whose mouth he described nature. Pastor and poet became one. For Petrarch, the experience of nature had not only become more personal, it had also become more antisocial. The solemn, even religious mood of the natural experience—Petrarch spoke of the "holy forest" and presumed to see the "lea of heaven, not an earthly pasture"—permits only the ordained servant of the cult of nature, namely, the poet himself. Shepherd, farmer, and nymph, the personnel of the ancient pastoral paradise, remained banished, so that "the shepherd's plump foot, the farmer's pitchfork never desecrate the still abode." Even the "guardian of the forest" stayed away from the spot.

From far away he could merely point to it in a way that was "entirely shy," as a pious man refers to the holy of holies in the temple. Human business and human action would have been disturbing encroachments in Petrarch's temple of nature. Here, nature itself ruled and took action, its works more perfect than all art. Without engaging himself in action, the poet collected impressions like a vessel: "in the center, resplendent, a hill of flowers no gardener's hand could have planted, purely created by nature's loving hand" (*Ep. Metr.* II, 17). The artificial paradise of the villa in Petrarch's time had not yet become united with the literary paradise of *locus amoenus*. The solitary was still alone in the country, being merely himself, devoted to his own soul and to its reflection in nature. Life in the country and the experience of nature in Petrarch's view formed an unsocial and non-societal ideal, in other words, an ideal existing beyond society (Figure 12).

It was very different for Doni. When he imagined nature as paradise, it was within the framework of the villa. *Solitatius* was here no longer shy and pious when he encountered the holiness of "natural" nature, since the urban *Occupatus*, along with urban *Civilità*, had transferred urban activity, the demonstrative consumer attitude of the urban dweller, and the loud, bustling lifestyle of the city to the country. For Petrarch, the person tired of the city sought refuge in the loneliness of nature, and he submerged himself in a preexistent paradise, the enjoyment of which demanded absolute "freedom" from material needs and awoke no social needs whatsoever in that person. For Doni, however, the city-weary *Occupatus* had traded one social condition for another. The villa paradise for Doni was no longer "innocent" or "natural" but rather was a man-made paradise supported by social institutions and therefore intimately bound up with their prosperity or ruin. Petrarch's *Solidaritus* found in pure nature a happiness that was believed to be lost, which he dreamed of in the city and sought in the country. Conversely, Doni's *Occupatus* looked for a kind of happiness in the villa that he lost in the city and recreated for himself in the country.

It was unthinkable in describing Doni's villa to say: "a hill of flowers no gardener's hand could have planted; purely created by nature's loving hand." Doni's interpretation of nature was "Latin," Petrarch's was not. The Roman could only experience nature in relation to people, that is, as a sphere of life created for and by people who populated it and gave it its social form. He had no notion of an "artless" nature in its original state. As early as Petrarch, the natural experience was less direct than in northern European literature, since it was filtered through a precisely structured literary screen, the stereotypes of which had already been given their principal contours by ancient poetry. Vitruvius's quotation about nature was once again current in Doni's statement "Ita, quod ultra natura laedit, arte erit emendandum [The unfavorable relationships that Nature provides must be artificially rectified]"–(*De Arch.*, VI, 1). Approximately a decade after Doni, Daniele Barbaro both paraphrased a maxim of Roman art theory—"Illud quod cecidit forte, id arte ut corrigas" (*Ter., Andr.* 4, 7)—and wrote the following about his villa in Tivoli in the dedication of the second edition of his *Vitruvian Commentary* (1567) to Ippolito d'Este: "nelle guali (opere ion Roma, et a Tivoli) la natura conviene confessare di essere stata superata dall'arte, et dalla splendidezza dell'animo (umano) [In the presence of these creations in Rome and Tivoli, Nature must confess to having been surpassed by the art and brilliance of the human spirit of invention]."

This sentence contained the essential idea of the villa as *paradiso artifiziato*, as expressed not only in the "d'Este," the Cardinal's villa in Tivoli, but also in the haute bourgeois "*Priuli*" in Treville and in the Venetian Prelate's "*Barbaro*" villa in Maser. Barbaro's judgment of the quality of the "*Villa d'Este*," based as it was on the authority of Latin aesthetics, could be transferred without difficulty from the real landscape art of Ippolito's Tiburtine villa to the illusionary paintings of nature in the Villa Maser. They put nature to "shame," as did the fountains, the serene architecture, the landscaped terrain, and the botanical elements of the Ligorio in Tivoli. Not only the artfully laid-out gardens of the central and northern Italian villas but also the painted villa landscapes satisfied (through the realization of an idealized, exalted nature) Aristotle's aesthetic postulate: ὅλως δὲ ἡ τέχνη τὰ μὲν ἐπιτελεῖ ἃ ἡ φύσις ἀδυνατεῖ ἀπεργάσασθαι (Art perfects what nature cannot realize) (*Phys.* II, 8, 199a, 15).

This is the source of the "ideal landscape" concept of the northern Italian villa masters, of the decorative depiction of nature inside their country residences as the evocation of a perfected nature. The Aristotelian and Vitruvian idealizations of nature's landscapes provided the aesthetic foundation for the acceptance of landscape painting into the canon of themes "worthy of being painted." Petrarch's rural paradise was adequately defined as "God's free nature." Doni's villa paradise, however, was depicted as "the unfree nature of man," since it was regulated, formed, ordered, and societally determined. The natural "painting" of the villa was not signed by God; instead, the paradisiac image of the villa bore a human signature. The person in the villa was no longer the "vessel" for the experience of nature, but rather nature was the vessel, the framework, and the background for human existence. For Doni, the villa was the definitive realization of a societal and sociopolitical ideal. Insofar as the paradise known as the villa was created by man in all its features, it was a "concrete utopia."

But this social dream had a repressive character. The dream realized was not one created by all for all; instead, it was created by the majority to be enjoyed by the minority. The "heaven of the rich" was only made possible by the sweat of the poor. The unearned income of the villa *padrone* was a prerequisite for the villa paradise of "fine society." The prerequisite for the villa paradise and for the profits of the villa, which has been dealt with so expertly and in such detail by northern Italian theorists, was, more or less, the unpaid work of the servants, the maids, and the tenant farmers. Petrarch's country paradise of free nature was open to all as long as they left both the city and urban standards behind them. Doni's paradise reproduced the urban relations of ownership and therefore of domination.

Since the villa paradise had the character of a social norm, a societal convention, it comes as no surprise that Doni dispensed completely with the seclusion of the *locus amoenus* with its ahistorical ideal atmosphere of the pastoral idyll and bucolic literature. He pushed aside not only the ancient forms exemplifying the dignified age of *santa agricoltura* but also the binding poetic models of classical antiquity and their elaborate ancient trappings, the Roman masks: "lasciando gli antichi, ché io non viddi mai [I do not linger with the forms of antiquity that I have never set eyes on myself]." Doni's villa paradise was richly peopled with human staffage. In other words, nature was but a mere facade, a backdrop for a social *spettacolo*. The new haute bourgeois ruling class "acted out" in the villa the old feudal way of life in the countryside as if it were on an amateur stage. A carriage (*carrette*) drew up before the villa; there were chivalrous cavalcades (*uomini onorati a cavallo*); there were open-air entertainments in sport and dance (*balli e molti piaceri*), picnics in the countryside (*conviti*), esoteric guessing games, tests of dexterity, card games and board games (*nuovi giochi d'invenzione reale e rare*), the performance of the latest easy *canzones*, and noble courtly love transformed into a bourgeois flirtation. These were the elements in the plot of the permanent *villeggiatura* game that reproduced the amusements for the original manorial class.

It would later be no coincidence that in 1556, the same year as Doni's portrayal of villa life in the Terraferma, an academy was established in Vicenza that was reserved exclusively for the nobility. Nor was it surprising that this association of the "more prosperous nobles, including most of Palladio's patrons" made the core of their program into the fostering of the nobility's tradition in order "to sustain the chivalric tradition in part by staging tournaments and other courtly festivities." Nor was it a coincidence that this noble Accademia dei Costanti was established only one year after and in direct rivalry with the "bourgeois" Accademia Olimpica, which was set up in 1555 in Vicenza and which had taken up the cause of fostering art and science, above all, theater, music, and mathematics.[105]

The simple shepherds and peasants who populated the rural paradise of antiquity and of Petrarch's thought were assigned a role and a place in the villa paradise as a class of domestic servants and farmhands living in the domestics' quarters. Peasants and shepherds (or the "bucolically inclined" poet of Petrarch's period) quietly lost in thought have resigned their place in favor of the rich and self-confident villa personalities who were full of the joy of life and who noisily showed themselves off while finding in the villa the gratification of all five senses. This civilian elite experienced its social self-understanding through the enjoyment of the villa life's superabundance. The *villeggiatura* became a social status symbol and the entertainment in the villa paradise became a demonstration of social power and social prestige. This is the same attitude that was later characterized by Veblen in his *Theory of the Leisure Class* as "conspicuous consumption."

As we have already noted, Doni made no mention whatever of the *campi*, or the well-cultivated field, as a new aesthetic dimension for the enjoyment of nature. There was not a word about the legitimation of the privileged existence of the villa landlords by the *santa professione degli agricoltori*. The *padrone* obviously abandoned his ethical alibi—the social "misfortune" of his own class as well as work itself—used to hide his parasitic existence behind the image of a devoted, socially sensitive *pater familias*. Days spent in the villa went by like pleasant summer dreams; each day was a festivity; each hour was an act of carefully routinized *villeggiatura* estate ceremonial, the rules of which could nevertheless be dispensed with in individual cases to suit the capriciousness of the young Venetian dandies and their ladies. Sport and games, mock chivalry fencing battles, and courtly love for the amusement of the *"belle donne,"* who were elevated to "objects of ostentation," appear to have been the aims behind all the directed social energies of the villa landlords.

Here we find the compulsion to engage in "meaningful activity" through "organized leisure," as evidenced by the ceremonies of the affluent at various moments in history, as Veblen demonstrated. All of this entailed the "investing [of] meaningless activity with the illusion of seriousness and significance. The less one still has to acquire, the more one feels the need to create a semblance of earnest activity, to appear socially engaged while remaining disinterested."[106] The forms within which this occurred were all derived from the rural lifestyle of the nobility as it had already developed by the time of the Middle Ages. What was new was the conscious orientation toward nature as the stimulant for spiritual sensations and aesthetic enjoyment.

The centerpiece of the villa tracts, of villa poetry, and of villa painting was the "pictorial assertion that the trees are green, the sky is blue, and clouds float" (to quote Adorno). This oft-repeated and solemn assertion forcibly directed the interests of the villa lords into those channels of social energy that opened onto a new and wholesale sensitivity to the delights of nature, to the charm and fascination of the landscape of the *locus amoenus*, enwrapped as it was in the villa paradise. This, too, was an enjoyment reserved for the rich. The poor laborer doing his daily work in the fields could also see the green trees, the blue skies, and the floating clouds above him whenever he looked up and wiped the sweat from his brow, but his look was not about the value or joy in the beauty of tree green, sky blue, or cloud white. Instead, he had to check whether the fruit trees were blossoming well, whether the cloudless sky meant drought or the cloudy sky presaged a dreaded hailstorm. "Nature, by virtue of the social mechanism of hegemony that defined it as the healthy opposite to urban society was thereby made incurably straight and was sold off."[107]

Doni, in various places within his villa tract, "exposed . . . the artificiality of the entire villa ethic," since "le forme son perdute, e non c'è ordine a trovar villa, che quieti l'animo [the old villa ideals have perished and one will no longer find a villa where the soul would find peace]" and mockingly unmasked "as hollow ceremony, the profound ancient sagas of the kings who cultivated their own gardens" (p. 39f.).[108] It is therefore only logical that in the description of the Villa Priuli he left out the obligatory references to the *campi* and to the art of *agricoltura*. This makes evident the objective distance achieved by Doni, who as a Florentine "foreigner" had a sharpened perspective that let him recognize how the work ethic of the villa *padroni* and the healing of *agricoltura* were but masks concealing the reverse side of the villa paradise, that is, the expropriation and domination on which it depended. Doni accurately portrayed the social self-image of the Venetian villa landlords around the mid-sixteenth century. His text forcefully prompts one to ask whether the owners of the Villa Priuli and their friends from the surrounding estates had any real need to use the alibi of the age—the dignity and the morality of *agricoltura*—as legitimation for what they did. They were so obviously and unquestioningly the lords of their paradise that sport, games, and dance, chivalrous leisure and social caball-ing, sufficed for them to preserve the appearance, to themselves and those dependent on them, that they were engaged in socially "meaningful" work.

Because Doni was largely free of the ideological conventions used by the villa writers of northern Italy, who were integrated into the system, he succeeded in drawing a picture of the life of the nobility in the paradise of the Venetian villas that did not obscure the subject behind a veil. The "second" successor generation no longer needed to acquire property and to expand it single-mindedly but had rather to preserve it and enjoy it with single-mindedness. In the end, they would devour it all without leaving a trace—including the moral capital that the "villa books" of the sixteenth century had so solicitously generated. Doni's description anticipates Goldo-ni's critique of eighteenth-century *villeggiatura*: In the final, deformed phase during which the number of bankruptcies grew and grew, even less propertied city patricians believed they had to prove their already shaken creditworthiness by spending senseless amounts on their *villeggiatura*; Alberti's old Franconian maxims about *masserizia* were forgotten and the income from the villa served only to finance expensive theater entertain-ment, *naumachies*, the pleasures of the ball, hunting, and festive banquets in the countryside.

Similarly, part of the profit was no longer used for investments in the farming operations and for their expansion through new purchases and the cultivation of land. As early as the seventeenth century, the *piaceri* of the villa spilled over to become the main thing that the villa was supposed to represent, thus dissipating the bounty provided by *santa professione degli*

agricoltori (the sacred profession of the farmer). The *spettacoli* imported from
the city into the villa soon surpassed urban delights in splendor and expense.
A French contemporary described the number of staff employed merely for
the introductory scene of a play performed in the villa: "On y compta
jusqu'à cinq-cent acteurs, savoir cent piquiers, cent femmes, cent cavaliers
montant des chevaux bardés, soixante hellebardiers, des chausseurs, des
estafiers, des pages, qui parurent tous dans la première scène du triomphe
[One could count almost 500 background figures, consisting of 100 lancers,
100 maids of honor, 100 knights on armored horses, 60 halberdiers, as well
as hunters, standard-bearers, and pages, all of whom were on stage in the
first scene of *Trionfo*]."[109]

The *villeggiatura* season was tripled in length during the eighteenth century to embrace spring, summer, and autumn. Goldoni reported that a
one-month stay in the villa cost as much as four months of life in the city.
The satiric verse in his villa plays complimented what Doni insinuated in his
description of the Villa Priuli, namely:

> Tutti gode un'intiera libertà.
> Dorme chi vol dormir; magna chi ha fame:
> Balla chi vol ballar; canta chi sa:
> Chi va solo in zardin, chi co le Dame.
> Chi a siè Cavalli strascinar se fa.
> Chi visita le razze, e chi el bestiame.
> Chi zoga al tavolin la notte, e'l dì.[110]

The "dream of the countryside," of paradisiac existence in an original
state of innocence, was envisioned collectively by the European aristocracy
and by the haute bourgeoisie during the eighteenth century. This dream
informed Rousseau's very "civil" social utopia to the same degree that it did
Marie Antoinette's Potemkinist village in the gardens of Versailles, complete with windmill, duck pond, and dairy. The fateful characteristics of
northern Italian villa life became even more distorted with the shepherd's
idyll, *petit hameau* romanticism. The philandering of the French rococo
lifestyle on which it was modeled contributed to the Venetian villa paradise
what the villa had already signified with its establishment in the sixteenth
century, albeit in obscured form, namely, a rural heaven of the rich.

The seeds of the Venetian *villeggiatura*'s destruction were sown here. The
end of the Rococo era, the ancien régime, and the political and economic
independence of Venetian capital also signified the end of the *villeggiatura*:
The farmers moved into the houses of the landlords to whom they had
previously had access only when dressed up in the costume of extras in a
play or as petitioners in the "exotic" Sunday state. In the villa comedies of
Ruzante, which were written for Alvisè Cornaro and were typical of early
"classical" Venetian *villeggiatura*, the *padrone* and his farmers appeared

together as servants of Diana.[111] The guest wing of the Vicentine Villa Valmarana "dei Nani," however, which symbolizes the end of the series of the brilliant Venetian villas, was decorated in the eighteenth century by Giandomenico Tiepolo. He painted rural genre scenes and peasant groups in traditional dress with the "exotic" figures of the farmers resembling the then-fashionable orientals and *chinoiserie* that were featured on the walls.

Doni captured the social condition of the Venetian villa at a point in time when the old class of feudal lords had obviously been succeeded fully by a new class of bourgeois landlords in the Terraferma. In accordance with the mechanics of social history, the "second" generation of rural "civil nobility" in rural areas were able to exchange the pioneer costume of the *cultivazione dei beni inculti* for the masks of a perpetuated Venetian carnival. They once again revealed the parasitic qualities that Machiavelli—in speaking as the ideologist of the "first" generation of civil landlords in the villa—had castigated in his *Discourses* from the beginning of the sixteenth century onward. To quote Machiavelli here: "With regard to the title of nobility, I say this—that one calls by this title those who live in leisure and overabundance from the profits of their estates without caring for agriculture or for any other occupation in life. Such people are corruptive in a republic, indeed in any country, particularly insofar as they also possess castles and subjects who obey them, in addition to their estates."[112]

There was a direct relation between Antonio Francesco Doni's text and the decorative paintings in the Venetian villas. Doni described the view out of the windows of the villa ("dalle finestre tu vedi") in precisely the same way that the theme would be treated in illusionist landscape painting in the villa. Doni's words exposed what the paintings were supposed to represent. The paintings illustrated what Doni's text meant. At the same time, the Doni perspective pointed to the interchangeability of actual views with artistically simulated ones from the villa, as characterized by the illusionist decorations of the Venetian Late Renaissance. In the one section about the Villa Priuli, Doni described not only the real view from the window but also how "paesi di Fiandra da buon maestri fiamminghi coloriti in Fresco [che] ti fanno stupire [Flemish landscapes painted by skillful Dutch fresco painters fill the viewer with amazement]."

The same frescos that "stupefied" viewers obviously had the character of an optical illusion, because only a few years after the Villa Priuli was built, the Villa Soranza was erected on the same site as a competing enterprise. And in the Villa Soranza—now destroyed—the young Veronese writer developed that illusionist system of decoration that he perfected ten years later in the Villa Maser (Figures 8 and 9). Carlo Ridolfi wrote about illusionist painting in the Villa Soranza that was intended to put the "Flemish" works of the nearby Villa Priuli in the shade.

FIGURE 13.   Villa Piovene Porto Godi, near Vicenza, end of sixteenth century

FIGURE 14.   G. A. Fasolo, *Villa Society and a Card Game*, wall painting, *sala centrale*, Villa Caldogno, near Vicenza, around 1570

The favorite themes of Venetian villa painting as described by Doni included not only landscapes representative of the villa paradise but also the staffage for that paradise. These pictorial figures were often alienated from and ennobled by the theater costumes of ancient history and ancient mythology, just as the villa landlords would frequently enough garb them in reality, in their "rappresentazioni sceniche" to beguile themselves and the requisitioned peasants with a delusion of the "pure" and organic social world of antiquity, the Golden Age of Diana, Ceres, and Bacchus.[113]

The wall paintings of Veronese, Zelotti, Fasolo, Farinati, Canera, Franco, Gambara, Maganza, and Tiepolo portrayed the reality of the villa paradise by taking happy, good-looking, well-dressed, and leisurely people, along with a cultivated garden setting (with fountains and waterfalls, tree-lined avenues, garden sculptures, magnificent carriages, noble horses, and hunting dogs), and combining them, always with a "decorative" aim in mind, to compose "beautiful pictures" (Figure 14). The same theatrical magic is inherent in villa life as a succession of festivities, just as it is peculiar to the great decorative paintings on the walls of the villa, which functioned as a representative backdrop for villa life even as it simultaneously portrayed this life. Thus, *the wall paintings are an important hermeneutic key to understanding the social structure of the villa.* Only if the sources of villa culture and its social background are ignored can these pictures be explained away as harmless and frivolous "wallpaper substitutes."

13

A Fresco in the Villa Maser

T HE VILLA'S MOST complete artistic expression as the *locus amoenus* and *paradiso terrestre* of the rich is to be found in Paolo Veronese's paintings in the Villa Maser. As has been shown, ancient ruins were an absolutely essential element for the idea of paradise entertained by the patron of this work, namely, the humanist and antiquarian Daniele Barbaro, who acted as a graphic symbol for this reactionary philosophy of history. In one frame of the Stanza di Bacco (Bacchus Room), the villa itself became an object of representation. Veronese's painting thus bore a striking resemblance to Doni's text. At the end of a central guiding avenue in the painting there is a large palace-like building with several stories. The building is flanked by tower-like *risaltos* as signs of domination and surrounded on all sides by twin-floored loggias mediating between architecture and free space. In front of the villa, there is a spacious forecourt divided up by architecturally encircled borders and small exotic trees in tubs. Numerous figures people the loggias, the forecourt, and the avenue. A landau carriage decked out in city fashion is pulling up in front of the portal, while the *padrone* and his family are greeting the new arrival from the middle balcony. A hunting lad with a spear has tied his mule to one of the orange trees and is awaiting instructions from his masters. In the avenue, a covered country-style carriage pulled by two beautiful white horses approaches the beholder. Two made-up ladies returning to the city from the *villeggiatura* are sitting in the landau and are being courted by elegant cavaliers on prancing horses. Close to the viewer stands a splendidly dressed hunter with a spear, who is watching over a pack of three thoroughbred dogs. The farming economy, the *fattoria*—the quarters for the servants and farm laborers, the kitchen gardens, and the farmland—are hermetically excluded. The rows of trees and the *habitazione del padrone* obstruct the view into the world of those whose work makes possible the leisurely life in the villa enjoyed by the *padroni* (Figure 15).

This type of picture—which could be called a "villa within a villa"—was much imitated in Venetian and central Italian villa decoration. This was

FIGURE 15.   Paolo Veronese, *Landscape with Ideal Villa*, wall painting, Stanza di
Bacco, Villa Maser, 1560–62

not without reason, since here the villa—translated into painting—bore the greatest resemblance to itself. Here, in the form of a painting, one finds the clearest expression of the social self-image of the landlords and the architecture and gardens within which the *villeggiatura* was both framed and ordered. In the Stanza di Bacco of the Villa Maser, the design of the fresco was an as yet undefined ideal villa. Later, in the Roman country residences, this "villa within a villa" type of picture would have more precise social contours. In the Villa Lante-Gambara in Bagnaia, in Ippolito's Villa d'Este in Tivoli, in Caprarola, the villa-castle, an entire series of villa views appeared as wall decor, as documentary treatments of the villa itself shown in *statu nascendi* with scaffolding and half-finished gardens, as depictions of other villa residences of the *padrone* in the surrounding area, or as painted landscapes illustrating the country castles of his friends. The lord of the villa thus saw himself permanently surrounded by graphic evidence of the extent of his landed property and of the scope of his building activity.

The illustrious examples of Maecenatism on the part of others in the *padrone*'s class, however, placed his own villa in line with them through their being integrated into the same artistic plan. The "villa within a villa" ensemble finally became an exhibition of the need for recognizing social status and prestige. Turner was right to see a "propagandistic function" in the painted landscape as wall decoration, and he wrote as follows: "The direct reference to lands possessed is analogous to the portraiture of this period, where the social status and profession of the sitter were stressed through emphasis on clothing as an unequivocal attribute. Both portraiture and landscape were concerned primarily with outward signs rather than with more personal or intangible qualities."[114]

In the course of the sixteenth century, the country estate became the secularized "princedom" of the urban haute bourgeois, who made villa building into the costume of his class, the lightweight hunting beret into his "civil crown." The richly decorated walls, however, portrayed apparel that had the same value as a social attribute, like the insignia in official pictures that marked out the *padrone* as banker, merchant, shipowner, Senator, antiquarian and humanist of great learning, cleric of high standing, man of letters, or man of affairs.

Ippolito d'Este, in his Tivoli villa, directly reproduced the Hadrianic *ars topiaria* (that is, the ancient notion of the villa as a "negative utopia" and as a "paradise of the rich") with garden art and decorative fountains. In the Villa Maser, this ostentation—as befitted the modest means of the Venetian villa *prelatizia*—had to be performed indirectly in a manner similar to that found in the frescoes of the Boscoreale villa.

In the Villa Hadriana, the Villa d'Este, and the Villa Maser, the villa itself displaced the idea of the city. The plastic decorations in the gardens and the

FIGURE 16.   Colen Campbell, Mereworth in Kent, designed in 1722

painted wall decorations not only displaced social reality spatially but also temporally, thus deflecting the present moment. This displacement was so perfected in the Villa Maser that the architecture and the paintings not only resembled themselves, they also reciprocally resembled each other. This identity of both form and content in the building and its interior furnishings explains the high quality of the Palladian country house as a *Gesamtkunst-werk*, so that "to the extent that architecture and painting can be compared, their styles were alike."[115]

The attempt to combine this "illusory utopia" and reality in the same equation so as to concretize "negative utopia" would appear to have suc-ceeded in the Palladian villa. The other side of the equation is the high artistic quality of these villas, a quality that no sociological method is able to address fully. *This, indeed, was the paradox of the Palladian villa, as Goethe himself rightly felt: Its "lie" operated by means of its artistic truth; its "truth" resided in its social lie.*[116]

14

Palladianism and Historicism

IN THIS CONTEXT, the history of Palladianism is illuminating. One would certainly not do Palladio justice were one to see him only as the inventor of new spatial forms, innovative spatial sequences, and original compositions for facades. He was as regressive as he was progressive, and a decisive aspect of his epoch-making influence was certainly the fact that a tendency toward *historicism* was particularly well developed in his case. It is a mark of all historically significant forms of art that they emerge when an epoch shapes its own self-understanding. It is when the forms with which an epoch shapes its environment artistically and in which the social relations are expressed illustratively are both brought into being that these attributes no longer come together in an obvious and genuine style. As such, claims to hegemony are aesthetically articulated, or legitimated, but there is no separate logic that produces the symbolism of hegemony in and of itself.

In such a case, one attempts to reclaim at least in part the intellectual spirit and sense of life of the "good old days" by means of the adoption of forms and styles from coherent and "unscathed" epochs with relationships of domination still intact. At the same time, in the eyes of the clients of the ruling class, the "good old" days also appear to be "good" *a priori*, because the relations of domination were evidently guaranteed without question or conflict.[117] Simultaneously, there is the perception of the aesthetic production of such earlier "unblemished" epochs as "beautiful," and from a historical point of view, this turns them into a set of normative principles for the ruling aesthetic.

Just as Palladio worked for clients who—as in the case of the Angelier-Cornaro Family of Venice and Padua—sought by means of adventurous name derivations (Corner = Cornelier) to assert claims for domination analogous to those of the ancient nobility, so it was necessary to use the forms of the classical art of antiquity as the forms appropriate to an apparently secure, dominant elite. In the case of Palladio, the process of patronage was not merely a purely formal or aesthetic one but also one that was avowedly political and ideological. In the Palladian epoch, the dignified and pompous orders, the acroteria, the atticas, the architraves, the rows of

90

FIGURE 17. Gian Francesco Costa, *Veduta del Palazzo del Godognola on the Brenta*, etching, mid-eighteenth century

FIGURE 18. Andrea Palladio, Villa Rotonda, Vicenza, 1566–70

statues, the porticos, and the peristyles of antiquity—all with their trium-
phal motifs and their festive spirit of decorative festoons, trophies, masks,
bulls' skulls, and putti friezes—were not themselves "ideally beautiful"
forms that satisfied a canonically determined aesthetic norm. These elements were also symbols of domination for the leading class of antiquity.

The reality of architectural practice impelled architects toward a concept,
toward an aesthetic norm, that possessed the *auctoritas historiae*. This was
clearly illustrated in the architectural language of Palladio's Villa Rotonda
(Figure 18), the incunabulum of the "classic" Venetian villa and the overex-
tended model for all European villas and even non-European villas as well
from the Baroque and the late Baroque through Neoclassicism right up to
the late Victorian period. Thus, one scholar could note the following:

> The "consecration of the house" is represented by the staircases, the
> pediment, and the statues. This is explained by Palladio's assumption that
> the Latin podium temple was derived from an Italian "Ur-house," so that
> he felt justified in characterizing his *casa di villa* (which was supposed to
> rejuvenate this elemental house) with such sacred and solemn formulas.
> To us, it might seem quite farfetched, but it shows what Palladio took the
> "villa" to stand for, namely, the house of the "golden age," a place of
> peace and of complete harmony between man and nature created by
> architecture. . . . Palladio's Rotonda [is] the typical work in that it dem-
> onstrates in crystal-clear terms what that other [ancient] villa embodied,
> that is, Palladio's dream of arcadia on Venetian soil.[118]

It now becomes more clear why, at particular moments and in specific
societies, Palladio's forms were reverted to, thus duplicating the historicism
that had already been developed in the Cinquecento. This has always happened
when a society with colonial, imperial, and capitalist tendencies has had to
legitimate itself through artistic production, thus seeking to articulate its claim
to hegemony by architectural means. Hence, one must speak, for example, of a
Palladianism with regard to the Polish, Scandinavian, and Bohemian nobility
during the Baroque and Neoclassical periods, in the Russia of Peter the Great,
in the England of the seventeenth through the nineteenth centuries (especially
with regard to Colen Campbell [Figure 16], Sir Christopher Wren, and Inigo
Jones), and in the houses of the Prussian Junkers of the eighteenth and
nineteenth centuries.[119] It also becomes understandable why the typical
"colonial style" has generally followed Palladian models—from Louisiana to
New England and from the Boer state of Cape Province to Indo-China and
Dutch East India—and also why the characteristic Victorian villas of the urban
haute bourgeoisie and of the new propertied class (the banking and industrial
"aristocracy" from the turn of the nineteenth into the twentieth century) so
often liquidated the inheritance of *Malcontenta*, *Rotonda*, or *Rocca Pisana*, in a
manner that was in most cases artistically fateful.

15

The Villa Ideal as Ideology: The *Sito Commodo* of the Villa as *Luogo Privilegiato*; the Villa as Patrician Legitimation

THE CONCEPT OF the villa as an "ideal" (as Rupprecht has termed it), permits a direct recognition of the villa as ideology. The basis of villa ideology was formed by the idealization of country life, of the agricultural mode of life. In social terms, idealization is synonymous with regression. Villa ideologues such as Cornaro, Barbaro, or Falcone considered the existing conditions unbearable and presented in opposition to them a moral norm, namely, that of the villa. This normative ethic, as illustrated in the normative aesthetic of the villa culture, was not connected congenially with real social progress but rather with historicism.

The classic Venetian villa referred to the models of antiquity in formal terms. The ideal of life of the *villeggiatura* (as based on Santa Agricoltura) raised archetypal modes of living to actuality, thus giving evidence of the retrospective social consciousness of an elitist class. The upper class had created this ideological base as their pièce de résistance for the purpose of deflecting attention away from their actual intentions and in order to legitimate their social practices.

In the sixteenth century and after, rulers tried to slow down urban emancipation and the rise of the city as a boundless metropolis by means of a retreat to the countryside. The phenomenon of the *villeggiatura*, which had already been prepared culturally and philosophically since the fourteenth century, was now followed by the articulation of clearly defined architectural types and by the postulation of an aesthetic norm for the construction of villas. The villa movement was deceptively legitimized by socioeco-

94

nomic arguments whose realization helped to secure dominion over others.

This problem can be illustrated particularly well by the example of the postulate concerning the ideal site for the villa, which could hardly be absent from any Renaissance architectural treatise. The authors often proceeded from one of the most beautiful landscape descriptions of ancient literature, such as the letter by Pliny the Younger to Apollinaris on the setting of the Tuscan villa,[120] which was elevated to the status of a canon. The villa theoreticians cataloged various demands with regard to the ideal location of the *casa di villa*, whose individual points became more and more circumscribed as binding stereotypes from Alberti through Palladio, Scamozzi, and Saminiato. The ideal plan was essentially structured according to four viewpoints: the *comodità*, the *sanità*, the *belleza*, and the *maestà* (or *magnificenza*) of the villa site.

Comodità was understood as the economic precondition. In the first place, the villa's structure always had to be connected to the estate's larger enterprise.[121] The entirely free-standing summer house for the seasonal sojourn, the typical "country house" of the eighteenth, nineteenth, and twentieth centuries, was a totally absurd concept for the sober calculating nobility of the fifteenth and sixteenth centuries. Accordingly, the villa structure had to be situated in an advantageous location with respect to the *possessioni* so as to enable rapid and effortless access to the agricultural places of production at any time in order to survey them and in order to instruct the rural workers.[122] In the selection of the building site, the *padrone* had to consider the natural conditions of the content from an economic point of view with respect to profitable forestry, cattle rearing, and crop rotation.[123] Scamozzi advised extreme vigilance in the purchase of land, since "le possessioni ben lavorate, e bene edificate [well-toiled estates with good buildings]" were evidence of the fact "che il lavoratore ha cavato buone entrate [that the owner had achieved good incomes]" (Book III, 15, 282f.). Here, the *padrone* could invest his capital without risk.[124] One prerequisite for a satisfactory income from agriculture in a Mediterranean country was the well-regulated use of water in the region.[125]

In an early capitalist society that was already completely directed toward a monetary market economy and that only witnessed the rural "barter trade" in distant places and on a modest scale, good transport networks from the rural place of production were essential to guarantee profits. In addition to the dense network of roads in northern Italy, there were the enonomical waterways of the closely knit canal and river system in the Po Valley. Pliny the Younger had already pointed out that for the *Tusculum*, the Tiber "flows right through the fields, is navigable in winter and during the spring carries fruits into the city" (Book V, 6). With reference to the *Laurentum*, he stressed the fact that it was not only approachable on one

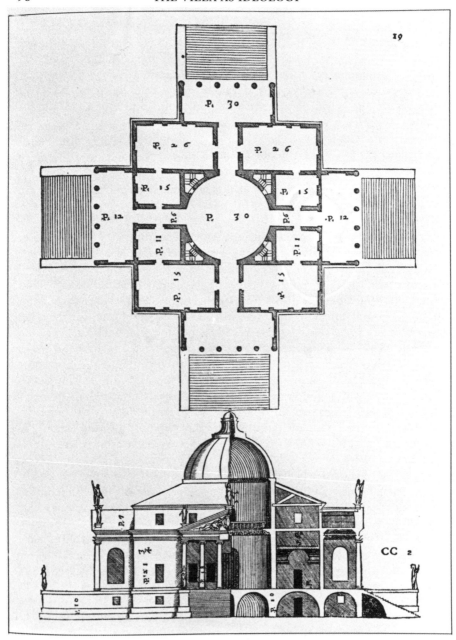

FIGURE 19.   Andrea Palladio, *Plan of the Villa Rotonda*, from *I Quattro Libri dell'Architettura*, Venice, 1570

country road but also on two main roads, that is, via the Ostian and the Laurentian (Book II, 17). Alberti wrote of the "viae claritas" (good road connections) of the villa (IX, 2). Palladio based his demands for a navigable river or for a country road on the following requirement: "le entrate con poca spesa in ogni tempo si potranno nella Città condurre [one should be able to carry goods at any time at little cost to the city]" (Book II, 12, 46) (Figure 17). Scamozzi introduced the term *urban market economy* without reservation when he stated that "[la villa] non sia tanto fuori del comercio degli huomini [The villa should not be located too far from a populated center of commerce]."[126]

The last facet of the *comodità* as a precondition for the building site of the villa led from the economic aspects to those of the *sanità*, that is, to the provision of physical and spiritual training by means of sporting events in the open air. It was the demand for the regional abundance of game and fish that not only reduced the cost of the *padrone*'s menu while enriching it as well but also served his physique through the hunt by hardening his "body, which is tired by urban life." At the same time, the new urban bourgeois class of rulers in the countryside clarified their claim to the old feudal hunting and fishing privileges and also to the chivalrous lifestyle to which the *ars venandi* (the art of the hunt) had belonged since the Middle Ages.[127]

The social and economic reasons for the villa ideal have been illustrated through the example of the ideal location of the *casa di villa* with its emphasis on *comodità*. All subsequent categories of hygiene, of aesthetic quality, and of dignity were already part of the ideological superstructure, which not only defined the villa as a factor of domination and as a new form of income but also as a guarantee of class privileges that extended beyond the material basis and immediate well-being.

For, the villa guaranteed the ideals of a class consciously seeking to practice the idea of *Kalokagathia*, which classical humanism had passed on and which had helped structure the villa as a framework for this end. The aims of this humanist philosophy of life were the formation of physical as well as spiritual "beauty" and the development of a "beautiful soul" through contemplation, none of which had been able to unfold without being disturbed in the city, owing to "questi tumuli, questi stepiti, questa tempesta della terra, della piazza, del palazzo [this tumult, this noise, this commotion of the city, of the marketplace, of the palace]."[128] The main aim was also the education of ideally beautiful youth, who were to carry on the chivalrous and feudal ideals within bourgeois clothing and in accordance with Cicero's treatise *On Old Age*. Alberti described the virtuous landlord as the "padrone e maestro di tutta la gioventù [lord and master of youth]," and the villa as the ideal school for youth.[129]

FIGURE 20.   Villa da Porto Colleoni, Thiene, c. 1490–1500

In the "unscathed world" of the villa, the *padrone* and his family were assailed neither by illness nor by melancholy. He lived "in daylight," enjoyed the advantages of the vigorous fresh air, of the cool breezes even in the summer, of healthy water, and of healthy nourishment. Alberti praised the villa as providing just such a setting when he wrote, "Nolo spectetur upsiam aliquid, quod tristiore offendat umbra. Arrideant omnia [No shadow should disturb the peace of mind by sad moods. Only happiness should rule]"[130] and when he claimed, "ivi si vivesse bene, sano, ivi fosse buon, aere e sana . . . pestilenza, febre e simili taro s'asalisseno [One should be able to live here healthily, the air should be mild and healthy . . . plagues, fevers, and such evils should only occur rarely]."[131]

The villa paradox took on even brighter outlines in the ensuing contrast with the background of the "dark" city.[132] Palladio too accented the contrasting qualities of the city through the enumeration of the hygienic and "psychological" advantages of the villa's ideal site and pointed to the physical exercises of riding and hunting that were demanded of feudal-bourgeois masters by rural life.[133] These demands, recognizable without difficulty as the paraphrase of the ancient ideal *mens sana in corpore sano* (a healthy mind and a healthy body), were evidently rooted in one of Palladio's childhood experiences. This was his encounter with the academy, which the Vicentine humanist Giangiorgio Trissino had established in his villa at Cricoli in order to be able to combine literary studies with physical training, *studia humanitatis*, and *palastra* in a pedagogical experiment based on the ancient Greek pattern and predicated on rural isolation.

Scamozzi followed his master Palladio. He demanded, "l'aria perfetta [vigorous, healthy air]" for the villa, "bontà dell'aria per potervi star sani [an advantageous climate as a guarantee for physical well-being]"[134] for the estate and praised, both with a dietary justification and with reference to Palladio's thoughts on physical training, the "tranquilità del corpo, e dell'animo nostro [tranquility of the body and spirit]" of life in the villa.[135]

Once again there was a concrete ideology behind the demand for physical training in the villa. The privileged class found its perfect identity in the pursuit of sports. It represented itself through sportive "work." *Sport as a social institution combined the old ideal of chivalrous leisure with the new ideal of the vita sobria*, thus allowing the privileged to attain the moderate and healthy life within the ethos of work yet without the smell of the peasant's sweat. Hence, sporting activities were to be salt only for the table of the rich. As Adorno observed in his critique of Veblen's *Theory of the Leisure Class*:

> The less one has to earn money for oneself, the more one feels compelled to achieve the appearance of serious, socially conforming, but nevertheless also disinterested activity. At the same time . . . sport corresponds to

FIGURE 21.   Castle-Villa Giustinian, in Roncade near Treviso, c. 1500

the aggressive and practical ethos of looting. It reduces to a common formula the antagonistic needs for both functional activity and the wasting of time.[136]

Of equal importance as exercising for the beauty of the body was the psychological strengthening of the body and the soul. Rural life also offered the idealized prerequisites for exercising the soul and the natural forces of the countryside that were, as Scamozzi said, the "effetti, che procedono da cause eterne [effects that proceed from elevated causes]." Conversely, the *artificial* forces of the city, which "effetti di cause molto men'nobili causes [derive from many causes] non possono contentare noì stessi, e molto meno l'anima nostra [can hardly satisfy us and our souls]."[137]

Aesthetic pleasures were certainly among the privileges that the *feudal bourgeoisie* enjoyed more often than did common people. The *belezza* of the region was enhanced by the notion of a prospect, by the skillful choice of the villa's belvedere site on higher terrain. The villa paradise did not merely rise above the "nether regions" of common existence in a humanist and literary sense but also in a quite concrete and material way. Moreover, the aesthetic privileges were rated at least as high as those concerning hygiene and climate. Scamozzi, the latest and therefore presumably also the most "self-conscious" of those authors who have been cited is the best aid here for the disclosure of ideological presuppositions. He talked revealingly of the *campagna commune*, which rose above the location of the villa as "il sito in collina, overo in luogo alguanto rilevato [the site on a hill or on slightly raised terrain]." He was concerned with the philosophical justification for the *dignità* and claimed that dominion was secured through an elevated location, even according to Averroes: "il luogo alto, à paragone del basso e come la forma paragonata alla materia, la quale—come si sa—precede tanto di degnità [the elevated site is related to the lower one in the same manner, as form is related to matter, which—as one knows—possesses much less dignity]."[138]

As the sphere of the common people, the *campagna commune* (which was the home of peasants, of tenant farmers, of agricultural laborers and, as such, was a *proletarian* town on the lagoon) was associated with brute matter. Nonetheless, being privileged from the outset by the nature of its site guaranteed the villa's participation in all higher values. Even the external milieu of the *casa di villa* had therefore to be taken into account with regard to the ideologization of villa life. Accordingly, Pliny had already expressed his opinion on his slightly raised Tuscan villa and on its landscape charms.[139] Alberti also rated the aspect of *dignitas* more highly than that of *utilitas* in the selection of the villa's site, especially where *dignitas* was related to the logic of hegemony. For him the uppermost arm of the patriarchal landlordship was the "pacifico stato e fermo reggimento [pacified state and secure power structure],"[140] so that "Tecta ingenuorum [the villa of the gentleman] velim occupent locum agri non feracissimum, sed alioquin dignissimum [should not be located on the most fertile, but on the most noble site of the estate]."[141] Over one hundred years later, Saminiato repeated this idea word for word, as it had lost none of its actuality.[142]

The villa situated in an elevated position (see Figures 5, 18, and 23) provided a double prospect: The villa *padrone* surveyed a wide stretch of land, which is to say his ascendancy over it was consolidated visually, and conversely the villa itself was assertively visible from afar, thus demanding attention even from the distant city. The villa maintained hegemony in relation to the countryside through its given artistic character and quite literally through its outstanding position. Hygienic, aesthetic, and climatic advantages were marshaled to justify the fact that the villa had taken the place of the old rural and feudal castle on the hill without there having been the least military and strategic necessity to do so. These justifications represented a classical form of "rationalization," that is to say, they had an ideological character because they hid what the villa really was: a masonry symbol of hegemony, a conspicuous "territorial matter." Thus, as far as the *sito commodo* was concerned, the viewpoint of the dual belvedere—with its associations of *honestas*, *dignitas*, *nobilitas*, *maestàs*, *magnificenza*, and *grandezza*—always came through next to the nonideological concept of *bellezza* in the writings of Alberti, Scamozzi, Palladio, or Saminiato and the other villa theoreticians.

For Alberti, the most important *amoenitates regionis*, which related to *bellezza* and which increased the aesthetic enjoyment (*voluptas*) of the panoramic view from the villa, were the following: "prati spatia circum florida et campus perguam apricus et silvarum umbrae et limpidissimi fontes ac rivuli et natationes [all around broad meadows and blooming fields, the open, smiling pastures, the cooling shadow of the woods, fresh springs and streams and ponds in which one can swim]";[143] Scamozzi expressed himself analogously.[144]

In only a short space, Walter Benjamin incisively sketched the social problem of the Italian villa as one involving the retreat of a privileged class, starting with the Renaissance conception of nature and with one of the leitmotivs of the art of the villa, namely, the idea of the panoramic prospect. To quote Benjamin on this:

> The fact that no gala box is as unattainable as the ticket to God's free nature, that . . . it . . . preserves its most comforting, tranquil, and sincere countenances for the rich man, as it enters through the large low-lying windows into his cool, shaded halls—that is the pitiless truth that the Italian villa teaches the person who passes through its gates for the first time in order to cast a view onto nearby lakes and mountains. What had been seen in the little Kodak picture fades into insignificance when faced by one of Leonardo's works. Indeed, the landscape hangs in the villa's windowframe as if God's hand had signed it.[145]

The villa had a constant visual presence and was already understood through its elevated position as a concrete embodiment of hegemony. Even today, our way of speaking reflects such claims (whether subconscious or preconscious) to domination, for example, when we say a building has a "commanding" aspect.[146] A connection between *habitaziona* and *fattoria*, or *fabriche per l'uso di villa*, that is to say, between the representative living quarters and the service yard (which had been called for since the fifteenth century and which was finally realized in the Palladian epoch) enabled the *padrone* to control the agricultural production processes comprehensively and at all times.[147] Scamozzi not only subordinated the plan, elevation, and illustrative decoration of the *casa di villa* to the idea of domination but also the entire architectural framing of the immediate and distant surroundings.

Scamozzi circumscribed the idea of domination with expressions such as *maestà, magnificenza, grandezza,* or *nobilità,* so that large courtyards on the front and rear elevation of the villa allowed the latter to appear "con maggior grandezza, e maestà."[148] The same applied to expansive garden layouts.[149] Similarly, the systems of road axes with which the *habitazione del padrone* reached out into the *podere* and beyond into the open countryside were also supposed to ennoble the buildings; the axes were not only to be broader and more straight than the "usual" country roads or lanes but also were to run along the top of built-up embankments so that they rose above the *compagna commune,* the flat land.[150]

In the middle of his *Nuova Cronica* (Volume 11) in the fourteenth century, Giovanni Villani sketched as follows a concise image of the beginnings of Tuscany's *villeggiatura*: "In the environs of Florence, there are many places with clean air, in beautiful surroundings, with enchanting views, with minimal fog and without rough winds, with clear water, where everything is healthy and good. Numerous buildings rise up there that have the character of mansions, and many feature bulwarks or have traits of castles. They are proud and magnificent buildings." In the middle of the fifteenth century, Alberti repeated Villani's words exactly when he wrote about the zenith of the Tuscan *villeggiatura*: "Posti in aere cristallina, in paese lieto, per tutto bello occhio, rarissime nebbie, con cattivi venti, buone acgue, sano e puro ogni cosa."[151]

In the sixteenth century, the same consciousness led toward a comparable social existence with the city flight of the Venetian *nobili.* Thus, the *villeggiatura,* whose ideological core we have tried to grasp in its demands for the ideal site of the *casa padronale,* represented a reconstruction of the original technical prerequisites for the regulation of patrician domains. One key is to reinterpret these efforts, along the lines used by Ernst Bloch in his critique of Jung, as attempts to *reconstruct* archetypical circumstances:

> The archetypical is often called prelogical or merely irrational, which is an error. C. G. Jung has put it into a headless unconscious of 500,000 years ago and has only allowed it to emerge from thence without any future, and entirely as *Regressio.* However, contrary to that view, not only have archetypal images always come forth anew from history but the really old ones too frequently exhibit an utterly bright, urgent utopian intention at the center of a myth. One might think here of transfigured memory—the Golden Age thought of as something submerged or as something that was still to proceed toward the future.[152]

Such archetypical structures of domination were easily made visible through the appropriation of land, more so than in the city with its "abstract" symbols. The distribution of land into a structure of dependency made it possible to practice the old ideals of domination in concrete forms. The dependent tenant farmer, who toiled the *padrone*'s land in the traditional form of the *mezzadria* and who usually had to hand over more than half of the profit, was constantly confronted with the *casa di villa*, in other words, by the concrete symbol of patronal hegemony. In the early sixteenth century, the villas of the Veneto were often still decorated with ornamental crenellation as symbols of sovereignty that were totally without function.[153] Thus the *villano* (or agricultural laborer) was constantly aware of his dependence.

The encirclement of the villa's *habitazione* and *cortile* by tall walls—which were increased further in height by towers, as in the case of the Barco della Regina or the Villa Giustinian in Roncade—ideally separated the place of production from the living domain and established a circle of respect around the *casa di villa*.[154] The *villano* could only pass through the sovereign enclosure if he had identified himself to the estate administration. The powerful, defensive gate buildings for the rural seats of the *Regina Conaro* and of the Villa Giustinian in Roncade were integral parts of villa development, and a separate *luogo per il portinario* (gatekeeper's house) still appeared in Scamozzi's ideal villa.[155]

As part of their claim to hegemony, many of the first "modern" country houses of the Veneto at the turn of the fifteenth century, which already corresponded to the definition of the classical *villa rustica* as a cultural institution, were still completely tied to the medieval traditions of the rural castle. The most well-known example is the Villa da Porto-Colleoni in Thiene (Figure 20). Significantly, the building was variously described by contemporary literature as well as by new research in quite different terms as a *villa*, a *castello*, or a *palazzo*. Certain characteristics, however, are unequivocal proof that it is a *villa* in the modern sense: the grand layout of the garden with fountains, a pond, and a cedar glade on the rear side, the opening of the upper floors onto the countryside, its free-standing location on the plain, the extensive number of farm buildings in addition to storage spaces for the stocking of the produce from the surrounding properties of the family, and finally the conscious architectural integration of *casa di villa* with its garden. In contradiction to this, though, the landlord's house was flanked by four scenic towers at the corners, with imposing pinnacled attachments at roof level, while battlements encircled the whole building for a decorative effect. The entire grounds of the villa, including farm buildings, sheds, *cour d'honneur*, and garden, were enclosed by moderately high walls, with these too being crenellated and articulated by defensive gate towers. This strange mixture of completely heterogeneous architectural ideas and the dialectical interplay of villa and castle, which can be

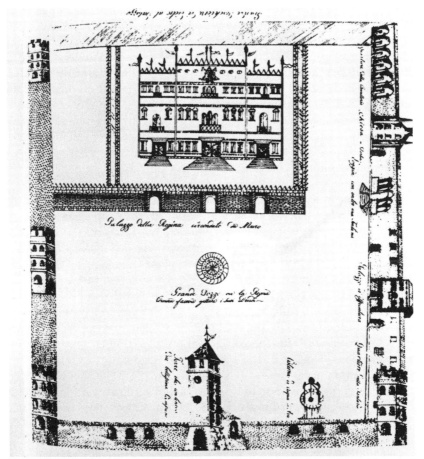

FIGURE 22. Barco della Regina in Altivole, near Asolo, country residence of Catrina Cornaro, Queen of Cyprus, 1491 (destroyed 1509)

grasped just as clearly in the villa castle of the *Regina Cornaro* of 1491 (Figure 22) and in the *Castello Giustinian* at Roncade (Figure 21) from the beginning of the sixteenth century, highlights the epistemological background of the villa's inception, which also determined the subsequent development of this architecture. Here, one must speak of the disguising of a modern notion of the *villeggiatura* by an architectural mask, in which the feudal conscience of history reemerged.

In later Palladian villas, the apparently still intact spiritual worlds of the Roman and Greek periods were elevated by classical building forms and by interior landscapes of ruins in order to meet the goal of reconstructing an ideal of the *aetas aurea*. In the case of the Palladian villa, the goal was to project the *negative utopia* back only to the cohesive world of the Middle Ages with its guaranteed structure of domination that was purportedly devoid of conflicts. The neomedieval forms of pinnacles, towers, walls, and gateways turned the building itself into a museum that was analogous to the conservative, museumlike image of the patron. Just like Caterina Cornaro's villa and that of Giustinian at Roncade, the Villa da Porto-Colleoni definitely has an affirmative character. Whenever architecture takes on such graphic features or such a representative character, in Sedlmayr's sense of the term, we are forced to ask: Who wanted to be represented here and to whom were such representations addressed?

Even as the first signs of alienation between the dominant and the dominated were visible here, it also seemed that this architecture was about the self-assurance of those who could still use pinnacles and towers as symbols of their social or political demands, although nothing needed to be defended here any longer except those very pretensions to privilege responsible for these forms in the first place. The walls between the towers and gate houses in the Villa da Porto-Colleoni, in the Barco della Regina, and in the Castello Giustinian are so thin that they would have been meaningless in military terms, but not in terms of propaganda. As the expression of a certain political tendency, they created the necessarily sovereign framework for the patriarchal residential villa, which was then in a position to supercede the castle as the hegemonic architecture in a pacified countryside.

In ideological terms, not only political but also artistic ideas discover themselves through social practice. *Wherever walls and towers merely have to defend ideas, wherever they have only to repulse political opposition at most and not military force, architecture as a guarantor of physical dominance—that is, the castle—turns into architecture as a form of ideological hegemony—namely, the residential villa.* The castle echoed in the rural palace of the da Portos was merely an aesthetic memory, even though it was an extremely lively memory according to the details as well as to the overall form. Here, the political reality of the countryside castle was maintained in the villa without loss of stature, despite the fact that the architectural forms appeared only as quotations in the interiors of the villa.[156]

Such politically loaded building forms are only possible on the basis of certain fixed building privileges. In spite of the Terraferma's extensive sovereignty, the authorities who controlled the hinterland politically and economically did not tolerate such architectural monuments of domination in every case. The da Portos were in fact a family who were obedient and loyal to *La Serenissima*. The Villa da Porto was therefore not only a monument of domination on behalf of the da Portos but simultaneously also a

FIGURE 23. Andrea Palladio, Villa Emo, Fanzolo, c. 1564

testimonial to the Venetian claim to power over the Terraferma. Strictly in accordance with the motto *pro summa fide summus amor*, political reliability was honored by granting political privileges. Architectural privileges were clear manifestations of these conditions. The Venetian procedure of playing off communes against feudal landlords resulted in the dispensation of such architectural privileges, that is to say, in a politics of construction whereby architecture became the medium of political and ideological disputations.

The fact that *La Serenissima* did not naively substitute for the existing political organization of the Terraferma its own sham republican version of politics (as a result of which the conflict between town and country would have intensified unbearably) provided evidence of their family-based policy in the countryside. Whenever Venetian nobles moved to the countryside, they also became aristocrats on paper. In return for money and political deeds, European sovereign households were mobilized to issue letters granting aristocratic patents to urban Venetian magnates. Yet the Venetian constitution contained no provision for hereditary titles nor did the Doge have the monarchical right to issue these nominal aristocratic titles. Thus, the rigid traditional power structure of feudal patronage was maintained in the Terraferma in spite of the changes represented by those who held these new forms of power.[157] It is also possible to give evidence of this practice of political construction *ex-negativo*, as recent research has shown. In disobedient communes, the medieval towers and fortifications that were monuments to nonconformity with feudal domination and to antirepublican loyalty to the emperor were razed to the ground. Furthermore, members of the old established rural aristocracy lost their right to decorate their country seats with the symbolic forms of castle architecture if they had conspired against the Venetian authorities.[158]

In his agricultural treatise of around 1300, Piero de Crescenzi attested to the character of this domination and to the elitist charm of the "firm" country seats of the northern Italian rural aristocracy. These latter positions determined undisguisedly the formation of the first real villas of the urban Venetian nobility in the late fifteenth and early sixteenth centuries and expressed themselves in more sublime, formal terms in the middle of the century. To quote Piero de Crescenzi on the vertical nature of this society:

> Ma se la nobilità de'signori et la potentía è tanta, che schiffino d'abitare con suoi lavoratori in una medesima coste, potranno agiatamente nel predecto luogo cosi disposto fare dimorare il loro luogo ordinato di palagi et di torri et di giardini secondo che alloro nobilità et possanza si converra.
>
> [It, however, the status and influence of the nobility are so great that they would be nauseated to live under one roof with their servants, then they

should disassociate their house from the rest by means of a palatial character, towers and gardens, as befits their status and their power.][159]

Consequently, we could hardly agree with Rupprecht when he declared as one of the decisive criteria of the northern Italian villa of the sixteenth century that it be "separated . . . from all architecture of domination in the countryside (castle, palace . . . monastery)" (p. 221). Nor could we agree with him when he wrote of Palladio's Villa Emo in Fanzolo (Figure 23) that it was "remote from any semblance of representation, from claims to importance or power and domination" (p. 221). Nonetheless, such statements are in accordance with the villa books themselves. For Petrarch "did not in fact condemn just the bad government" in the city, "but all forms of domination" (p. 210). With Lollio too, "domination and injustice flowed together in his conception of the city; it is indicative that he mentions *Città* and *Castella* at the same time" (p. 229).

Petrarch certainly cannot be accused of equivocation. In a manner similar to that of later villa theoreticians, he sought to realize his ideal of the *vita solitaria* in the countryside. Yet his flight from the old social ties of the city was not aimed at new social ties in the countryside, which might have appeared more positive. Rather, his was a flight *from all social interdependencies per se*, from any form of politics, and this flight had no other aim than the defense of the monadic self. Petrarch fled to the countryside because it appeared to him to be the domain of the totally apolitical. His position was that of the radical individualist who was to embody a form of asociality as a proud stylization of the "outcast," or perhaps even as a form of anarchism. Petrarch was antiurban, as were Falcone, Lollio, and Gallo, but this was not due to his political thought process. Indeed, far from it; his animosity toward the city was merely an expression of his total opposition to sociality as such. Petrarch thus found his self-understanding simultaneously "outside" of the political and in reaction to it.

Certainly by the time of Lollio, however, the apolitical *vita solitaria* had transformed itself into the highly political *vita rustica*. The ideal of the *vita rustica* was the theoretical background to distinct political tendencies and to definite political manipulations. This equivocation, which was called ideology and which constituted a fluent language for the forms of the Renaissance villa, divulged itself in the case of Lollio, Gallo, and Falcone. The antagonism between the theories of agricultural humanism concerning the *vita rustica* and the postulates of the architectural theoreticians (such as Alberti, Palladio, and Scamozzi) on the *villa rustica* and the contradiction of a rural philosophy of life with a rural building theory were both canceled by the concept of the villa as ideology. Lollio, Gallo, and Falcone praised life in the countryside as existence in an "empire of freedom" where the domination of some people over others was apparently nullified. Yet, Alberti and his successors, such as Palladio, Scamozzi, and Saminiato, demanded and practiced a villa architecture that had as its aim the perpetuation of just such a system of domination by a few people over the majority. The ideology of life in the countryside along with flight from the city unveiled itself here. The political and artistic styles of the age matched each other in these architectural treatises, and this identity was but a consequence of the dialectical thought about the state in the Renaissance. The resulting configuration went as follows: politics as a work of art, the work of art as an expression of politics, or hegemony as stylistic phenomena, the phenomena of style as hegemony.

Only those who uncritically accepted the contradictions between the moralizing villa books and the theoretical ideal of the villa, that is, only those who accepted a coin as both one-dimensional and undialectical (in spite of the fact that the coin's sides showed divergent positions at academic face value) could contend that the villas of the Quattrocento were "remote from any semblance of representation or divorced from claims of importance, power, and dominance." Two things could be concealed behind such a contention: first, an unconscious reconstitution of academic research by an ideology that has reproduced itself assiduously and continuously from the fifteenth century until today; or second—and far worse—an art history that serves as the "lackey" of a cultural ideology whose aims have not changed fundamentally since 1550 but whose concerns have only become more transparently untenable ever since.

In the idealization of the patriarchal structure of life in the countryside within villa ideology, there appeared almost Manichean traits. The world was simply interpreted in the manner of a "terrible simplification" as a crude conflict between light and dark. This view was without differentiated transitional stages and it featured the bedeviled image of an ominous and impure life in the city versus the desired ideal of a bright and honest life in the countryside. For as Heide Berndt (1968, p. 13) has observed: "Within the organic society of feudalism, the city was an alien object because it represented a different socializing principle than did the . . . large households of the feudal landlords: The city is essentially a market settlement, it is an 'exchange-economical opposite' to the 'exchangeless interior of the Oikos' [the feudal farmstead of the master]."

The art theorists presented the relation between town and country in a similarly effective and tendentious light/dark manner. Scamozzi saw the "cause eterne" as the driving force behind the rural form of life while seeing the "cause molto men'nobili"[160] as the driving force behind urban culture. To Alberti, the city was the birthplace of "vizio, bestialità, perversità, falsità," and "scandalo" (vice, bestiality, perversion, falsity, and scandal).

Hence, he fled from "questi strepiti, questi tumulti, questa tempestà della terra, della piazza, del palagio."

His concept of the *tumultuoso* anticipated surprisingly well the concept of the chaotic, of the anarchic, as Oswald Spengler labeled the infamous mode of life in the proletarian metropolis of the industrial age. The life in the countryside guaranteed that the *homo rusticanus* (the rustic dweller), that is, the "veri, buoni, uomini [true and good human]" in the villa would be "nuina malinconia, piacere, diletto, onestà, contentamento d'animo [Free from melancholy, in addition to having piety, happiness, honesty, and peace of mind]." The rustic dweller lived in a "proprio paradiso."[161] Palladio also saw the relationship between town and country in antagonistic terms. As such, he believed that the "agitationi della Città" were opposed by the "sanita del corpo, ristauro e consolatione dell'animo, contemplatione, beata vita" of the countryside.[162] This iconology also linked the agrarian domain of Ceres with the idea of *virtù*.[163]

The socially and historically advanced *vita urbana* on the threshold of emancipation and enlightenment was discriminated against in favor of the *vita rustica*, whose patriarchal structures and paternalist authority still appeared to be intact, or at least easily reconstituted and reclaimed. In scientific terms, one could call this process a "regressive metamorphosis," since the social situation in the city, where liberating tendencies were already emerging, brought forth a reactionary idealization of things that were apparently long since past and had begun to be surmounted. It was not the countryside that developed the "classical" Venetian villa, as well as the superstructure of the *vita solitaria* as *vita rustica*. On the contrary, all initiatives in favor of the *villeggiatura* appeared as the reverse of the utopian if analyzed by "critical theory."

Villa ideology actualized the old dream of the Golden Age, of arcadian and bucolic existence, so that, as one scholar has noted: "Saturn's golden empire, which had passed away in prehistoric times, descended no further into the past; it became the present and entered the gate to the villa. Both positions, the Christian and the antiquarian, coincided in the changed goal of the *hic et nunc* of the villa."[164] That is to say, the art of *agricoltura* was the medium that allowed a transformation of the *aetes aurea* into a "regressive utopia" to take place. Ensnared by *agricoltura* and converted from Petrarch's *Solitarius* to Gallo's *santa professione degli agricoltori*, the villa *padrone* became immersed in an ahistorical sphere of ideal existence. His consciousness led him to reject the social reality of the city. The social existence of the city, with its historical "then and there," was repressed in favor of the ahistorical—even prehistorical—*hic et nunc* of the villa in the countryside.

The arcadian ideal as a social form of existence was concretely realized in the *usanza nuova* of the classical Venetian villa and in the social organization of the Po Valley estates. Thus, one translated the Padania ideal of the *aetes aurea* from prehistorical terms into historical ones, from the Greek legends of arcadian peasants and shepherds into the Roman republic of such men as Cato, Cincinnatus, and Manius Curius. This new world of the Venetian Renaissance had already idealized Cicero in literary terms. As a precursor of the Venetian villa ideologues, Cicero was just as "nonnaive," just as "sentimental" as, for instance, Alvise Cornaro, whose *Vita Sobria* or *Barbaro Epistle* of 1566 would have been unthinkable without the knowledge of Cicero's treatise, entitled *On Old Age*. The quite divergent view of the relation between town and country put forth by Thomas More has been discussed as follows by Herman Bauer: "Utopia is the ideal of the *Zoon politikon*. . . . It always portrayed a functioning state system. Thereby it also differentiated itself unequivocally from all arcadian and bucolic dream ideals. . . . Arcadia has as its goal the flight from the bad and hostile city. Utopia has as its the goal a flight from the same city, but again it is to another, better city."[165]

The arcadian, therefore regressive, utopia of the villa is the exact opposite of the concrete utopia, which modern philosophers such as Ernst Bloch have proposed as a social model for the future. The conflict between emancipation and reaction was concretized as the confrontation between town and country and converted by Cornaro along the best Ciceronian lines into the generation gap between young and old (thus trivializing it). As such, this latter view represented itself as an authoritarian conflict that was, however, not openly carried on in the *villeggiatura* and whose solution was therefore undermined. The conflict became more acute despite, or precisely because of, its disguise through the removal of the concrete base for urban conflict by diverting it to the countryside.

It was there that antiquated conditions were reconstructed in a totally historical manner by calling upon the humanist legitimation of the antique *renovatio*. As such, conditions no longer corresponded to the preliminary stage for the democratization of the cities, since, as others have noted:

> The villa is a world at rest with itself. Evil has been banished to the distant city. It was precisely because of this that the domain [of the villa] could become a paradise. This paradise [is founded] on the trust in the stability of the moral individual. Consequently, the domain of the villa and the life in it are static; any dynamism and tension are absent, and there is no goal toward which any movement might be going.[166]

The tendency toward social stasis, toward an archconservative consciousness, appeared quite undisguised in the villa books. Falcone wrote the following in 1559 about the villa: "Pianta è semina secondo l'uso del paese, è non essere curioso d'novita [Plant and sow, as it is the tradition of the country, and beware of the introduction of novelties]."[167] Alberto Lollio saw in tradition, in conservative historical consciousness, an argument for the supremacy of rural life in opposition to urban forms of existence: "La vita rustica [è] molto più antica, et assai più nobile della urbana [The life in the country is much older and therefore much more noble than that of the city]."[168]

Only a few critical intellects seemed to have seen through the conservative jargon of villa ideology. By 1557, the Florentine Antonio Francesco Doni, who with his villa treatise only played the role of an outsider within the contemporary villa literature, had already uncovered the antiemancipatory character of the life in the countryside, the masquerading of and the fixation with archaic social roles in the villa culture. Hence, he disclosed the ideological background of the link between the villa and *studia humanitatis*, that is to say, the social legitimation of the *villeggiatura* through the irretrievable authority of ancient history. As such, he noted that "le forme son perdute, e non c'è ordine a trovar Villa che quieti l'animo"—"lasciando gli antichi, che io non viddi mai."[169]

We repeat: The villa movement disguised conflicts of authority, reconstituted archetypal conditions, and saw itself as a counter to urban emancipation. From this point of view, then, the villa—which art history has deemed a progressive, far-reaching cultural form when seen in aesthetic terms only—otherwise unveils itself de facto as a reactionary phenomenon. It is not possible, however, to locate the previous illustrated relationships in terms of direct dependence on the consciously articulated intentions of the dominant class of the sixteenth century. Without a doubt, the interdependencies of that period that can be read within the material of the historical facts and extracted from the literary documents now appear to us more immediate than was really applicable to the development of the *villeggiatura* from a vantage point within contemporary history. It would now make little sense to make a political accusation on the basis of a social, historical, and ideological interpretation of past villa culture.

16

The Dream of the Country in the Nineteenth and Twentieth Centuries: Spengler, Tönnies, Riehl, and the Gründerzeit Villa

EVEN AT THE turn of the twentieth century, the conflict between town and country was regarded as a critical problem from the point of view of cultural philosophy, architectural theory, and political analysis. Thus, it could be observed that "the proposals of the nineteenth and twentieth centuries to reconcile this conflict, whether they came from Marx, Howard, Kropotkin, or Le Corbusier, resolve the characteristic elements of town and country into something that is, in principle, uniformly new. A real detachment from these elements is not possible either in the villa or anywhere else—except through an inner exile reminiscent of Petrarch's."[170]

Riehl, Spengler, and Tönnies tackled the problem of contrary standpoints. Surprisingly, their alternatives to the solutions of Marx or Kropotkin often bring to mind the agricultural humanism and villa ideology of the Cinquecento. They saw in the modern big city a melting pot for strengthening the proletariat and a decay of the old urban forms for maintaining domination and for sustaining elites. They interpreted this decay as disallowing the ascendancy of small, highly privileged groups over the masses: "Maintaining the domination of big landowners makes it possible to depict the common people as a 'unified work of art' (to quote Riehl) that has a hierarchical structure."[171]

One found the primal picture of the state in the community, since the social value of property belonging to individual citizens of the community was respected and taken for granted to a greater extent in the village than in the city. In the end, the domination of the big cities was entirely equated with the "domination of the proletariat." Riehl by no means interpreted social contradictions only as historical developments; he also interpreted

114

them as natural, that is, as "elemental" and thus unalterable facts. In a way reminiscent of Alberti, Tönnies wrote that "in the big city, therefore, in the capital and especially in the metropolis, family life is in a process of decay."[172] This socially and politically motivated black-and-white caricature of town versus country went as far back as the conservative Prussian censorship of art in the nineteenth century. Schiller's *Wilhelm Tell* was felt to be unacceptable. Thus, the most inflammatory passages were stripped of their socially critical, hence explosive, force.

Oswald Spengler, who based legitimation of the late bourgeois practice of domination on bourgeois cultural ideology, believed that the expansion and emancipation of the big city were jointly responsible for the "death" of all culture. For him, the "original sin" began with the disintegration of feudal domination and of the corporate state. He saw the petty bourgeoisie in the cities, that "shapeless class," as the prime mover of this process of destruction. No offense seemed more odious to him than revolt against the ruling class, and he identified the idea of freedom with the concept of "rootlessness" and claimed: "It lends expression to the fact that within the town walls the plant-like attachment to the country has come to an end and the ties running throughout country life are torn. Its essence, therefore, is a negating element."[173]

In another passage, Spengler's physiognomic view of the metropolis came surprisingly close to the distorted picture of the city characteristic of the villa ideology of the Italian Renaissance from Petrarch and Alberti to Falcone. However, the language he used became, at the same time, "quainter" and more threatening than that of his Italian predecessors. In addition, there were the keywords "hearth," "pious sentiments," "center," "family," "affinity for the country," which also appeared in the villa books of the Renaissance. Subsequently, those anti-intellectual words of warning were used by the totalitarian ideology of fascism to underpin their archaic, barbaric, and inhuman vocabulary with such phrases as "blood," "feeling," "intellectual nomad." To quote another author on this rhetoric:

> [It] is no longer houses in which Vesta and Janus, the *penates* and *lares*, possess some kind of pagan place but rather mere dwellings created not by blood but by purpose, not by feeling but by economic entrepreneurial spirit. As long as the hearth in the pious sense is the real, important center of a family, then the last tie to the country has not disappeared. Only when that also is lost and the masses of tenants and overnight guests in this sea of houses lead a wandering existence from shelter to shelter, like the hunters and herdsmen of old, is the intellectual nomad fully developed.[174]

Surprisingly, such positivistic prejudices have even been handed down to and become an established part of post-Freudian psychoanalysis. Thus, Erich

Fromm, unconsciously paraphrasing a biblical saying and still completely adhering to the notions of idealistic ethics, could write critically about the modern form of society and culture as if the modern field of social philosophy, the concepts of "the reality principle" and the "achievement principle" were unknown to him as historical, genetic, and psychological categories:

> In the face of his creation [man] can really say it is good. But what should he say in the face of himself? . . . While we were creating wonderful things, we failed to make beings out of ourselves for the sake of whom this immense effort seems to be worthwhile. Our life is not one of fraternity, happiness, contentment, but a life of intellectual chaos and inner uneasiness.[175]

Not only is there a suggestion of the biblical saying "For what is a man profited, if he shall gain the whole world, and lose his own soul?"[176] Here, one is also immediately reminded of Alvise Cornaro's anticity bias that led to a comparison of the rustic "vita ragionevole e con ordine" with the urban "vita senza ragione e senza ordine." Marcuse has pointed out here how the revisionist cultural critique succumbs to the "power of positive thinking."[177]

In the period of industrialization since the mid-nineteenth century, mechanisms of domination have emerged that bear a very obvious similarity to conditions during the sixteenth century, that is, to the beginning of capitalist forms of economy. Large "dominating" industrial plants in the heart of the town or within the city limits seem to resemble, both in character and in power structure, large *latifundia*. One might regard large-scale industry as a "substitute" for large-scale rural landholdings, though the two forms of capital accumulation did not, by any means, necessarily exclude one another in the nineteenth century. The rural *padrone* and the industrial magnate view the employment of dependents as a guarantee for their lavish lifestyle and for their substantial demands within society, an aspect of which is neglected to a certain extent when the *villeggiatura* is examined only from an aesthetic point of view. Both rural and industrial magnates have a tendency to maintain tradition and to form dynasties. Furthermore, they each develop specific forms of "family pride," of uninterrupted succession and permanent expansion of their dominion, which is played down as a necessary "realignment of boundaries."

One may assume that for the dependent worker it does not make much difference whether he or she is employed in agriculture or in mechanical production. In any case he or she has virtually no share in the ownership of the means of production and no self-determining role in the process of production. By virtue of permanent settlement on the *podere* or in immediate proximity of the factory *latifundium*, which was required by the employer, the worker is restricted in his or her freedom. A system of loans, interest to be paid, lease charges, and attachment of wages for services provided by the employer have extended dependence beyond the immediate work process to the private sphere, thus reinforcing it. The Krupp workers' settlement programs demonstrated this in the nineteenth century, as did the methods for settlement of the Venetian *beni inculti* in the sixteenth century. The "more humane" form of dependency in the villa system of the sixteenth century was, in the end, a "more repressive one," because it was less discernible. In the dependence on the *padrone* as a seemingly "good father" and as a commissioner of *divina providenza*, divine providence, false feelings of obligation and guilt developed in relation to a pseudoreligious background. This prevented the formation of a dynamic, that is, socially militant and socially revolutionary, class consciousness. As has been noted:

> Not entirely without criticism does Heinrich Freese describe the Krupp settlements in his brochure *Concerns of Manufacturers (Fabrikantensorgen)* as follows: "With deep regret I saw that Krupp consumer establishments were the size of big-city shops and noticed that the work force was entirely excluded from the management. Everything is brought into being one-sidedly. Everything that happens, happens from the top, and everything that is created remains the property of the company." The 3,208 Krupp workers' accommodations have the disadvantage "that the worker is now not only dependent on the employer by virtue of his work but also by virtue of his domicile, and if he loses his job, he also forfeits the much-praised apartment" (H. Freese).[178]

It is not surprising that factory owners transferred their place of residence to the immediate proximity of the production plants during the initial phase of industrialization. It is not surprising either that these buildings had a villa character and that they frequently even had a historical link to Palladian models. As in the case of the *casa di villa* of Garzoni, Giustinian, Soranzo, Barbaro, or Cornaro, they were located, so to speak, right in the middle of the *possessioni* and preferably at an especially prominent site so that they were literally elevated above the "depths" of ordinary existence—usually rendered noble through the artistic and patron-like ambitions of the owner.

The claim to domination of the "directors' villas" manifested itself in monumental arrangements and in the decorative use of forms of fortification as ornaments devoid of meaning. The battlements, oriels, little towers, half-timbered walls and wall boundaries of *Gründerzeit* villas were linked to the apparently "ideal world" of the Middle Ages and preserved a late romantic as well as hyper "German" historical consciousness. The classic column arrangements, however, the atlantes and hermes, the pompous portals and classicist gables in Renaissance style document a humanist claim to education and refinement in which the

FIGURE 24.   The Krupp's Villa Hugel, Essen, 1869–73

clattering concepts of Doric, Ionic, and Corinthian had the same value as Czerny études, flower watercolors, and Scott's chivalric novels. As was the case with the "historically" oriented Palladian villas that followed the *casa di villa degli antichi*, so the *Gründerzeit* edifices often even combined several historical styles (Figure 24).

As in the villa of the Renaissance, a *glacis* of garden and tree park created the necessary distance from the production area without lessening the tendency toward constant surveillance and demonstration of power. It was not until the concentration of far too many expansive manufacturing plants (with their related climatic, hygienic, and aesthetic disadvantages) that the urban magnates were forced to move to prestigious green areas and villa zones outside of the city at the beginning of this century. As the system was increasingly perfected, there was no longer a need for continuous presence. The responsibility could be delegated to paid directors who frequently continued to reside in physical proximity to the production sites and, as "majordomo" of the industrial age, basically performed the same task as the stewards of the Renaissance, who constantly remained in the villa, near the *fattori*.

One does not do justice to these edifices if one simply dismisses them as typical *Gründerzeit* kitsch—even if approached through the architectural ideology of "new functionalism," "functionalism," and "antihistoricism." This purely aesthetic judgment of quality follows a normative type of aesthetics that bases its canon on the "actual" historical epochs in which such forms still had a "genuine" and "effective" message, when the political and the architectural style of the period corresponded to one another. If one sees only the kitsch in the *Gründerzeit* villa, then it is "nullified" in two respects. First, one overestimates its artistic claim by measuring it against a canon of "originality" that it, of course, cannot live up to; and second, one underestimates its social claim if one views and judges its threatening ornamental masks only aesthetically. It is not necessary to pursue Veblen's attack on culture with single-minded rigor (that is, to assume that every culture is a form of barbarism, advertising, and exhibitionism denoting power, prey, and profit) in order to perceive the aspect of a threat, of repression, and an "aggressive barbarism," which lead directly to the false "archaism" in the art of the Fascist system for total domination behind the historically masked ornaments of nineteenth-century architecture.[179] The prestigious structures of the big cities of the fin de siècle—the villas, town palaces, town halls, railway stations, insane asylums, and hospitals— dressed themselves up in the stylistic robes of classic ancient temple facades, of medieval castles and sacral Gothic architecture, of Renaissance and Baroque palaces.

Bourgeois art history limited itself to revealing the theatrical falseness, the sham and circus trumpery, the tawdry, half-educated stage spectacle behind these sumptuous robes. However, it is not enough just to hear the false theatrical thunder resounding in the barbaric ornamental machines of the *Gründerzeit*. Cultural critique as a "pure" critique of taste remains completely inherent to the system in the manner of a tasteful theater review, so that it merely blames the architect of the *Gründerzeit* for furnishing a poor and unfaithful Palladian, Scamozzi, or Sansovino performance, for putting on a tasteless "production." In the previously quoted passage on the contradictory character of Palladian architectural ornamentation (that is, on the aspect of "persuasion," of "truth and falsehood" in its classically dressed edifices), Goethe went a decisive step beyond this bourgeois art critique intrinsic to the system. Veblen ultimately took the most radical position. As Adorno noted: "The real temples, cathedrals, and palaces are as false for him as are imitations of them (of the nineteenth century) . . . [since] he explains culture on the basis of kitsch, not the other way around."[180]

In other words, repressive attitudes and ideologies of domination did not first manifest themselves in the "imitations" of the nineteenth century but were already evident in the "originals" of the sixteenth. Nevertheless, the ideological "substrata" in the *Gründerzeit* villas became even more apparent than in the northern Italian country houses of the Palladian epoch (Figures 18 and 23) to the extent that the copy (especially when there is a substantial gap in quality) overemphasizes or even caricatures essential features of the original. For it is the magic of apparent originality in Palladian architecture, the high degree of artistic quality at first glance, that is able to make the ideological critique seem unjustified and violent. "The presence of his works is so impressive" (Goethe), that by virtue of its "great form" it veils the historical irony of its "double historicism." After Veblen, one would have to designate the *Gründerzeit* villas as "imitations of imitations." For even Palladian architecture does not find its identity, its "truth" in itself, but through a mask of the classical architectural ethos. When Palladio and Scamozzi demanded *maestà, magnificenza, grandezza, nobiltà,* or *degnità* in the ideal villa, this referred to the same demand on architecture as an expression of image, power, or profit that today carries the label of "conspicuous consumption."[181]

In the ideological superstructure of the rural and industrial magnates of the sixteenth and nineteenth centuries, this is comparable, in particular, to the formation of a work ethos that in the cloak of patriarchal concepts is closely connected to national terms and to the symbolic figure of the paternal patron. In the role of the "chief servant," the latter avowedly stylizes himself as the trustee of all the social concerns of those dependent on him. The Venetians' national maxim of *pro summa fide summus amor,* the ethically based program of *cultivazione dei beni inculti* (the self-view of an

Alvise Cornaro, who on his *podere* "brings up water, improves the air, settles people, increases the population, and perfects living conditions so that he can claim with complete justification to have given God, altar, and church more souls for worship"), embodied the same attitude that stood behind the Krupp workers' welfare programs, which counterbalanced and diluted the urge for social and political emancipation on the part of the dependent persons through a patriarchal "system of appeasement." For Alberti and Palladio, the patriarchally organized *latifundium* was a place *perpascere la famiglia* ("to put the family out to pasture," that is, to maintain the family life without interference), an area where the *negotio famigliare e privato* was guaranteed to go undisturbed.[182] Accordingly, ideologically fetishized concepts such as "Kruppian" or "the big Krupp family" have been lovingly preserved until today.[183]

17

Theodor Fontane's "Villa Treibel"

IN HIS NOVEL entitled *Gründerzeit, Frau Jenny Treibel*, Theodor Fontane created a literary monument with added value as a historical source. The story, which takes place shortly after 1874,[184] describes the replacement of the feudal elite of the high nobility by the advancing big urban merchants and industrialists during the Prussian fin de siècle as the social "background" of the conflict between the middle class and the upper class (Corinna and Leopold).[185] However, Fontane does not merely describe, he analyzes perspicaciously. The beginning of Chapter 2 is particularly informative in that the apparently one-dimensional description of the Treibel villa becomes transparent and makes visible the abovementioned social, as well as genetic and formal, analogy between agricultural villa and industrial villa, the analogy between *latifundia* of the sixteenth century and factory grounds of the nineteenth century.[186] The same motivation of a social demand for admiration as in the Venetian Cinquecento lies mutatis mutandis behind the Treibel family's flight out of the city. Treibel, a distinguished businessman, has abandoned the bourgeois townhouse and has settled halfway between the "proletarian" sphere of the city (the milieu of the petty bourgeoisie and the middle class) and the "feudal" sphere of the country (the milieu of the lords of the manor).

In other words, he settles in a suburban area in the middle of his factory grounds, in a genuine "villa" that elevates the production site to an "industrial *latifundium*" and dominates it, thus enabling constant supervision of the production process and at the same time a pseudofeudal lifestyle in a framework of relative individual freedom denied by the city. The building is situated on a river and it has two stories. As a radius of respect, the garden and park lend him "dignity" over the production plants. Hygienic disadvantages—such as the factory smoke—must be accepted to ensure a visibly dominant presence. Even the Venetian *nobili* did not shy away from residing cheek by jowl with servants' quarters and stables. Feelings of social resentment are shown by the heroine, who herself has risen to the upper class from the proletariat and is, as are all parvenus, especially guarded about her rights. She regrets that the villa lacks a separate servants' and tradesmen's entrance.[187]

Analogies with the Late Renaissance go even further, however. In the Treibel's villa, the "dining room" (or *sala*), into which a "reception room" (or *vestibolo, entrata*) leads, is also the "heart and bosom of the house" (cf. Alberti and Scamozzi). Stucco work and historical reliefs give the drawing room a refined appearance. Only the foremost artists could meet the socially elevated cultural standards of the *"padrone's"* spouse (Professor Franz Reinhold Begas). The drawing room is situated along the main axis, the axis of symmetry, of the house and this axis is, at the same time, a prospect axis, a "view channel." From the drawing room the view opens up "to the large, parklike back garden," which was an important Vitruvian requirement for the *compartimento* of the ideal villa in antiquity and in the Renaissance.[188] As was true during the Renaissance, a "splashing fountain" functions as a stimulating aqueous element, part of the obligatory accoutrements of garden and villa. The fountain closes the circle of elements defining the villa, *terra (podere)*, *aer* (open, spacious constructional form), and *ignis* (sun).

As in the fictitious estrade of the *salotto* in the Villa Maser, where (as a sign of refined taste) the parrot, small Bolognese dog, and monkey lend a peculiar exotic flair, the Treibel's *fontana* would not be complete without a colorful cockatoo. Corinna lacks only a peacock. The Treibel's drawing room fulfills all the functions of the Palladian dining rooms: feudal prestige (*feste*), sumptuous dinners (*conviti*), family ceremonies (*nozze*), cultural events on behalf of the ideological legitimation of upper-class social practices (*apparati per recitar comedie*). Adolar Krola's musical lecture at the conclusion of the dinner belongs here. As in the Cinquecento, nature and architecture, greenery and stone all communicate so that the garden is an integral part of the house and can be reached directly from the dining room in the sultriness of summer. The latter is indeed a direct and commensurate extension of the garden and vice versa. After dinner, the company proceeds to the obligatory "garden promenade."

18

The Dream of the Countryside
as a Timeless Ideology

IDEOLOGIES ARE CHARACTERIZED by a tendency to seem self-evident and to be markedly resilient, even when the economic and social relationships originally responsible for them have long since passed. For this reason, Rupprecht's study serves less as a conclusion than as a point of departure when it states: "The form that in the villa once united *agricoltura* and *litterae*, economy and ethics, *rusticitas* and *humanitas* is gone. People are no longer looking for paradise in the countryside."[189]

In fact, a broad trail leads from the "German ideology"[190] of the nineteenth century and its converse, Fascist *Blut und Boden* (blood and soil) barbarism in the twentieth century, back to the agrarian ideology of northern Italian humanism and, even beyond that, to an ahistorical conception of country life as an archaic domain of the good life: ideal, sober, and void of conflicts. Then, the belief that "man is good" was still valid, not the misguided critical extension of this belief into the insidious view that "only the good man is good." Spengler, Riehl, and Tönnies were not the only ones to set up the curiously anachronistic field markers for Heidegger's ideology of *Pracht des Schlichten* (splendid simplicity). Even such heterodox contemporaries as Alfred Krupp, Karl Jaspers, Konrad Adenauer (West Germany's first chancellor), and Ben-Gurion (Israel's first prime minister), as well as anonymous members of the Weimar ministerial bureaucracy also maintained these views. One can even read something along similar lines in a recent theoretical paper on Albrecht Thaer and Justus von Liebig's agricultural research at the end of the nineteenth century: "Of course, the soil has always been tilled for its utility. The radically new situation that is represented by Thaer's case is, however, characterized by the fact that agriculture is now coincidental only with utility, that there is no other criterion but profit. . . . [Liebig] showed that it has now become possible to combine boundless material blessings with a dismaying submission of ethical elements."[191]

With "dismaying submission of ethical elements," art history is disclosed as deeply ideological, even when it is given credit for being free from ideology. The academic subject of sixteenth-century agricultural humanism—which is not recognized as part of the ideological superstructure but on the contrary is assigned to the domain of "pure" philosophical and cultural history—becomes totally imploded, thus striking back at the subject being researched. Thus, the mainstream analysis has remained necessarily system-immanent. This is largely the predicament of today's art history, which deceives itself by militating against the unmasking of its own immanently ideological character, by characterizing such critiques as ideology obtruding from the outside onto the subject. With the introduction of ideological and historical critiques into the discipline, traditional art history suspects a covert and partisan attack on the fetish of autonomous scholarship. The mainstream position necessarily rejects such ideological critiques as leading to a supposed ideologization of itself. It is probably not a coincidence, since this blind inhibition prevents a hermeneutic approach to the villa as ideology, just as it precludes consideration of the abovementioned problem. In such circumstances, academic polemics are not held back. A recently published review, for example, stated that the results of modern economic history are "results that have contributed nothing to the knowledge of Palladio's villa architecture." This blanket judgment was followed by another sweeping claim: "A similar overestimation of socioeconomic facts for the history of Venetian villa architecture can be found in virtually all recent publications."[192]

Such conventional criticism reveals an attitude that is symptomatic for positivist art history. With the rejection of a sociological and historical framework, the traditional scholar then mounts a high horse, albeit possibly without bridle and saddle, in order to ride a proper aesthetic that is isolated from history, supposedly self-mirroring and purportedly value free. Yet such an ostensibly value-free art history, which operates "for the sake of the history of form," is just as fraught with ideology as was the *l'art pour l'art* movement of the late nineteenth century. This initially emancipatory stance protesting late bourgeois society and its models for aesthetic legitimation simply leads to resignation, however, thus terminating with a negative affirmation of the existing order of things and a betrayal of its own protest, which ends up in the pocket of the bourgeois culture industry. This has evidently been the fate of all artistic subcultures of late capitalist society, whether they operate under the label of *Bohème*, as at the end of the nineteenth century, or whether they lose themselves through commercial integration, as happened to the Beat Poets, Pop Artists, and other underground cultures of the 1960s.

"Classical" art history does not as yet appear to have moved beyond the critical implications of impressionism. As an "impressionistic" scholarship addressing the "natural history" of forms, this position falls far behind that of Jacob Burckhardt, even in those instances for which its refined analysis of aesthetic phenomena was produced. In all respects, Burckhardt's studies of the Italian Renaissance (which were published over one hundred years ago) certainly dealt with economic and social history as closely connected with the history of form. In writing on aesthetics, W. F. Haug sharply criticized traditional art history:

> In aestheticism what had been repressed by capitalism returns alienated, and this means removed from all concrete historical relationships of meaning. Its opposition is a fundamentally loyal one. The counterforce of the aesthetic, which it sets up, remains an empire of inconsequential sensibility, of the "eternal return of the same renunciation." At the heart of it, the protest simply reveals itself as an affirmation of its own importance, as an existence in isolation to history. As it does not develop in any period of history, its abundance is void. How close are the following two statements: "There is no meaning to it all" and "Everything has an aesthetic charm"![193]

Because of their resilience, ideologies are resistant to all attacks by critical thought. This especially applies to the ideology of the "wholesome" life of the countryside as associated with the elemental existence of forever-fit farmers and shepherds. The virus of blood, soil, and homeland grew in the same cultural soil as did agricultural humanism along with the *villeggiatura* of the sixteenth century, and it even brought forth strange, if less scintillating, and more sober flowers in modern existential philosophy. Heidegger, for whom the human being was not the "master of what exists" but rather the "shepherd of existence,"[194] orientated himself in his philosophical jargon to an ideal of "archaism." In claiming that "the oldest of the old follows us in our thoughts and yet it comes toward us,"[195] he secured safety for his philosophical deeds behind the modest dry stone walls of the peasant's house. Thus, to Heidegger: "Philosophical work does not proceed as the solitary activity of an eccentric. It belongs right at the center of the farmer's work."[196]

A parallel with Alvise Cornaro's maxims of the *vita sobria* comes to mind quite informally here. Philosophy has finally reached the level of the church spire when country roads are elevated to the level of a regulating measure, so that "humans attempt in vain to order the earth's sphere through their planning if they do not fall into line with the country road."[197] As such, it is nothing but an embarrassing regression if modern philosophy, by making loneliness in the countryside into a moral imperative, falls back on Petrarch's *vita solitaria*, for "solitude has the innate power not to individualize us but to displace the whole of existence into the distant vicinity of the essence of things."[198] In response to this situation, Adorno made such philosophical language the subject of his criticism and laid bare the false consciousness behind these veils. In commenting on the consequences of Heidegger's position, Adorno observed the following: "By means of his polished [and hardly rustic] figures of speech and far removed from all social consciousness, he makes agricultural relationships into . . . an ostensibly wholesome life, the opposite of the damaged existence, and the farmer is equated with something that is monolithic and entirely protectively enclosed and that proceeds with a firm rhythm and unbroken continuity."[199]

Modern urbanization too has coined a number of catch phrases whose ideological roots can be traced quite easily right back to the sixteenth century and beyond. These include such phrases as the satellite town, the villa suburb, the green area, functional zoning, the residential village, the modern anticity cluster village, and Broadacre City (Frank Lloyd Wright's idea), all of which are based upon hostility toward the city, especially its metropolitan concentration, and are organized in favor of city flight by means of owner occupiers, decentralization, and green strips. The history of modern urban architecture is simultaneously the history of the contemporary architectural ideology, as conveyed through the Athens Charta (1933), the Emergency Decree of the Weimar Republic on Housing Policy (1931), the Eighth International Architectural Congress (1951), the First Housing Law of the Federal Republic of West Germany (1950), and the Second Housing and Single Family Dwelling Law (1956). Through their language, the bills and texts of contemporary architectural congresses as well as building regulations already involuntarily and ideologically reveal the multifarious mechanisms for manipulating consciousness that led to these laws and congresses in the first place. They are self-representations of a society that thinks it can master the future by means of the past. Impassioned forecasting becomes an alibi to divert attention from the sad architectural present and to compensate for various frustrations by projections into the future. The aims of the forecasts, however, remain necessarily misguided as long as neither the architectural past nor the architectural future have been addressed incisively.

Konrad Adenauer thought the metropolis was the breeding ground for the "alienation of the human" and necessarily led to the "corruption of true humanity." This view was based on an authoritarian Christian structure and an old rural Franconian image of the world that focused on the family's link to nature. Similarly, connecting the garden and mother earth to a moral maxim of social and political activity can be retraced to Petrarch's *vita solitaria*, Alberti's *cena familiaris*, or Cornaro's *vita sobria*, to name the archetypal formulations of this view.

Such antiquated and misguided concepts found false realization after 1949 in the irrational political practice of "green plans" and in widespread subsidies for agriculture. Certainly, the immediate considerations regarding specific rural electoral constituencies were not the decisive ones, since there were motivations behind the subsidy policies with deeper roots. *Ein Volk* (a people)—or so Spengler reflected on the countryside during Sunday election speeches—that abandons its farmers in the age of total urbanization and industrialization and that sacrifices its dream of the countryside is cut off from its roots, which have provided a mysterious driving force. They should give themselves over to clear, seemingly cohesive, ties as if sprouting from an archaic consciousness that can be directly interpolated with *religio*, in the Latin sense of the word. Through ideology, these politics have gained a metaphysical standing on the national agricultural level, as well as on the European level, as has been shown already with the example of the *villeggiatura* of the sixteenth century.

The urban dweller refuses to acknowledge that the dream of the countryside is no longer fabricated by himself and is dreamed on his or her behalf by others, that is, through the products of the culture-industry, as in the *Heimat* (vernacular) film, trivial literature, pop song lyrics, and in the advertisement packages of German developers. The latter in particular include guarantees of existential protection through a "healthy" conception of the world and of oneself in relation to the straw-thatched cottage, the peasant's parlor, and the open dry-stone chimney. Within the regulated freedom that the framework of leisure permits, the urban dweller heads for the countryside as if returning to the paradise of childhood and compares the reality of the countryside with the view of it that has been carefully promoted by the consciousness industry. This is done not in order to exchange the hell of the city for rural paradise at some future point but in order to return to the city as if coming back from a national park or from a reservation of indigenous peoples. In the West, the rural sphere has become a museum of itself. For, as Adorno has observed:

> The subsidies paid to the farmer are the raison d'être of what the eccentric jargon supplies to the subsidies' meaning. . . . Those who are tied to their locality by the force of their labor like to make a virtue of necessity and seek to convince others that the constraints on them are of a higher order. . . . Stable careers, which are in themselves only a phase of social development, become transformed . . . in a normative way through the appeal to a false eternity.[200]

Alfred Krupp already divulged his ideological cover in 1865 when he put forth his cynical justification for a workers' housing program in the countryside. Accordingly, he said: "Who knows, after a few years when a general revolt seizes the country, a rebellion of all classes of workers against their employers, who knows whether or not we will be the only ones who will be spared, if we can still set everything in motion." In 1931, on the eve of the totalitarian regime in Germany, the goal of an organized and ideologically embellished urban flight was proclaimed by an emergency decree in an even less disguised and utterly petit-bourgeois manner. It was intended "to make the urban worker more settled by means of close ties to soil and property, to deproletarianize him and to make him less prone to crises by means of his own additional food supply."[201] The petit-bourgeois arcadia that was brought out of the cupboard in 1931 was nothing but a trivialization, a caricature of the tacit aims for redeveloping the *beni inculti* in the Terraferma and for propagating the new classicist villa ideal, thus actualizing the old dream of the countryside. Here, arcadia was a regressive utopia, a perversion of utopian concepts.

Hostility to the city found an especially clear literary definition in an autobiographical account by the French writer Marc Augier of collaboration in Sigmaringen and Berlin during the last days of the Vichy government. Marc Augier, who was a student of Jean Giono (the political leader of the French youth movement and later the mouthpiece of French Fascism, together with Alphonse de Chateaubriant and Jean Fontenoy), escaped the inferno of burning Berlin for the solitude of the Austrian alpine world in the winter of 1944–45. He described his experiences in unmistakable jargon:

> No planes, no sirens, no bombs. The spirit of the mountains was revealed to me as never before. To be far from the war was actually meaningless. But I stood outside sin, outside the sin of the urban dweller. I had returned to the fountainhead, to the foot of the glacier, from which the first human race had set off. They had descended to the plains, where life seemed so much simpler. The hunter became a farmer. Always escaping from the strains that God had demanded of him, the farmer first built villages, then cities. One day, the humans built Berlin. The fall of Berlin gained a new meaning. Without a doubt it only marginally preceded the fall of Paris, New York, and Moscow. The fires of heaven came upon the earth to chastise the cities for their pride. Sodom and Gomorrah repressed the eternal return . . . with the archinstinct of an animal, my generation divined that it was the city that had brought forth sin. Our outdoor clubs, our youth hostel network, our mountaineering and camping organization signify the first departure from the city. Nobody will be able to halt this development.[202]

The poet, whose masquerade as the proper sportsman, mountaineer, and skier suited Augier well, looked down from the heights of the Austrian Olympia onto the metropolis from which he had fled, as Lot once viewed Sodom. The Berlin sea of fire appeared to him as an analogy for the Dead

Sea, which had covered the site of the destruction of Sodom and Gomorrah according to Moses' account. The metropolis became the first victim of a "divine" judgment in the sacrificial temple of nature. Augier's text might be extended with countless other extracts merely through perusing this packaged ideology of urban hostility and its confluence with the youth movement as well as with National Socialism. The message of the Italian villa books by Alberti or Petrarch became submerged in these later developments as a literary tradition and at the same time was unquestionably also present as an ideological tradition. No further comment is needed to show that the former resembles the latter in a way that makes their unintentionally comical link seem threatening.

19

Satellite Town and Penthouse

A HOSTILE VIEW toward the city, a belief in flight from the active urban domain of work to a secure natural surrounding, is an idea that can be deduced from the satellite town. In this respect, we are only concerned with architectural mass packaging, with organized "urban flight" en masse. No alternative can here be suggested to the satellite town, but the most problematic aspect of the satellite town is its close link to the tradition of ideologically motivated hostility to urbanization, and this should be illustrated.

Ebenezer Howard's concept of the garden city (*Garden City*, 1898; German publication in 1907) was still determined by the then-predominant image of the city at the turn of the century. This view held that the city was destroyed by industry and dirtiness and was based on the fear that the city could suck the countryside dry, that it would imprison humans in gloomy destitution and bar their way back to nature. Ebenezer Howard's idea of the garden city was soon expanded into a politically relevant plan for the "social city." The relation between the early socialism of Fourier's vision and the ideal urban design of Howard's predecessors as well as of their contemporaries (from Robert Owen in 1820 through Jean Baptiste Godin in 1860–1880 to T. Frotz in 1896), along with the alliance of social reformism, the workers' movement, and the garden city movement of Howard's successors (B. Kampffmeyer in 1903, Theodor Fischer and Bruno Taut in 1917–1919, and the German Garden City Society in 1902) immediately brought the haute-bourgeois conservative forces to their feet. Already at the beginning of World War I, there were threatening and cynical polemics from the official municipal side that were directed against the garden city and the supposed danger that within it the working class would construct system-destructive forms of proletarian self-organization and self-identification. Defenders of this reactionary view held that

once these garden cities are everywhere, what do you think, gentlemen, that you will confront in those gardens? Red roofs and red window frames on the front, red carnations, roses, and red poppies on the gables, red cabbage in the vegetable gardens, and they will allow only red robins to live in the trees. Thank God that there are still men whose faces will turn red with shame and anger at such a sight, and who will attack such a red transformation![203]

CIAM, which was founded in 1928 by a group of architects to which Le Corbusier belonged, falsified the conception of Howard and his students both in functionalist and in formalist terms, thus constricting it with the purpose of stabilizing the system in accordance with a maxim about the fundamental domains of "living, working, leisure." In this way the division in theoretical urban praxis within the daily functions of city existence was first manifested.[204]

Seen merely from a superficial point of view, a satellite town such as Northwest City near Frankfurt appears to be an outlying self-contained town quarter that is not integrated with the city. But, in actual fact, this is not a functioning city, on a smaller scale, that is outside the metropolis. Rather, it grows parasitically on the city while taking on few of its functions and representing the city only very partially. The social advantages of urban existence are rigorously denied in favor of an expensive flight to fenced-in nature—a nature, which, as a panorama in conflict with the ever-changing image of the television sets, looms in front of standardized windows. The desire for a nonregimented existence,[205] for a contrasting solitude and silence, becomes merely the negative side of such inactive living centers because of their thoroughly organized form. All that remains is the almost pathological call to consumption. For this purpose, the consumer industry has reserved the center of the satellite town and of suburbia for its tasteless shopping-center advertisements.[206]

If for Mitscherlich the compromise solution for the affluent citizen was the purchase of a plot of nature that could be fenced in and used for play by the rural inhabitant, then the city "transplanted" in nature was now to mediate the image of its own proximity to the surrounding green, as the symbol of a "wholesome" world. As one commentator noted, "Qualities are assigned to green vegetation in a way that borders on the manic. It remains quite incomprehensible why trees and bushes should have such a favorable therapeutic influence on mental illnesses."[207] Thus, a bogus alternative to the city is presented as the "place of work," deformed as the city is by exhaust and dirt, by impetuosity and unrest. One deludes oneself with the image of a possible division and then produces it in the consciousness of the masses. This is the idea that one could free oneself from all this "horror" by fleeing to a "better world," that is, to "our" world, in which the central heating system need only deliver the regulated warmth. It was along these lines that the following remark was made: "The Märkisches

Viertel of Berlin, a monstrosity featuring so-called grand gestures [has been created] through the play of floor heights. . . . The absence of genuine concepts that were still present in the garden city ideas (cooperatives, shared responsibilities, identification of the inhabitants with their city) is disguised poetically with the words 'To emphasize the individualism of the single dwelling within the arrangement—that is democracy. . . . The remainder is applied sunshine'" (Stranz, in *Bauwelt*, 1968).[208]

This bears no relation to the satisfaction gained from an "experience of contrasts filled with many sentiments"[209] that "drives the urban dweller back to nature and the rural inhabitant into the city."[210] Distorted by manipulation, the fundamentally stimulating experience becomes embedded in an architecture that is surrounded by nature and remains sterile and that is more likely to reject nature than to integrate with it, since "nature, having thus been seized by the social mechanism of domination as a curative antithesis to [urban] society, is all the more drawn into the incurable and then sold off."[211]

The soon perceived and much belabored problem of suburbia is not at issue, nor is that of the solid free-standing homes in the countryside with their very consciously formulated ideology of settledness, which mitigates the defensive feeling of being the owner of the property and soil.[212] It is not the privileged few but rather entire groups of bourgeois clerks who are concentrated in the satellite towns, so the effect is both more general and less evident. In the presumed bliss of the countryside, a breath of individuality is still available (behind a garden fence, of course), while the sensation of deindividualization present in the "organic" world is produced en masse through the forms of monotonously uniform architecture. At the same time, the proximity to each other of these very freehold bungalows, which fills the gap in the subconsciously mediated security system, is not renounced even though it acts only as a cheap compromise—a compromise that a class-oriented society evidently takes into account, yet only to help shroud class differences. It is through this sense of immediate neighborliness that a false proximity to the socially superior is mediated. A feeling of happiness by turning away from the city to the community ends with sentiments of deceptive togetherness.

Anonymity notwithstanding, there is a perverted sense of social unity, a kind of suburban esprit de corps that finds expression through naive or unwittingly cynical and certainly ideologically based catch phrases such as "arranged society," "social symmetry," or "social housing." The dream of escaping to the countryside, which was perhaps still dreamt of in individual terms, has become reconstituted as the organized dream, the channeled flight. The particular manifestation of this lies in an architecture that is intended for the mass depopulation of the cities and that results in the "poison of monotony" (Neutra). The already habitual alienation in the workplace is reproduced in planned urban architecture that conforms to standardization and a "rational" grid, which once again unmasks itself as a purveyor of ideology. As Wolfgang Pehnt has observed of these developments,

> Meaninglessness and a lack of identification brought the garden city then and bring the satellite town today into the whirlpool of hypnotizing forces of the metropolis. Certainly, there is a concern with finding solutions. Planners are trying to replace unsatisfactory terraced housing and the crushing effects of monotonous slab blocks in both Germanies with more distinctive spatial structures. The symptomatic misunderstanding, however, still resides in the assumption that the monotony in housing can be solved by formal means alone, that is, stimulation by means of a sensuous complex environment was intended, but what was achieved was a plurality of heterogeneous formulae that were predominantly directed by aesthetic considerations.[213]

The city proper therefore remains located in the sphere of work, in the domain of concretized production, which many evidently still believe to be divisible from the domain of living and leisure. Thus, the current sphere of production and consequently its guiding principle are conserved as unchangeable constants. As such, actual norms and directives emanate from the domain of work rather than from elsewhere. This situation determines the imposed norm of "happiness" in the private family domain and forms the resulting architectural configuration, which is not permitted to transgress the boundaries of the domain of work, to which architecture remains immanently related in a most fatal manner. Horkheimer wrote the following about the historical and undiminished prerequisites at the turn of the century for the dividing of work time from leisure time, the social sphere from the private domain:

> Life outside the office and the factory was intended merely to rejuvenate one's energies for the office and the factory; thus, after-hours life became a mere appendage to work, as though it were the comet's tail of production, and the latter was measured in temporal terms as "leisure time." . . . If the latter extended beyond reproduction towards the regaining of expended energies, then it was regarded as *uneconomical*, unless it was used for the further development of work.[214]

A distorted picture is the only alternative offered and it doubly disfigures as well as veils the actual form of life in the city. On the one hand, the city is still discriminated against as an apparent "threat" to the bourgeois family order. On the other hand, however, what remains at the core of the cities—which, after all, are shaped by commercial transactions—are banks, department stores, entertainment centers, and the like. These entities are overlooked as the actual source of conflicts, so that they become largely transposed into a realm of benevolent "neutrality." How such desolation looks can be seen very clearly, for example, in the banking quarter of the city of London [particularly after the Thatcher-sanctioned private development of the 1980s—*the translators*].

In this context belongs the current widespread practice of locating the university campus at the edge of the city. This has occurred especially in the United States and in the United Kingdom. These relocated centers have been developed so students can shape their own little town in the countryside and thus keep away from the concrete urban source of conflict. This division is all the more serious because it has been carried out with such particular consistency that the urban domain has remained suppressed for years. Cities are therefore not destroyed but rather are hollowed out. The city's inner sphere is depopulated, thus killing off the urban *nervus rerum*; human potential is incapacitated by means of what Marcuse has termed the "one-dimensionality" of mainstream Western thought.

In the case of the penthouse, first created in the United States and now increasingly seen in Germany, it may be asked whether the dream of urban flight and the desire for undisguised status symbols do not apply to the penthouse in the same way that our research has shown they apply to the villa. This question is answered by various criteria that are specific to the penthouse. The penthouse is situated high above the netherworld of common existence and on top of the flat roof of the tower block. As such, it satisfies the demands both for a *luogo privilegiato* and for a *sito elevato*, which were postulated by Renaissance theoreticians such as Scamozzi with regard to the villa as hegemonic architecture.

The building line of the penthouse strongly continues the load-bearing lines of the building so that ideally broad terraces result on all four sides. Not only do these terraces permit the unchecked entry of light, air, and sunshine into the penthouse but they also act as filters and abate the noise, bustle, and fumes of the city. Just as was the case with the villa landlord, the privileged owner of the penthouse is given assurance of a healthier, more hygienic life.

Besides the function of surveying and overseeing, which the penthouse shares with the villa owing to a *sito elevato*, there is also the idea in common of a prospect, or *belvedere*. The grand terrace of a villa *belvedere*, which featured trees, garden surrogates, and potted palms, served to screen the view of the surrounding area. Similarly, the city is kept outside the "wholesome" domain of the rooftop penthouse villa in the heart of the city. Simultaneously, the obligatory rooftop plants signify a delight in and a proximity to nature that are characteristic of the villa; that is to say, this practice announces the determination—if only scenographic and artificial, nonetheless demonstrative—to create an island-like artificial paradise right at the heart of the chaotic, hopeless urban world. Although this paradise was once sought outside the city, there are now new means of construction that allow its realization right in the city center. The owner-occupied house in the countryside and the haute-bourgeois suburban villa have wandered back from the city's edge to its center on account of the penthouse fashion, and the attendant ideological values have accompanied this move.

In its contemporary form, the penthouse too is *antiurban*, at least as long as it remains a privileged site for a few wealthy individuals. Its social function is not a public one but a purely private one. It does not serve any new urban tasks, nor does it compensate for the inescapable isolation of the city dweller in the industrial age. On the contrary, the penthouse further intensifies this isolation. In addition, it has a socially repressive character by virtue of its monopoly status symbols, thus provoking resentment amongst the underprivileged inhabitants of tenement blocks. As such, the penthouse can be ascribed to a special moment of class-based cunning. In an arranged society where life in the countryside is no longer a class privilege, former values find themselves assuming new architectural form in a fateful new way. Just as the penthouse stands high above the city, so the villa stood outside the city.

A few of the ideological implications that formed the background for the Renaissance villa, the suburban villa of the Victorian era, and the owner-occupied residence of more recent times continue to exist for the penthouse. For example, the flat roof of a tower block, just like a piece of ground elevated above the plain, can be rented or bought. Accordingly, some are able to obtain a small, enclosed, private domain as an "exhibition of power, loot, and profit" (to cite Adorno on Veblen) conveniently and conspicuously located right in the heart of the city. For what would the merit of such an exhibition be if it were not constantly in everyone's view? In sum, the idea of a penthouse is central and functions almost like a "Columbus" egg[215] for a renewed urbanization and rehumanization of the city, especially in the wake of the Charter of Athens, which concerned the disentangled and alienated spheres of dwelling, working, and recreation.

But as long as penthouses remain the prerogative of the privileged and as long as the urban projects of the avant-garde town planners remain mere hypothetical projects (because they run afoul of the taboo against challenging "ownership relationships vested in private property and embedded in the soil of cities, which make every creative, far-reaching redesign impossible"),[216] architecture will be marked by hegemony and repression. If penthouses are defined as the ornaments atop large capitals of the tower blocks, then in Veblen's sense, "the ornaments [become] threats owing to the way they resemble the old models of repression."[217] As luxurious objects of ostentation, as clear demonstrations of surplus capital, penthouses act like all "deceptive pictures of uniqueness in an era of mass production . . . [that is, as] replicas of highly industrialized mechanization that tell us something about themselves."[218]

It follows from this that the penthouse in its present condition shares an essential attribute with the historical villa, as well as with the modern villa of the industrial era, but above all with the factory villa of the Victorian industrial magnate or with that of the Renaissance *fattore*, namely, its use for "surveillance." Penthouses, which are located on the rooftops of office towers, department stores, banks, and administrative units, frequently remain the prerogative of owners, directors, leading employees, or business friends of these establishments. As a privilege, these structures are a guarantee for the claim to hegemony by these politically and financially ascendant elites. Only for these reasons do they shorten the route from the private domain to that of work. The material symbol of the livelihood for a merchant, that is, a department store, is then crowned by the status symbol of his private life, namely, a penthouse. This is reminiscent of how the Renaissance landowner placed his *casa padronale*, the villa, at the center of his property as a sign of domination.

The question regarding the practical motivation for building and inhabiting the penthouse leads to the same result. Only a metropolis that is strong in capital has the following: first, affluent buyers or tenants for such dwellings; second, tower blocks that can carry parasitical penthouses; and third, the chaos of "rush hour" traffic that validates this concept of the magnate's "villa" in the green belt *ad absurdum*. There are no general humanizing principles that have led to the conception of the penthouse, no desire for humanization, rehabilitation, reinhabitation of the business centers desolate after work hours; there are only pragmatic reasons for these inadequate changes. The advantages the penthouse unquestionably gives belong only to those very few who have transplanted the villa to a city rooftop; the countryside villa assumed the role of a weekend retreat a little closer to heaven than ordinary mortals normally go. A historical moment is reproduced with the penthouse, since in medieval cities the houses of patricians were grouped around the market with its higher property cost. The medieval city had already mapped the social gradient onto the topographical structure. The powerful lived at the secure city core, within the first ring of defense, while the social *pariahs* lived on the edge of the city. In this respect as well, the penthouse is only a modern variation on the ideology of "negative utopia" with its preference for existence away from the city.[219]

Faced with tall architectural complexes located in the centers of the metropolis and crowned with penthouses instead of with crenellations, the historian is involuntarily reminded of the family towers in Italian medieval towns, which were undisguised symbols of domination with their potent, projecting forms. All of this would seem ironic to the observer if he or she were ignorant of the social and political force that these buildings once represented. Such a townscape has been preserved up to the present as a quasi-museum in San Gimignano, Tuscany. There the closer the building is to the center and the higher its towers, the more important the social status of its inhabitants. Although they are in a more anonymous, pluralist form, the tower blocks of Berlin, Frankfurt, and Düsseldorf, as well as the skyscrapers of New York, do not represent anything other than what was represented by the towers of San Gimignano, which, however, stood in a more directly competitive relationship with each other. In anecdotal form, local history reports a continuous rivalry over increasing the heights of the towers in relation to those of the neighbors. Everyone wanted and still wants to be higher up.

Hegemony and its visible expression through architecture are not only regulated by abstract ideas but also by concrete constraints. With changing social conditions and historical circumstances, the constraints change, and beginning with architecture, these new forms are accommodated in material form. An archaic tendency is always unmistakable in the reconstruction or preservation of patriarchal dominance. Does this archaic tendency not evidence its own persistence in the penthouse's adaptation to life along the lines of medieval family towers?

20

Further Reflections
on the Villa (1971)

OUR CONSIDERATIONS WITH respect to methodology inevi-
tably lead to reflections on the concept of the villa, the history of this
concept, and the scientifically objective dimension of artistic quality in
relation to this concept. To start with, we distinguished between a historically subjective concept of quality—specifically, that which was regarded
as artistically "valuable" in the respective historical periods—and a more
contemporary subjective view of quality. The "historical" concept of quality usually appears objectivized in relation to the "contemporary" concept.
Hans Sedlmayr outlined this problem and the related methodological dan-
gers and sources of errors in very definite terms within the comprehensive
reference framework of an "objective science of history":

> Recognizing the peculiarity of our own "modern" era . . . creates a new
> way of eliminating one source of errors when researching older epochs,
> particularly the Renaissance; this source of errors arises when one's own
> standpoint is not taken into account and views and concepts of our own
> era are thus unwittingly projected onto the older epochs, misrepresenting
> and distorting them. . . . [It is possible] to eliminate the distortions and
> "discoloring" of this reflection to the extent that the "structures" of one's
> own time mirror can be determined. The extent to which this is possible,
> that is, the limits of such a method, is a central epistemological problem
> in the objective science of history that can be clearly demonstrated by
> using the very facts of art.[220]

In other words, to what extent does the currently dominant ideology of
history, the contemporary ideologically framed scientific concept, influence
the picture of the past as drawn by research? And, conversely, to what
extent is an examination of art in its historical dimension delimited by
ideological structures of the past that continue to have an effect on the
present, thus turning the entire putatively objective examination of history
into a mere bundle of ideologies? To formulate the question in exaggerated

139

terms by using a concrete example, we should ask whether any art historian who is commissioned by the present owner of a Venetian villa (whether from an old and established aristocratic family or a nouveau riche one from Milan's industrial upper class) to write a historical monograph on the building is at all able to draw an objective picture of this work of art. Can he or she do full justice to its historical, social, and aesthetic quality? To what extent is sycophantic writing the necessary result of such patronage? This example was chosen deliberately because the art history of Venetian villas in particular supplies a wealth of material that is illustrative of the "class-based scientific" nature of the study of art. The monograph published in 1960 on the Villa Barbaro-Volpi in Maser (*Palladio, Veronese e Vittoria a Maser*) and jointly written by a number of prominent experts on Italian culture is an obvious case in point.

On the Preconditions for Artistic Quality

In Karl Marx's *Grundrissen der Kritik der politischen Ökonomie*, one encounters the following guiding principle: "In the case of the arts, it is well known that certain periods of flowering are out of all proportion to the general development of society, hence also to the material foundation, the skeletal structure, as it were, of its organization."[221] Here, Marx is referring less to the problem of generally understanding artistic production than to the resulting effect of art. For Marx, it is often not such a complicated matter to determine the relationship between art and society. The difficulty for him is based more on the fact that the artworks of the past "still afford us artistic pleasure and that in a certain respect they serve as a norm and as an unattainable model." Thus, Marx draws a clear distinction here between the relationship between art and society in these respective historical periods and our subsequent relationship to the works of art of these same past epochs. The historical aspect of art seems to be of more interest to him, that is, art both as a conveyer of what we conceive in our consciousness as history and as a formative "model" influencing our historical consciousness.

The specific question as to why works of art "still afford artistic pleasure" implies the more far-reaching question regarding the social usefulness and necessity of art in general. Yet the overall critique of ideology must be particularly emphasized here as one moment of social enlightenment. For it is the ideological content of works of art in their historicity that is undoubtedly the precondition for Marx's second statement that "in a certain respect they [can] serve as a norm and as an unattainable model."

From the point of view of epistemology, the difficulty entailed in the more important second problem does not reveal itself until we analyze the dialectics of art and society in past epochs. The origin and context of what now counts as a "norm and model" is not to be found in the meaning (usually unmediated) that art has for us today. The essence of a work of art can be grasped in its totality only if it is interpreted in terms of its historicity and its conditions of creation. If one does not view the aesthetic enjoyment of art as an autonomous process, then the enjoyment afforded to us by the artworks of the past is greatly shaped by the ongoing ideological content that they communicate to us. Therefore, the pleasure derived from art of the past, which has long ceased to be a "disinterested pleasure," can only be understood by knowing the effect that the works of art had at the time of their creation.

The bourgeois "aestheticized" concept of art is characterized principally by the strict ideological demand for absolute "quality," so that the concept of quality is rendered dogmatic in nature by displaying very little of the causal (that is, the social) conditions of artistic quality. The picture of quality was and is generally based on nonaesthetic values oriented to the interests of the ruling class. "Quality" in an artwork originates in the consciousness of those who perceive it, and this consciousness has always been a component of ideologized social practice. Those who seek the preconditions for artistic quality beyond social consciousness and the pre-vailing ideology must necessarily and implausibly propound the existence of an aesthetic quality unaffected by social developments. The preconditions for artistic quality, however, can only be conceived of within the framework of conscious social practice.

The preconditions for artistic *value* can thus be found primarily in a nonaesthetic sphere, since "the feelings invoked by art are real and, in this respect, nonaesthetic."[222] As has already been observed, "Works of art owe their existence to the social division of labor, to the separation of intellectual and physical work."[223] The consequence of this fundamental fact and basic condition of artistic reality is that artworks can never be detached from their dialectical relationship with social reality. Even if, as O. K. Werckmeister has noted of artworks, "their aesthetic quality makes one forget 'that they are made' (Adorno)" and that they appear as "a pure objectification of the spirit in matter; regardless of the natural context or of art's necessary social mediation through work,"[224] their real point of reference can exist only within a certain social reality that causes artworks to "appear" as they do in the first place.

The significance of the above for scientific analytical practice, taking the example of a sociology of art, is that this practice, "which is seriously concerned about its function as social critique in contrast to pure com-munication research [and it should be added, art history], must get used to the idea of defining the mediation between art and society both inside and outside of the aesthetic framework."[225] The contemporary conception of quality, which is hypostasized as a criterion, must not affect the critical elaboration of the *historical* concept of quality. Knowledge of the historical concept of quality is an absolute requirement if the significance of art in its historical development is to be even approximately defined. The picture of quality, which seems to be more closely linked than art itself to other forms of ideology (such as religion, myth, philosophy, law, and epistemology), is "ideology" to the same extent that art is an element of the ruling ideology. In the desire for qualitative differentiation in order to recognize "absolute" quality, external categories unrelated to art are imposed on the artwork even though quality is purportedly measured by using purely aesthetic categories. The relationship between artistic and social reality is here reproduced with all its contradictory features in the very concept of quality.

The attempt to come up with an "autonomous" and supposedly unbiased history of artistic forms has not only made form into the sole bearer and mediator of quality but also turned form "in-and-of-itself" into a presumed quality per se. This concept of artistic quality was oriented to what "preceded" and then "superceded" it as a consequence of a rigid conception of development akin to Darwinian biology. Remarks such as "not yet" or "no longer" became favorite set phrases for an art history that believed in an evolution of autonomous artistic forms in competition with biology itself. The problematic character of the actual ideological interaction between art and quality was ignored, being relegated to a supposedly nonpolitical sphere.

The required categories were obtained from the comparative analysis of form and style. On the basis of pseudoscientific problems, art was degraded to the level of an inexpensive and handy treasure chest of quotations and thus integrated into the prevailing ideology of history as a "collection of quotations." The logical development of this integration was the notion of an ahistorical status (*Geschichtslosigkeit*) for autonomous artistic forms and autonomous aesthetic quality, with which traditional art history (not without blame) is confronted today in fields such as those of museum curating or the preservation of historical monuments.

This issue of analysis concerns the various interpretations of form and content: the evaluation of the relationship between the analysis of form and the analysis of content in general, all in relation to aesthetics in particular. According to Henri Lefebvre, "the Hegelian demand contracts and limits the content and makes it unworthy of the spirit."[226] For the work of art, therefore, this means that "the confinement of the content of art to a number of aesthetic definitions" reduces this content "to an abstract form" (ibid.). In other words, Hegel reduces content to abstract thought "by claiming to grasp it 'totally' and exhaustively" (ibid.). Elsewhere, Lefebvre continues with his critique of Hegel along the following lines:

Truth is no longer grasped as a unity of form and content; it is determined by the correspondence of form with itself, by the inner coherence of form, by the formal identity of thought. And intellectual freedom is not defined as an appropriation of the content by "becoming conscious"; it defines itself as the liberation of mind from content as such—experience, life, action—by means of the concept and the idea. Thus the form is not criticized with respect to the content or derived from its unfolding.[227]

Form, therefore, which Max Raphael says is "defined as such as an a priori entity and posed as an aesthetic demand on the contents to be created,"[228] possesses priority of meaning as well as expression over content and satisfies the demand for creativeness before content. At the same time, any "analysis of the form of the work of art, and what form means as it manifests itself in the work of art" is "meaningful solely in relation to its concrete material" (Adorno, *Aesthetische Theorie*, p. 433).[229] And it is not just at a point "where form appears to be emancipated from every content given to it [that] forms take on their own expression and their own content of their own accord" (ibid.). The fundamental division of form and content brings forth the ideology of the new content, so that the division becomes a form of ideological articulation. As Adorno has noted, "Vulgar materialism and a no less vulgar classicism concur in the fallacy that there is some sort of pure form. The official doctrine of materialism also overlooks the dialectics of the fetishized constitution of art" (Adorno, ibid.). This happens quite aside from the vigorous denial of any materialistic and fetishistic character to art on the part of traditional bourgeois art history.

In our study of the Venetian villa, it is said at one point (following Arnold Hauser) that the "preconditions for artistic quality lie beyond the alternatives of political freedom and nonfreedom." This does not mean, however, that the preconditions and effects of artistic quality lie beyond the *dialectics* of political freedom and nonfreedom. According to the dialectical view of historical materialism, the concept of artistic quality is not a constant but a constantly changing variable in the historical process. As we have established, the respective determinants of quality do not follow the categories of an autonomous history of form. As is the case with a superstructural phenomenon like art, the notion of artistic quality therefore has a dialectical relationship to the economic base—to the sphere of production and to the circulation of goods—thus exercising an effect on the manifestations of ideology based on that substructure. Every discussion about questions of aesthetic quality must, therefore, necessarily start from these basic questions of economic substructure and lead back to them.

In the recently published *Aesthetische Theorie*, Adorno comments on the possible "opposition" that works of art may possess by virtue of their "rationality": "The opposition of artworks to domination is a mimesis of the latter. They must adapt themselves to the behavior of domination in order to produce something qualitatively different from the world of domination."[230] Opposition to or contradiction with a social system by a work of art can, according to Adorno, only develop out of precisely that system of domination and, moreover, can be understood only from within this standpoint. In order to "produce something qualitatively different from the world of domination," artworks have to integrate what they aim to destroy. The perceiver of an artwork recognizes through self-consciousness what the artwork cannot due to its material restraints and its "aesthetic appearance," namely, a comprehensible and nonabused form of opposition.

In the dialectical relationship to society, the contradictory position that a work of art can take with respect to the social order becomes a mimesis that, according to Adorno, is the basic determinant of specific artistic quality. Adorno also distinguishes between the directly time-dependent (that is, contemporary) effect of the artwork and its long-term historical effect. The time-dependent notion of quality, however, is also bound up with the question of the historical facticity and normativity of the artwork, which is an aspect that does not seem to correspond to the context for situating meaning (*Bedeutungszusammenhang*) as described by Adorno. Thus, the dialectics of class-related social differences can be found directly reproduced in the work of art: "The feudal dialectics of domination and servitude have taken refuge in works of art whose mere existence possesses a feudal element."[231]

This thesis should now be examined more closely by taking the example of the "classic" Venetian art of villa design in the Palladian epoch. We must then ask to what extent Palladian villa architecture already embodies feudal values by its "pure existence," to what extent it either openly reflects societal conflict or acts instead as a proven mask for societal conflicts so that the contradictions of *realpolitik* are manifested through it in a one-dimensional and distorted way. Is the Palladian villa only a representation of certain trends toward the reconstitution of feudal structures of domination or is it already a "refuge" for the "feudal dialectics of domination and servitude" to such a degree that it also retroactively embodies "the feudal element" under different economic and ideological conditions?

We have attempted to clarify this question for the period of origin of the northern Italian villa. However, we were not able to answer the question in a manner that dealt with the entire problem involved. For this reason the fundamental historical part of our study is supplemented in the final chapters by a study that is intended, through the use of selected examples, to show ways in which a certain cultural ideology is able to achieve an autonomous existence (*Verselbständigung*). The purpose here is to demonstrate the extent to which ideological constants can represent links between historically different forms of social (and thus artistic) practice. For example, the comparison between the medieval Italian noble tower and the penthouse as signs of domination should not be understood as a formal historical treatment; rather it should be considered an attempt to explain the obvious kinship between these two sets of formal structures in proximity to their ideological structures. Determining the degree of ideological self-sufficiency should enable us to gauge the extent to which a work of art is able to convey the social structures that it represented during a certain period, even when that historical movement has been superceded by another.

If one pursues this question far enough, it might just be possible to ascertain why past works of art continue "in a certain respect [to] serve as a norm and as an unattainable model" (to quote Marx) even for us today. Through this learning process, it will also be possible for us to unchain ourselves from such traditional models. It would be wrong to interpret the "unattainable model" conveyed to us by a work of art as an inevitable fact in the anthropological sense. Rather, this presumed "inevitability" is itself part of a common cultural ideology that is based on an erroneous conception of history, thus producing in turn an unacceptable account of history. According to Henri Lefebvre, every ideology is "a conglomeration of errors, illusions, and mystifications that can be explained by starting with what ideology distorts and converts, namely, history" (Lefebvre, loc. cit.). It is important here for us to examine the distorted and discolored elements we encounter (as "history" in the form of ideology) with respect to their original ideological purpose and social significance. It would be undialecti-cal and not especially fruitful to attempt to determine the ideological aspect of artwork simply on the basis of its aesthetic appearance and in light of our present social condition. The historical dimension of a work of art would still not be taken into account and one would necessarily obtain an incomplete, indeed a misleading, picture of it.

In sum, it can be said that the works of art of the past "afford us artistic pleasure" inasmuch as they increasingly become a dominant structure of consciousness. Furthermore, it must still be determined when in history there were processes in which aesthetic practice came to be seen as independent, thus penetrating consciousness without being linked to so-called renaissances.

Marx attempted to see such a pre-Renaissance development in Greek art and believed that the fascination of Greek art, which is so difficult to define, must be sought in its historical quality as manifesting the "childhood of mankind." This statement must be qualified, however, insofar as this subjective and anthropological notion, which goes back to the views of Winckelmann, Goethe, and Hegel on classical Greek art, is not a product of the exact dialectical and materialist view of history as developed by Marx himself in his *Critique of Political Economy.*[232] The specific quality of the Palladian villa can be grasped only by applying the hermeneutic approach described, if, as our study was intended to show, one begins with an *objective* concept of quality that also reflects what Adorno termed the "dialectics of domination and servitude." This qualitative context was fundamental for attaching importance to the villa as the visible expression of a "negative utopia." Such an assessment of a work of art does not furnish information only about the object itself. This becomes particularly evident when the assessment of quality is discriminatingly voiced against so-called triviality, kitsch, and imitation. A critical examination of the ideologically based concept of quality is an important hermeneutic tool for understanding the societal function and social structure of aesthetics. The critique of ideology can show that the work of art as an "aesthetic appearance" has an utterly social function that is certainly not restricted to any apolitical realm. "Quality" as a criterion for value is to be seen in fundamental terms not as an abstract, intellectual phenomenon but rather as a social one. Any assessment of artistic quality using the sociology of art will have to take this as a methodological precondition if it does not wish to fall behind traditional art history as a mere "aestheticist" sociology of art. In this regard, Lefebvre writes of "Marxism according to Marx" that "it is not an aesthetic but rather contains a theory of works of art, along with their preconditions, their genesis, and their disappearance."[233] However, this does not release post-Marxist theory from an obligation to devote its attention to the field of aesthetics but only implies that *it cannot deal with aesthetics as if it were simply a bourgeois theory.* There is no point in emphatically rejecting artistic quality a priori on behalf of an approach to epistemological theory and to the critique of knowledge or in supposing that a sociological equivalent could take its place.

Viewed in this context, Marxism is not a new form of "aesthetics" detached from practice. Rather, Marx sees the aesthetic objectifications that have unfolded in history—works of art or art as such—in a dialectical context that is constantly changing and that by no means excludes the criteria of aesthetics. Accordingly, aesthetics, and thus aesthetic "quality," are more totally grasped within the framework of social-historical changes and no longer remain a mere component and result of "purely" philosophical speculation. There is thus no justification for the frequent reproach by conventional scholars that a nonaesthetic "viewing of art" is being pursued, since completely different concepts and interpretative frameworks are quite obviously involved here. These differences manifest themselves most clearly wherever attempts are made to define the relationship between art and society, since as Arnold Hauser has contended, "The complete sense acquired by a work of art for a later generation is formed by the accumulation of various interpretations."

Just as we stated at the beginning that artistic quality cannot be measured by standards based on an "autonomous" history of forms and styles, so this applies generally to those ideologies rooted in the collective social consciousness, which only seem independent. Since with regard to the sphere of production and the material processes of exchange between people, they have no autonomy, artworks cannot have an "autonomous" history either. From the point of view of the history and critique of ideology, however, this does not in any way mean that the categories of artistic quality in past epochs were not subjectively oriented through social consciousness to the formal or stylistic criteria of works of art. The quality attributed to an artwork often developed and was even determined in relation to either ideological opposition and rejection or in relation to affirmation and imitation with respect to the formal vocabulary of the preceding style. The more one identified the social consciousness of past epochs with their objectifications in the sphere of artistic language, the more important it became on the level of artistic language to identify one's own desired forms of life and interests with supposedly "cohesive" epochs of the past. The fact that higher demands (because evidently less of a problem and obviously more illusionary) were frequently based on purely formal identification instead of on actual content is in turn an indication of the ideology pervading the prevailing consciousness.

In the case of the development of the *villeggiatura* in the sixteenth century, this identification was undoubtedly no longer "purely" formal. It is not difficult to recognize from the "direct language" of the contemporary "villa books" and treatises on architecture the intention of achieving a self-conscious and long-sought identification with antiquity, even though it had to be achieved on the basis of completely different political and economic conditions and with the help of architecture that had painted and sculptural decoration. It is difficult, however, to decide how the various subdomains of the dominant ideology at that time exercised reciprocal influence and how they were related to practice. Outside the aesthetic sphere, it is philosophy, religion, mythology, law, and morality as "intellectual powers" that force a "negative utopia" toward social reality. One has to presume that the criteria of artistic quality and its evaluation in many cases started directly from these intellectual domains, that is, without a concrete relation to the social base. The notion of artistic quality does not therefore appear detached from practice. The relationship between art and society cannot be made comprehensible, however, until the various aspects of the ideology are known and taken into account, since the relationship of art to society is couched in its own terms while also being determined by them.

We have interpreted the Palladian villa as a distinctive expression of feudal order and have presumed also that it adapted to these feudal structures to a great degree with the help of independent formal and aesthetic structures. *If one thinks dialectically, however, then the villa must, at the same time, also have incorporated and embodied something of the actual and current social contradictions, against the background of which it came into being.* If, on the one hand, the villa encompasses the "feudal dialectics of domination and servitude," then it also confronts, on the other, the emancipatory possibilities of the city and the urban bourgeoisie pressing for an understanding of itself. *According to Adorno's theory of "a work of art as a negation," the villa is a definite manifestation of feudal order, yet in its negation, the villa also bears the contradiction of itself within itself.* By integrating its own negation within itself, the villa has become a perfect artistic expression, a vivid material illusion of the backward-oriented social ideals of an aristocratic ruling class.

In the Venetian villa, the social contradiction does indeed appear initially to be artistically "overcome" and resolved due to the "density" of its ideological content. However, it has to carry within itself its own contradiction, which is inherently in accordance with its dialectical relationship to social reality. If the villa's mimesis of "domination" consists in the fact that it has to present something "qualitatively different from the world of domination"—so as to harbor any "opposition" in Adorno's sense—then one could perceive this sublimated opposition in its paradoxical representation of the "world of the rulers" as a utopian and unfulfillable dream in relation to the very domination presupposed by its own existence. This in turn facilitated, if not enabled in the first place, an analysis and exposure of this dream.

In the Villa Rotonda near Vicenza (Figure 19; see also Figure 18), which is unquestionably the high point in the historical aesthetization of the "dream of rural existence," what is meant becomes obvious. Vested in the highest artistic quality, *utopia here finds its most unified and convincing artistic representation as a contrasting image to its own actual social reality.* Living in the "rotunda" can only remain an unfulfilled and unfulfillable ideal. By virtue of its own absoluteness and perfection, it has the hermetic character of a work of art that, at least for the viewer today, seems to be transformed through the aura of inaccessibility associated with a "shrine" and is no longer like a "house" in the customary sense. Insofar as the villa represents the artistic idealization and aesthetization of the social ideal and illusion of a certain class to such an extent that utopia alienates itself more and more from actual practice, *the villa turns into its own unresolved contradiction.* The negation of the work of art becomes visible here because the brittleness of the relationship between practice and consciousness comes to light with particular clarity in the villa.

The villa has become a "self-contained" system that, in common with other systems, shares the fact that "it is left behind by the movement of history."[234]

We have seen the significance of a view of quality for the conventional concept of history and for the formation of historical consciousness in relation to aesthetic practice. Any sociology of art that considers itself a science of history must take this situation especially into account. For the science of history has a part "in the dialectics of historical enlightenment that dismantles historical traditions as historical consciousness expands."[235] For Brecht and Trotsky, enlightenment toward socialism will "only take place through highly qualified, highly diversified art. The question of quality will be politically decisive for genuine socialist art."[236] Accordingly, one cannot dispense in a "presocialist" era (in which the historical sciences have the function described by Habermas) with the knowledge of what artistic "quality" has effected and continues to influence in the historical process.

Finally, another aspect of artistic quality that goes beyond the historical should be mentioned, namely, the question of to what extent the processes of historical development can be seen with respect to their total, contradictory character in an artwork. Does a work of art subjectively possess "quality" for us if it reveals social interdependencies with our historical consciousness as *typical* so that insight into the actual course of history is possible through an analytical examination of the work of art? The work of art possesses subjective quality for us when it comprehensively "represents" history, when the societal contradictions can be perceived in it beyond all doubt, regardless of whether it takes sides. It is left to critical analysis to question the work of art to the point where the analyzed work "reveals how this manifestation is bound up with the structure of [capitalist] society and its possible negation."[237] From this standpoint, it seems entirely secondary whether a work of art behaves in a conformist manner or not, whether it opposes or affirms the existing social conditions, since "the relationship between art and society has its beginning at their starting point and in the latter's development, not in direct partisanship, but in terms of what is now called commitment. Also in vain is the attempt to perceive this relationship in such a way that one invariably construes nonconformist positions of art throughout history and sets them in opposition to affirmative positions. There is no shortage of artworks that could be incorporated only in an already fragile nonconformist tradition by force and whose objectivity is, nonetheless, deeply critical of society."[238]

Notes

NOTES TO INTRODUCTION

1. See, for example, the recent remarks in this regard by Andreas Beyer, "Die Villa als Wille und Vorstellung," *Frankfurter Allgemeine Zeitung*, February 8, 1991, p. 33.
2. Jürgen Habermas, "Über Titel, Texte, und Termine oder Wie man den Zeitgeist reflektiert," in *Der Autor, der nicht schreibt*, Frankfurt, 1989, p. 4.
3. For a representative collection of articles by most of these scholars, see Monika Wagner, ed., *Moderne Kunst*, Hamburg, 1991, or W. Busch and B. Schmoock, eds., *Kunst: Die Geschichte ihrer Funktionen*, Weinheim and Berlin, 1987. Klaus Herding's contribution has been addressed by Adrian Rifkin in "Bicentennial Literature on Art and the French Revolution," *Oxford Art Journal* 13, No. 2 (1990), pp. 113–117.
4. Peter Bürger, *Theory of the Avant-Garde* (1974), translated by Michael Shaw, Minneapolis, 1984; and Andreas Huyssen, *After the Great Divide: Modernism, Mass Culture, Postmodernism*, Bloomington, IN, 1986.
5. Michael Müller, Horst Bredekamp, Berthold Hinz, Franz Verspohl, et al., *Autonomie der Kunst: Zur Genese und Kritik einer bürgerlichen Kategorie*, Frankfurt, 1972.
6. Erwin Panofsky, "Three Decades of Art History in the United States," in *Meaning in the Visual Arts*, Chicago, 1955, p. 322.
7. James Ackerman, *The Villa: Form and Ideology of Country Houses*, Princeton, 1990, p. 287.
8. Ibid., p. 286.
9. For an important anthology of the "new art history," see the one published by Humanities Press: A. L. Rees and F. Borzello, eds., *The New Art History*, Atlantic Highlands, NJ, 1988.
10. When parts of the book were published in an English translation in the British architectural journal *9H* (No. 5, 1983, and No. 7, 1985), the latter title was chosen by the translator, W. Wang.
11. See Raymond Williams, *The Country and the City*, London, 1973; Alex Potts, "'Constable Country' Between the Wars," in *Patriotism*, Vol. 3, edited by R. Samuel, London, 1989, pp. 160–186; Neil McWilliam and Alex Potts, "The Landscape of Reaction," in *The New Art History*, pp. 106–119; John Barrell, *The Darkside of the Landscape*, Cambridge, England, 1980.
12. T. J. Clark, *Image of the People*, London, 1973, p. 10. Nochlin's excellent essay of 1971, which was published in *Art and Sexual Politics*, edited by T. Hess and E. Baker, New York, 1989, pp. 1–43, is famous for its emphasis on *institutional mediation* along gender-based as well as class-based lines of such categories as "genius."
13. Ibid., p. 11. For a recent assessment of Clark's place in British cultural studies, see Perry Anderson, "A Culture in Contraflow—II," *New Left Review*, No. 182 (July/August 1990), pp. 90–92.

151

14. Ibid., pp. 12–13.
15. Ibid.
16. Among the more famous books by members of this group are the following: Thomas Crow, *Painters and Public Life in Eighteenth Century France*, New Haven, 1985, and Serge Guilbaut, *How New York Stole the Idea of Modern Art*, Chicago, 1983.
17. See, for example, Donald B. Kuspit, "Critical Notes on Adorno's Sociology of Music and Art," *Journal of Aesthetics and Art Criticism* 23, No. 3 (Spring 1975), pp. 321–327, or Donald B. Kuspit, "Dialectical Reasoning in Meyer Schapiro" (1978) in *The Critic as Artist*, Ann Arbor, 1984; David Craven, "Towards a Newer Virgil: Mondrian Demythologized," *The Journal of Fine Arts* (University of North Carolina—Chapel Hill) 1, No. 1 (Spring 1977), pp. 14–31 (Republished in *Praxis* 2, No. 4 (Summer 1978), pp. 235–248); or Patricia Mathews and T. Gouma-Peterson, "The Feminist Critique of Art History," *Art Bulletin* 69, No. 3 (1987), pp. 326–357.
18. For a critique of mainstream art history in the 1970s, see David Craven, "Hegemonic Art History," *Kritische Berichte* 10, No. 3 (Summer 1982), pp. 54–60. For the two best overviews of left art history in the period, see Alan Wallach, "Marxism and Art History," *The Left Academy*, Vol. 2, edited by Bertell Ollman and Edward Vernoff, New York, 1984, pp. 25–53, and Karl Werckmeister, "Radical Art History," *Art Journal* 42, No. 4 (Winter 1982), pp. 284–291. For the best overall assessment of the place of Benjamin and Adorno in modern criticism, see Terry Eagleton, *The Ideology of the Aesthetic*, Oxford, 1990, Chapters 12, 13.

NOTES TO TEXT

1. G. Mazzotti (1957), especially pp. 5–11 (Introduction), pp. 47–48 (*From Castles to Villas*), and pp. 383–385 (*Life in the Villas*).
2. M. Muraro (1966), especially pp. 58ff.
3. G. Fiocco (1965), especially pp. 66–73 (*Il disfacimento dei beni feudali di Terraferma*) and pp. 88–89, Note 6.
4. J. S. Ackerman (1966), esp. pp. 48–54.
5. F. Sansovino, *L'Avvocato*, Venice (1559), cited by M. Muraro, *Civiltà delle ville venete*, hectograph of the lecture at the Biblioteca Hertziana in Rome (1964), Note 31, p. 39.
6. Marino Sanudo, *Vite de' Duchi di Venezia, Muratori XXII*, passim. See J. Burckhardt (1928), Book I, Ch. 7, p. 67. This is an objective statistic and not an index of, for example, the number of men capable of bearing arms or the number of taxpayers or households, as was often used for population figures in Milan or in Florence, for example. If we take the present-day population of Venice as a gauge and also take into consideration the fact that the external location of the city virtually disallowed any expansion of the area for living, for trade, or for commerce, then the figure for 1422 already represents the limits of the possible, even if one considers that the shipfaring citizens of Venice were absent from the city for the greater part of their time.
7. Marino Sanudo, op. cit., and *Muratori XXII*, Col. 958–960, 963, 1215f. See J. Burckhardt (1928), Book I, Ch. 7, p. 68. Each of the gallions alone carried a

regular crew of 200. On the structure of Venetian trade, cf. Scherer, *Allgemeine Geschichte des Welthandels I*, 326 A, and Lewis Mumford (1961), p. 371.

8. There are no indications of a significant and autarchic volume of business to compare with that of maritime trade. Various single and apparently independent branches of industry and trade, such as the emergent glass industry in Murano during the fifteenth century or the fish and mussel farms in the lagoon, remained economically unimportant fringe phenomena, mainly serving the needs of the city itself.

9. Burckhardt, following contemporary sources, states the private wealth of three particularly rich Venetians: Doge Andrea Vendramin—170,000 ducats (1475); Lodovico Patavino, patriarch of Aquileja—200,000 ducats (around 1460–1470); Antonio Grimani—100,000 ducats. J. Burckhardt (1928), p. 529f. (addendum to p. 76, Note 3).

10. J. Burckhardt (1928), p. 529 (Appendix), following Francesco Vettori.

11. Francesco Sansovino (1581), 151f. Recent Italian research especially has directed much attention to the history of Venetian trade in the fifteenth and sixteenth centuries in general and to the economic, political, and agricultural preconditions for the Venetian *villeggiatura* and reclamation of new land in particular. Cf., among others, J. S. Ackerman (1966), Chapter 2 ("Villas"), pp. 48–54; F. Braudel, *La vita economica di Venezia nel secolo XVI, Civiltà veneziana del Rinascimento*, Florence (1958), pp. 81–102; R. Cessi, *Alvise Cornaro e la bonifica veneziana del secolo XVI*, Accademia dei Lincei, classe scienze morali . . ., Series 6, 13, Rome (1936), pp. 301–323; M. Cipolla, *Studi di storia della moneta*, Paris (1948), Vol. 2, esp. p. 109; G. Cozzi, *Il Doge Nicolò Contarini. Richerche sul patriziato veneziano all'inizio del Seicento*, Venice (1958); H. Kretschmayr, *Geschichte von Venedig*, Stuttgart (1934), passim; Gino Luzzatto, "Per la storia dell'economia rurale in Italia nel secolo XVI," in *Festschrift für Lucien Febvre*, Paris (1953), Vol. 2; G. Luzzatto, *Storia economica dell'età moderna e contemporanea*, Padua (1958); G. Luzzatto, *Storia economica di Venezia dal XI al XVI secolo*, Venice (1961); M. Muraro, *Civiltà*, esp. pp. 39ff.; M. Muraro, *Treasures of Venice*, Geneva (1963); G. Pavanello, *La laguna di Venzia*, Venice (1925); E. Sereni, "Prodromi dell' agronomia," in *Miscellanea in onore di R. Cessi*, Valpadana, Brescia, Mantova (1956), Vol. 2; A. Stella, "La crisi economica veneziana della seconda metà del secolo XVI," *Archivo Veneto*, Series 5, Nos. 58–59 (1956), pp. 17–69.

12. M. Muraro (1966), p. 539.

13. C. Malipiero, in *Archivo Storico* Vol. 7, Part 2, p. 709f., reveals the extent of the grain trade and the exact grain prices in the city of Venice in 1498—at the beginning of the "permanent crisis."

14. *Archivo di Stato di Venezia, Provvedimenti sopra beni inculti*, Series 299. The translation is taken from M. Muraro, *Civiltà delle ville venete*, hectograph of paper (1964), Note 33, p. 40.

15. This was preceded in 1506 by the Magistratura dei cinque Savi alla Mercanzia, in 1501 by the commissioning of the Magistrato alla Acque, and by the appointment in 1542 of a *publico mattematico alle acque*, i.e., an official responsible for hydraulic engineering in the city and the Terraferma. In the fifteenth century, there was already a senatorial commission with the title Officiales Supra Canales, as well as an Officiales Paludum. On the reorganization of the Venetian Beni Inculti, cf. especially Muraro, *Civiltà*, pp. 14, 34, 38, 41, 43; and V. Miozzi, *L'antico veneto Magistrato dei Beni inculti*, Rome (1921); R. Cessi/N.

Spada, *La difesa idraulica delle Lagune venete cel secolo XVI*, Venice (1952); G. Griffo, *Sommario di tutti decreti concernenti i Beni inculti*, Venice (1958); D. Beltrami, *Saggio di Storia dell' Agricoltura delle Republica di Venezia durante l'età moderna*, Rome/Venice (1955); and G. Ferrari, "La legislazione venziana sui beni communali," in *Nuovo Archivio Veneto*, Series 19, Vol. 36.

16. After nine years of intensive activity, three Senate nobili were appointed *provveditori sopra luoghi inculti*, responsible for implementing the 1563 Terminazione del Magistrato dei Beni Inculti and the "piano generale per la sistemazione e regolazione di tutte le acque scorrenti fra i Colli Berici e gli Euganei," i.e., the new cultivation of the Padania. Cf. M. Muraro (1966), p. 539.

17. The Venetian Magistrato dei Beni Inculti confiscated land lying fallow, taking possession of it for the state and handing it over to settlers from the city. The Venetian state gave preference during the cultivation of these areas to Venetian citizens wishing to settle in the Terraferma, while the big established landowners fell increasingly far behind. Exact figures dating from the eighteenth century state that at that time the established feudal landlords in the Terraferma possessed only 8 percent of the land, while 38 percent was in the hands of the Venetian nobili. Cf. Muraro, *Civiltà*, Note 22, p. 34.

18. As early as 1300, Giovanni Soranzo, the fifty-first doge of Venice, became a citizen of Treviso, allegedly for the sole reason of being able to acquire land in the Terraferma, in the Marca Trivigiana. It is also documented that in 1317 one of his sons was a *padrone* in the Treviso region. G. Mazzotti, *Le Ville Venete. Catalogo*, Rome (1967), p. 37. Letters to their property managers in Venice, written in 1504–1514 and 1553–1556, respectively, by Andrea Alpago and Andrea Berengo, Venetian citizens resident in the Orient (Damascus and Aleppo), provide an insight into the continuation of the conquest and settlement of land in the Terraferma until well into the sixteenth century. See G. Fiocco (1965), pp. 88–89. For an account of property relations in the Terraferma during the fifteenth and sixteenth centuries, also cf. Vittorio Lazzarini, "Beni carraresi e proprietari veneziani," in *Miscellanea in onore di Gino Luzzatto*, Milan (1949), and the same author, *Proprietà e feudi in antiche carte venziane*, Rome (1960).

19. For Tommaso Mocenigo, whose name is bound up with the completion of the settlement and conquest of the Terraferma in 1405, averting the danger of Venice becoming isolated from the continental hinterland was a supreme maxim clearly guiding his policy-making. This was at a time when it was becoming increasingly clear that the complex structure of Venice's foreign dominions could not be maintained indefinitely. Cf. G. Fiocco (1965), p. 66ff.

20. The Terraferma had no part in the Venetian state government, which, with all the associated privileges, trade monopolies, and influence on foreign policy, remained firmly in the hands of a few *Serenissima* families eligible for the Senate. Over the centuries, these families had developed a caste spirit and isolationism of almost British character.

21. The Garzoni and Cornaro families are good examples of this process, which was particularly marked in the Padua region where the feudal landlords were maneuvered into a politically and economically hopeless situation. After trials for high treason in which they were branded as *ribelli* against those in power, and after economic action that bankrupted them, their *latifundia* were lost to the state. The Venetian patricians, who could avail themselves of sufficient

liquid means by shifting capital away from maritime trade, acquired the feudal properties at the state auctions. On the Garzoni family, cf. B. Rupprecht (1965), p. 2f.; on the Cornaros, cf. G. Fiocco (1965), pp. 89–95. The Angelieri-Cornaro patrician family established itself in the course of the fifteenth and sixteenth centuries more and more as rural patricians: "si sostitui alla classe feudale nella proprietà terriena del Padovano [they penetrated the established feudal class by acquiring land in the Padua region]." G. Fiocco (1965), p. 66ff. The bastions of the Cornaros were in Este, Codevigo, Fosson, Campagna, and Luvigliano. The Garzonis had recognized this trend even earlier, and with acquisitions achieved with astonishing determination in 1442, 1455, 1462, and 1465 they expanded their empire to include Pontecascale, Arre, Conselve, Vanzo, San Siro, Aguà, Pontelongo, and Pontecchio. The Giustiniani, Barbaro, Soranzo, Priuli, and Dal Bene families were similar cases in point.

22. Guiseppe Ceredi, Cristoforo Sorte, Alvise Cornaro, and Cristoforo Sabadino wrote well-known tracts dealing with water-raising works, dam-building, regulating river flow, and land drainage. Even an architect as engaged as Palladio found the time to concern himself intensively with the development of the Archimedes screw, while Marcantonio Barbaro, one-time governor of the Terraferma, took pleasure in learned disputes about such machines, experimenting with them and utilizing them in suitable locations. Frequent recourse was made to models originating in ancient art theory and technology (Vitruvius, Pliny the Elder). Cf. Temanza (1778), pp. 315–317, and Muraro, *Civiltà*, Note 35, pp. 42–43.

23. M. Muraro (1966), p. 540.

24. B. Rupprecht (1966), p. 228.

25. One year after the first edition of Piero de Crescenzi's agricultural tract entitled *Opus ruralium commodorum* (Augsburg, 1471), which signifies the beginning of the Italian "villa books" series, the first editions of agricultural tracts by Cato, Varro, Columella, and Palladius were published in Venice. The best-known publication of these authors was organized by Aldus Manutius (Aldo Manuzio) in 1514 in Venice under the title *Libri de re rustica*. Reprints were published repeatedly until the late eighteenth century, one appearing in Venice in 1792–1797 under the title *Rustici Latini Volgarizzati*. Cf. Rupprecht (1966), pp. 222–223, following Vittorio Niccoli, *Saggio storico e bibliografico dell' agricoltura Italiana*, Turin (1902).

26. M. Muraro (1966), p. 540.

27. Extracts quoted from M. Muraro (1966), p. 541. Complete texts in *Opere di M. Sperone Speroni*, Vol. 5, Venice (1740), pp. 329–330. Also B. Rupprecht (1966), p. 228, and G. Fiocco (1965), p. 193.

28. M. Muraro (1966), p. 539, following *Parti . . . de' Beni Inculti*, No. 21. With regard to the cultivation of the land, "si debbia procedere con tre ordini, a imitazione del Nostro Signor Dio, che nella fabbrica del Mondo divise prima i cieli della materia confusa, poi separò essa terra da l'acqua, et infin fece in detta terra nascere le cose particolari, degli animali, degli arbori, e dei grani; così con tre divisioni si può condurre ogni retratto a fine. Il primo, levando le acque di sopra la terra [one must progress in three stages, in imitation of God the Father, who in the creation of the world first separated heaven from earth, then earth from water, and finally brought life into being on the earth—the animals, the trees, and the corn. By dividing in three in this manner, every work can be

brought to completion. The next step is then to drain the land]." (October 10, 1556; Venice, Bibliotheca del Museo Correr, M.S.P.D., C.977, n. 21). Quoted from Muraro, *Civiltà*, p. 16.

29. Quoted in the following: G. Fiocco (1965), p. 179. See also M. Muraro (1966), p. 542. A clue to Alvise Cornaro's activity as an agronomist, villa landlord, and cultivator of the land is provided in an obituary written in 1566 by Giacomo Alvise Cornaro in honor of his grandfather and preserved as a manuscript in the Austrian National Library in Vienna. Printed in G. Fiocco (1965), pp. 200–203 (following S. Cicogna, *Iscrizione Veneziane, S. Giobbe*, Venice (1959) pp. 751–754). Cornaro showed an early interest in matters relating to cultivation of the land. He had a large (200-*campi*) swamp area drained, an enormous undertaking in terms of manpower and material. It was completed after only two years: "reduse tuti a coltura, et ritornò il buono aere a quella villa e luogo nel quale tanto era lo aere triste [brought everything to cultivation and returned good air to this villa and location, thus negating the sad air of before]." The population of the demesne grew in leaps and bounds from 40 to 2,000 souls. Towns were also established and settled here—such growth cannot be explained solely in terms of migration from the countryside. Cornaro restored the local church, built a stone mansion in solid style (*casa di villa*), and established a large economically organized farm as well as a settlement for farm laborers. He produced a code(s) of arbitration for the estate, thereby creating a rural-patriarchal legal order that earned his farm the title of Villa della Pace. His agents gave the leaseholders and laborers instruction in modern rational methods for growing produce.

30. V. Scamozzi (1615), Book I, Vol. 3, Ch. 15, pp. 282–283; Book I, Vol. 3, Ch. 12, p. 266.

31. B. Rupprecht (1966), p. 228, following Falcone.

32. Reprinted in G. Fiocco (1965), Appendix "Lettere," pp. 194–197.

33. Cf. Guido Piovene and Remigio Marini, "L'opera completa del Veronese," in Classici dell'Arte, Vol. 20, Milan (1968), Appendix "Documentazione," p. 84f.

34. A. Hauser (1958), p. 19.

35. H. Marcuse (1968), p. 65.

36. Ibid.

37. Interview in the German news magazine *Der Spiegel* 23, No. 12 (1969), p. 161.

38. L. B. Alberti, Grayson edition, p. 156. *Masserizia*, a key term frequently used by Alberti, refers to the economic virtues the paterfamilias should display, i.e., thrifty management of the estate's economy, clever capital administration, a modest standard of living in accordance with the financial situation of the family as a production unit: "La masserizia è utile, necessaria, onesta, e lodata [thriftiness is useful, necessary, honorable, and praiseworthy]" (p. 166). This quality is even raised to hallowed heights at times: "Santa cosa la masserizia [Thriftiness is next to godliness]" (p. 163). Anticipating Cornaro's ideal in life, Alberti identifies *masserizia* with "sobrietà del vivere [moderation in the standard of living]" (p. 176) and associates it with the notion of rational organization of time in agricultural production: "masserizia del tempo [economy of time]" (p. 186).

39. B. Rupprecht (1966), p. 243. Alberti gives a pertinent description of the "villa patriarch," whose authority keeps the large rural family "sotto un tetto . . . in mezzo padre di tutti ogni sera acerchiato, amato, riverito, padrone e maestro di tutta la gioventù, la quale cosa suole essere a voi vecchi troppo supprema letizia

[the father in the center, surrounded each evening by all, loved, honored, lord and teacher of all youth—this seems always to be what provides the greatest joy of all for you old people]" (L. B. Alberti, Grayson edition, pp. 191–192). The ideological tendency to confront the country with the city, urbane anonymity with the ideal of security in the rural family, becomes quite evident in Alberti's socially critical statements: "Gli onori di fuori non pascono la famiglia in casa—da natura l'amore, la pietà a me fà più cara la famiglia che cosa alcuna [The outward show of deference does not feed the family in the house—Love and piety seem to me to be of greater value to the family than all else]" (L. B. Alberti, Grayson edition, p. 185). "La villa utile alla sanità, commodo al vivere, conveniente alla famiglia [The villa is wholesome for the family, allows a comfortable existence, and guarantees a healthy family life]" (ibid., p. 200).

40. G. Falcone (1559), pp. 12, 36, 66–70. In Agostino Gallo (1550), the sections dealing with the patriarchal family regime and the role of the woman point in much the same direction—collections taken from ancient and contemporary tracts and incorporated into his "villa book." See B. Rupprecht (1966), p. 243.

41. L. B. Alberti, Grayson edition, pp. 186, 195.

42. G. Falcone (1559), pp. 186, 195.

43. B. Rupprecht (1966), p. 227.

44. G. Fiocco (1965), pp. 12, 36, 66–70.

45. A. Hauser (1958), pp. 30–31.

46. This is reflected in the decorative systems of the period. Commencing with Cornaro's Paduan city villa on the Santo (Mediterranean area of the Odeo), culminating in the Palladian villas at Emo or Barbero (Stanza del Cane and Stanza della Lucerna), religious themes penetrate the decoration by profane and private farmers. Conversely, city palaces belonging to the church—such as the Veronese Vescovado (*salone*)—are decorated with pictures depicting the rural and profane, a series of illusionist ideal landscapes such as one would only expect to see in a villa.

47. Daniele Barbaro had the world-ordering and fate-determining forces of classical paganism and of Christianity depicted on the *salotto* ceiling of his villa in 1560–1562. This included the following: the *Divina Sapientia* and *Provvidenza* united with the astrological deities and the signs of the Zodiac, all arranged in a horoscope that symbolized the separate houses of individual nativity and the ultimate order of things. The Muses on the walls in the adjacent *sala a crociera*, which signify the *Nuovo Parnaso*, likewise function as guarantors of harmonic order in the Pythagorean cosmos.

48. V. Scamozzi (1615), Book I, Vol. 3, Ch. 12, p. 270.

49. It hardly seems coincidental that the architectural formalism of the Palladian villa can only be compared with the *Ordo* concept of medieval monasteries that were, apart from the castle and the farm house, the only buildings to be constructed continuously from antiquity to the Renaissance. The monastic motto *ora et labora* is more than just superficially related to Barbaro's and Cornaro's ideal of *sancta rusticitas* of holy agriculture. To elucidate the relationship between monasteries and villas would be well worthwhile.

50. In other words, these were (1) the extensive portico-vestibule and the salons "à feste, à conviti, ad apparati, per recitar comedie, nozze e simili sollazzi [for festivities, dinners, comedy, recitals, wedding ceremonies, and similar entertainments]" in Palladio (1570), Book I, Ch. 21, p. 52, on the nymphaes, grotto spaces, and garden rooms; (2) the *abitazione* with *camera*, *anti-camera*, and

postcamera next to the *sala*, with kitchens and laundry chambers; (3) the *"fab-riche per l'uso die villa"* with the stables, grain stores, tool sheds, wine and oil cellars, threshing floor and servants' quarters, poultry court and dovecot. The most complete account of the different parts of the functional area of the villa was given by Scamozzi, who listed the following: the *corte, portici, cucina, stanza dal torchio del oglio* (oil press), *cantina, granari, stalla da bestiami, bagno luogo da tenir il latte* (milk chamber), *sale, caralleria* (horse stables), *luoghi da riporre i fieni & i stranni, e le paglie* (fodder store for hay, straw, and chaff), *luoghi per la castaldia, ò fattore di villa* (custodian's quarters and offices of the domain), *stalle da capre, stanza da serba frutti, e semenze* (rooms for samplings and seeds), and finally the *luogo per il portinario* (gate keeper's house). See V. Scamozzi (1615), Book I, Vol. 3, Ch. 15, p. 285.

51. Ibid., p. 285: "Per risparmio della spesa, e comodità del padrone—fa una bella vista—à tutte l'hore il padrone puo vedere tutte le sue cose [For reasons of cost reductions and the landlord's comfort—it makes a good impression—the pa-drone can constantly control all his business]."

52. A. Palladio (1570), Book I, p. 46: "[La fattoria] non sarà troppo vicina alla case del padrone, nè tanto lontana, che non possa esser veduta—nè quelle à questa, nè questa à quella sia di impedimento [The farm buildings should not be too close to the master's house, nor should they be so far away that he may no longer oversee them. Neither should the farm buildings impede the master's house or vice versa]."

53. Here the ordering concepts are quite evidently conveyed, as they had already been updated in the Florentine surroundings of Marsilio Ficino's academy and in the Tuscan *villeggiatura*. This was true in the circle of Daniele Barbaro (the publisher of Aristotle) in which an attempt was made to balance Platonic idealism and Aristotelian substantivism.

54. L. B. Alberti, Grayson edition, p. 359: "Alla possessione se manca la casa, meno gli manca, che se alla casa mancano e'terreni [If the properties lack the master's house, then this lack is less serious than if the master's house lacked properties]"; p. 194: "E senza quelle spese non mi pare la villa sia . . . atta a pascere la famiglia [And without such incomes the villa appears to be unsuit-able as a means of existence for the family]"; p. 195: "la possessione in prima fusse atta a darci tutto quello bisognasse per pascere la famiglia, e se non tutto, almeno insieme le più necessarie cose: pane, vino [The property should pri-marily produce all those things that are necessary for the family's needs, and if not all, then at least most: bread, wine]."

55. V. Scamozzi (1615), Book 1, Vol. 3, Ch. 15, pp. 282ff.: "possessione, che sono di maggior spesa, she di rendita al padrone [properties that require more investments than they yield in income] perchè sarebbe tenuta pazzia [because that would have to be considered madness]."

56. A. Palladio (1570), Book II, Ch. 12, p. 282ff.

57. V. Scamozzi (1615), Book I, Vol. 3, Ch. 15, p. 45: "Noi altrove la [agricoltura] mettesimo fra le Arti molto necessarie alla vita humana. . . . Da Senofonte fu chiamata Arte nel genere suo, sopra à tutte l'altre. . . . Platone disse, che essa era data per donno d'Iddio a gli huomini. . . . & Attalo diceva, che non era la più liberale, nè la più dolce cosa, che l'Agricoltura, intendendo l'uso della Villa [We consider agriculture to be one of the most necessary arts for human existence. Already Xenophon described it as an art, which, due to its nature, was superior to all others. Plato emphasized that it had been given to people as a gift by God, and Attalus said that there was neither a more liberal nor a more

comfortable activity than agriculture, for which the villa was used]."
58. G. Zarlino, *Supplementi Musicali*, Venice (1556), p. 57. Some exaggerated
claims have been made about the perception of this order, as, for example, the
following: "Under a Renaissance dome, a Barbaro could experience the faint
echo of the inaudible music of the spheres." R. Wittkower (1952), p. 124.
59. A. Hauser (1958), p. 28.
60. J. Carter and P. H. Muir (1967), p. 75.
61. L. B. Alberti, in *De re aed.*, Book V, Ch. 17, called the *sala* the *forum* and the
"womb of the house." Scamozzi cited Aristotle, *Lib.*, XII, *Animal*, in calling the
sala the "cuore nell' corpo dcll' edificio [heart within the body of the build-
ing]." See V. Scamozzi (1615), Book I, Vol. 2, Ch. 19, p. 304.
62. L. B. Alberti, *De re aed.*, Book I, Ch. 9: "Domus pusilla urbs [the house is a
little city]."
63. Ibid.
64. A. Palladio (1570), Book II, Ch. 12, p. 46.
65. Ibid., p. 66.
66. Ibid., p. 69. The whole passage reads as follows: "Io ho fatto in tutte le fabriche
di Villa . . . il Frontespicio nella facciata dinanti; nella quale sono le porte
principali: perciochè questi tali Frontespici accusano l'entrata della casa, e
servono molto alla grandezza, e magnificenza dell'opera; facendosi in questo
modo la parte dinanti piu eminente dell' altri parti: oltra che riescono commo-
dissimi per le Insegne, overo Armi de gli Edificatori, le quali si sogliono
collocare nel mezo delle facciate. Gli usarono ancho gli Antichi nelle lore
fabriche . . . Vitruvio . . . ci insegna come si devono fare [In all villa buildings . . . I place a frontispiece on the main facade, where the main entry is
located, so that the frontispiece highlights the primary entrance and under-
scores the meaning and the beauty of the architecture; in this way the main
facade is projected forth more than the other sides. Such frontispieces are
especially good places for the villa lord's coat-of-arms, which one normally
locates in the center of the main side of the building. In this manner the ancient
architects also proceeded in their buildings. . . . Vitruvius gives instructions
concerning how this is to be done]."
67. Fritz Burger wrote in 1909 on the frontispiece of the Villa Maser: "Within this
simple . . . configuration, the Greek pediments and columns appeared slightly
outdated as the decoration for large surfaces—just like a superfluous poetic
phrase within an objective demonstration" (F. Burger, 1909, p. 107). Goethe
was quite clear-sighted in his assessment of Palladio's villa and palace facades,
particularly if one equates his notion of "lie" with the modern concept of
ideology. J. W. von Goethe, *Italienische Reise*, Part 1, September 19, 1786 (1962
edition), p. 44.
68. A. Hauser (1958), pp. 7ff.: "It is not more than a wishful dream and an echo of
the idea of *kalokagathia* that social justice meets artistic truth somewhere. . . .
[Thus] quality can by no means be approached from a sociological viewpoint."
69. They went from being symbols of absolute rusticity in the country house of
Alberti or Piero de Crescenzi to being allegories for *arte della pace el della
conservazione* in the countryside.
70. Like the Basilica of Constantin and the Arch of Titus, Septizonium and
Collosseo, the Pantheon, the Column of Trajan, et al.
71. A. R. Turner (1966), pp. 205ff. and Konrad Oberhuber, "Hieronymus Cock,
Battista Pittoni und Poalo Veronese in Villa Maser," in *Munuscula Discipulor-
um: Kunsthistorische Studien, Hans Kauffmann zum 70 Geburtstag*, edited by

Tilmann Buddensieg and Matthias Winner, Berlin (1968), pp. 207–223, figs. 161–189.

72. Rudolfo Pallucchini, "Gli affreschi di Paolo Veronese," in *Palladio, Veronese e Vittoria a Maser*, Milan (1960), pp. 75–76. Also included are contributions by B. Berenson, P. Ojetti, H. Honour, F. Franco, and A. Medea.

73. On the geography of the Po Valley and the Veneto, see above all, Otto Maull, "Länderkunde von Südeuropa," in *Enzyklopaedie der Erdkunde*, edited by Oskar Kende, Vol. 26, Leipzig (1929), pp. 197–211, 209–211, and also Herbert Lehmann, "Das Landschaftgefuge der Padania," in *Frankfurter geographische Hefte*, No. 37, Frankfurt (1961), pp. 87–158, and by the same author, "Zur Problematik der Abgrenzung der 'Kunstlandschaften', dargestellt am Beispiel der Po-Ebene," in *Erdkunde Archiv für wissenschaftliche Geographie* 15, No. 4, Bonn (1961), pp. 185ff.

74. Pliny the Elder, *Nat. Hist.*, Book XXXV, pp. 116–117.

75. Only a brief discussion of the historical relationships between the three architectural monuments can be given here. Pirro Ligorio, the creator of the garden for the Villa d'Este in Tivoli, was also the first one to excavate Hadrian's villa systematically. The Villa Hadriana and the Villa d'Este are located only a short distance from each other. Around 1550 Hadrian's villa was first excavated and the construction of the Villa d'Este was begun. Furthermore, Palladio and Barbaro, the creators of the Villa Maser, were on good terms with Pirro Ligorio and Ippolito II, the architect and patron of the Villa d'Este. The commencement of construction on the Villa Maser in 1560 coincided with the second phase of construction on the Villa d'Este in the 1560s. The concept of the "Rometta" in the Renaissance villa of Tivoli appears to have been directly inspired by the landscape gardens of Hadrian's villa in Tiburtio, which were equipped with Hellenic monuments and natural motifs.

76. Karl Schefold, *Pompejanische Malerei. Sinn und Ideengeschichte*, Basel (1952), p. 35. Palladio was familiar with the Villa Hadriana and its Greek backdrops, at least from Latin sources. In his guide to Rome, *Antichità di Roma* (1554), Vicenzo Lucrino discussed Hadrian's villa at length.

77. Martin van Heemskerck, *Römischen Skizzenbuch*, Rome (1535), Vol. 2, fols. 87v and 85.

78. Palladio (1570), foreword to first and second books.

79. E. Bloch (1964), p. 132ff.

80. J. W. Goethe, *Italienische Reise*, Part 1. September 16, 1786.

81. J. Burckhardt (1928), p. 167, following Petrarch, *Epistolae Familiares*, Vol. 6, p. 2.

82. H. Bauer (1966), p. 93.

83. M. Horkheimer, *Utopie* (1930), p. 94.

84. H. Bauer (1966), p. 93.

85. Niccolo Machiavelli, *I Tre Libri de'Discorsi sopra la prima deca di Tito Livio* (1531), reprinted in Berlin (1922), p. 303. Cited by Max Horkheimer, *Machiavelli und die psychologische Geschichtauffassung*, Vol. 3 in *Gesammelte Studien*, Frankfurt (1930), p. 12.

86. Ibid. Cited by Horkheimer (1930), p. 12.

87. M. Horkheimer (1930), p. 81.

88. Ibid., p. 78.

89. Ibid., p. 80.

90. This theory was developed by Horkheimer in the chapter on culture in *Studies on Authority and Family*, Institute for Social Research, Vol. 5, Paris (1936).
91. M. Horkheimer (1930), p. 81.
92. Ibid., p. 82.
93. A. R. Turner (1966), p. 212.
94. M. Horkheimer (1930), pp. 86–87.
95. Ibid., p. 87.
96. Ibid., p. 88
97. Ibid.
98. Ibid., p. 81.
99. M. Horkheimer (1930), *Machiavelli*, p. 18.
100. See B. Rupprecht (1966), pp. 235–39, on Gallo.
101. Ibid., p. 236.
102. Ernst Robert Curtius, *Europäische Literatur und lateinisches Mittelalter*, 4th edition, Bern and Munich (1963), p. 204.
103. B. Rupprecht (1966), p. 241.
104. Antonio Francesco Doni, *Attavanta—Villa* (written before 1537), edition in Bologna (1566) under the title *Le villa del Doni*; quoted here following the Florentine reprint (1857) with the title *Attavanta—Ville di M. Anton. Francesco Doni Fiorentino*, pp. 72ff. (*Villa, che fu del Magnifico Signor Federico Prioli alle Tre ville*).
105. J. S. Ackerman (1966), pp. 31–32.
106. T. W. Adorno, "Veblens Angriff auf die Kultur," in *Prismen*, Frankfurt (1955), p. 91.
107. M. Horkheimer and T. W. Adorno, *Dialektik der Aufklärung. Philosophische Fragmente*, Amsterdam (1947), p. 177.
108. B. Rupprecht (1966), p. 247.
109. G. Mazzotti (1957), p. 284.
110. Ibid.
111. M. Muraro (1966), p. 542.
112. N. Machiavelli, *Discorsi* (1922), p. 11f. Quoted here following Max Horkheimer (1930), p. 17.
113. The frescoes in the villas of Roberti in Brugine, da Porto-Colleoni in Thiene, Foscari-Malcontenta, Campiglia in Albettone, or Caldogno and Giusti in Magnadola contain lively images of life in the *villeggiatura* society of that period. Examples include the festive lunch outdoors or in the open loggia, the card and board game (Tric-Trac) played in the late afternoon, the open-air concert in the countryside organized by the landowning family, the evening dance.
114. A. R. Turner (1966), p. 200.
115. J. S. Ackerman (1966), p. 40.
116. Some elements from R. Bentmann's Ph.D. dissertation on the Paolo Veronese paintings in the Villa Maser (Universität Frankfurt) have been integrated into Chapters 9, 10, 12, and 13.
117. It is thus that the building ideas of the *"ancien regime"* of Ramses in Egypt is to be understood as a vulgarized sense of scale based on a misunderstood monumentality.
118. Erich Hubala, *Renaissance und Barock*, Frankfurt (1968), p. 49.
119. The land expansion and agricultural policies of the Prussian feudal gentry at the end of the eighteenth century are described by Theodor Fontane in his

novel *Vor dem Sturm* (1878), which is set in 1812–1813.

120. Pliny the Younger, *Epistulae—Gaius Plinius Caecilius Secundus: Plinius des Jüngeren Werke*, translated by Dr. C. F. Schott, Vol. 1, *Briefe*, Stuttgart (1827), p. 6.

121. In light of what Pliny and Alberti wrote, we can assume that a manor house without a landed estate was possible but a villa without surrounding lands was not. Scamozzi indirectly made this clear when he described *spesa* (expenditures) beyond the *rendita* (estate's income) as economic insanity (*pazzia*).

122. In *De re aed.* (Book 5, p. 17), L. Alberti (1966) wrote of the *casa del padrone* that "faciles ad se ex agro porrigit aditus [it allows easy access from the agricultural areas]." Palladio said that the villa should be "comodo alle possessioni, e nel mezo di quelle [in a favorable position on the estate and in the center of it] con industria et arte dell'Agricoltura accrescer le facultà [in order to increase the estate's income through the labor and the art of agriculture]." Scamozzi elaborated on the principle of controlling the farmland by the central *casa del padrone* even further in *Idea* (1615), Book I, Vol. 3, Ch. 12, p. 270: "The manor house must be in the middle of the property . . . so that the landlord can reach all parts of the estate with ease in order to supervise the farm estate."

123. Pliny praised Tusculum for its profitable mountain forests and for its good grazing grass, in *Epist.*, V, p. 6. Alberti wrote on behalf of a "naturally fertile site" capable of bearing in abundance in the Grayson edition, pp. 188, 191. Scamozzi too emphasized the "good quality of fruit" produced on the ideal villa in op. cit. (1615), II, p. 11.

124. Saminiato argues in much the same vein that "good land can produce any kind of juicy fruit or exquisite wine" in op. cit., p. 233ff.

125. Pliny praised the good water supply in Tusculum in *Epist.*, V, p. 6. Palladio (1570) wrote along these lines that "for the highest use and adornment of the villa, one should be able to water the landed property, the gardens and orchards, as water is an essential prerequisite for an honorable existence" (Book II, Ch. 16, p. 11). Both Scamozzi (1615), Book II, Ch. 6, pp. 117, 119, and Saminiato, in op. cit., pp. 233ff., underscore the economic significance of water supplies for the estate.

126. In his *Idea* (1615), Book III, Ch. 12, p. 270, Scamozzi wrote of the ideal site as one "not too far from frequently used main roads and near navigable waterways, so as to be able to transport people and things comfortably." Saminiato calls for a "wide access road" and a "site near the city" (pp. 233ff.).

127. Pliny praised the good hunting on his Tuscan villa (*Epist.*, V, p. 6). Alberti insisted on "fishing and hunting grounds" (*De re aed.*, Book V, p. 17), as did Scamozzi (1615), Book III, Ch. 2, p. 224, Saminiato (op. cit., pp. 233ff.), and Cornaro (cited in M. Muraro, 1966, p. 541).

128. L. B. Alberti (1430–1440), Grayson edition, p. 200.

129. Ibid., pp. 188ff. Alberti wrote of the home and the family as pedagogical institutions: "There is nothing that seems to me of greater priority to family life than the upbringing of the young" (p. 187).

130. L. B. Alberti, *De re aed.* (1450), Orlando-Portoghesi edition (1966), Book IX, Ch. 2.

131. L. B. Alberti, Grayson edition, pp. 188ff. He praised the "fresh air" and the villa as "conducive to good health" in all respects (pp. 197, 199).

132. Ibid., pp. 200ff.: "What a blessed form of existence villa life is; oh bliss yet to be discovered. One lives here free from troubles and melancholy."

133. A. Palladio (1570), Book II, Ch. 12, p. 45: "Through the physical exercise gained by walking and riding on the villa estate, the body stays healthy and robust."
134. V. Scamozzi (1615), Book II, Ch. 6, p. 119.
135. Ibid., Book III, Ch. 12, p. 266: "A healthy climate always prevails over the villa and consequently all food is better and of higher nutritional value."
136. T. W. Adorno, *Veblens Angriff auf die Kultur* (1955, 1969), p. 91. Along with the idea of *sobrietà del vivere* on behalf of a healthier more frugal economy (*masseria*), Alberti also argued for exercise and a sensible diet. As Alvise Cornaro would later, Alberti called for the affluent to "make a science of nutrition and of moderation in eating as well as in drinking" (p. 175).
137. V. Scamozzi (1615), Book III, Ch. 12, p. 266. See also Saminiato, op. cit., pp. 233ff.
138. V. Scamozzi, Book II, Ch. 6, p. 119.
139. Pliny, *Epist.*, Vol. 5, p. 6: "The sight of this landscape with mountains gives great pleasure. . . . one does not believe that he or she is seeing real countryside but thinks that this is a beautiful and idealized painting of it."
140. L. B. Alberti, Grayson edition, p. 188ff.
141. L. B. Alberti, *De re aed.*, Book V, p. 17.
142. As Saminiato stated (op. cit., pp. 233ff.): "One should not choose the most fertile but the most distinguished point of the villa estate as the site for the *padrone*'s residence."
143. L. B. Alberti, *De re aed.*, Book IX, p. 2.
144. V. Scamozzi (1615), Book II, p. 119: "The beauty of the site consists of the most charming views of hills, both near and far."
145. Walter Benjamin, *Illuminationen, Ausgewählte Schriften*, Frankfurt (1961), p. 320.
146. The relevant quote in Alberti is in *De re aed.*, Book IX, Ch. 2, p. 17. Scamozzi formulates this point even more sharply: "Nature creates such elevated points so that they are conspicuous to all and raised above all others in beauty, form, and charm. Apart from the fact that they can be seen from afar, it also seems that they invite us to admire and extol them. Furthermore, their height permits a comfortable panoramic view of the surrounding area." Similarly, Saminiato endorsed "a long, broad road leading to the main entrance of the villa" as the *via regia* pointing toward the prominent villa (op. cit., Book I, Ch. 8, pp. 33ff.).
147. Here we should recall Scamozzi's demand that the cultivated lands be directly adjacent to the *casa del padrone* "so that the landlord can survey his business at any time" (1615, Book III, Ch. 15, p. 285).
148. V. Scamozzi (1615), Book III, Ch. 22, p. 323.
149. Ibid., p. 324: "Cultivated lands and decorative gardens are not just useful for practical purposes but also for increasing the significance and beauty of the *padrone*'s residence."
150. V. Scamozzi (1615), Book III, Ch. 21, pp. 322–323: "The road axes that lead to villas and lordly mansions should be broader and more beautiful than all others, since they are symbols of sovereignty."
151. L. B. Alberti, Grayson edition, p. 195.
152. E. Bloch (1964), pp. 132ff.
153. This was true of Barco della Regina, the Villa Giustinian in Roncade, the Castello da Porto-Colleoni in Thiene near Vicenza, the ideal villa in one of the Stanza di Bacco wall paintings in the Villa Maser, the Villa Grimani Marcello

in Montegalda near Vicenza, and the dei Vescovi in Luvigliano.

154. At the Barco della Regina, the radius of supervision was actually doubled. Here there was also an inner *glacis* that was inscribed by an outer ring with a clock tower, reinforcement battlements, chapel, demesne office, and administrator's house. This architectural idea goes back at least to the fourteenth century, to the wooden model of the ideal villa in Piero de Crescenzi's agricultural treatise of around 1500 in Venice (Figure 3).

155. V. Scamozzi (1615), Book III, Ch. 15, p. 285.

156. The observations concerning the Villa da Porto-Colleoni are based on the results of a trip to the Veneto under the auspices of the Frankfurt Art Historical Institute, which followed a seminar led by Wolfram Prinz. The results of the research on Venetian villas from the pre-Palladian period have been published in *Kunst in Hessen und am Mittelrhein* 13 (1973): 7–45.

157. We owe this information to Michelangelo Muraro, who (along with Cevese, Fiocco, and Mazzotti) is one of the main experts on Venetian villa culture. See also M. Muraro, *Civiltà delle ville Venete* (1964), Note 23, p. 35, on the partly rural and partly urban Venetian aristocratic families that resided around Vicenza and elsewhere in Veneto and that were torn between loyalty to the kaiser and to the republic at the time of the League of Cambrai.

158. See Fernando Rigon, *Villa Spessa e S. Anna di Carmignano*, Dissertation at Padua, 1967–1968. It is summarized in the *Bollettino del Centro Internazionale di Studi di Architettura 'Andrea Palladio'*, Vol. 10 (1968), pp. 325–331. Rigon provides numerous sources and references along with valuable historical and sociological material on the political and economic situation of the early Venetian *villeggiatura*.

159. Piero de Crescenzi, *Opus ruralium commodorum*, Vol. 1, Vicenza (1490), p. 7.

160. V. Scamozzi (1615), Book 3, Ch. 12, p. 266.

161. L. B. Alberti, Grayson edition, pp. 179ff; 200; 199f.

162. Palladio (1570), Book 2, Ch. 12, p. 120f.

163. V. Cartari, *Imagini* (1647), p. 120f.

164. B. Rupprecht (1966), p. 26.

165. H. Bauer (1966), p. 26.

166. B. Rupprecht (1966), p. 244.

167. G. Falcone (1902), p. 14.

168. Alberto Lollio, *Delle orationi di M. Alberto Lollio. Aggiuntavi una Lettera del medesimo in laude della Villa*, Ferrara (1563), fol. 219r.

169. A. F. Doni, *Attavanta-Villa* (circa 1557), reprinted in Florence (1857), pp. 72, 21.

170. B. Rupprecht (1966), p. 249.

171. H. Berndt, *Gesellschaftsbild* (1968), p. 25.

172. F. Tönnies (1887), p. 286.

173. Ibid.

174. Cited by T. W. Adorno, "Spengler nach dem Untergang," in *Prismen*, p. 54.

175. E. Fromm (1950), p. 1; quoted in H. Marcuse (1968), p. 257.

176. Matthew 16:26.

177. The "well-adjusted" person is accused of having betrayed his or her "higher self" and "human values"; for this reason he or she is haunted by "inner emptiness and insecurity" despite "triumph" in the "struggle for success." Those who have achieved "inner strength and integrity" have better fortune even though they may be less successful than their "unscrupulous" neighbor.

H. Marcuse (1968), p. 257. These words depict to a surprising degree the same distorted image of urban life as drawn by Petrarch, Alberti, and the villa books of the Cinquecento. The surprise is caused by two factors—the "anticipatory" moments in Petrarch and Alberti and the revisionist viewpoint taken by E. Fromm.

178. Franziska Bollerey and Kristiana Hartmann, *Gartenstadt—Trabantenstadt. Eine gesellschaftspolitische und formale Analyse*, hectograph of the talk given on July 4, 1970 at the Twelfth German Art Historians Convention in Cologne, the Art 1871–1918 Section. *Großstadt und Industrie*, p. 8. Cited following H. Freese, "Fabrikantensorgen," in Berhard Kampffmeyer, *Flugschrift*, No. 2. *Die Vermählung von Stadt und Land. Ein soziales Experiment*, Berlin (1903), p. 21.

179. Veblen noticed one aspect of kitsch (in the nineteenth century) that the aestheticians had failed to see, one that could contribute toward understanding the shock-inducing catastrophe that so many architectural styles and interiors of the nineteenth century signify for us today, namely as expressions of oppression. From Veblen's perspective, "ornaments become threats through their tendency to resemble old models of repression," while the characteristics he calls "archaic" are equivalent to "approaching horror." T. W. Adorno, "Veblen's Angriff auf die Kultur," in *Prismen*, p. 88f.

180. Ibid., p. 89. Adorno corrects Veblen's one-sided approach to cultural criticism by observing that Veblen "noticed that the knight's castle and the railway station were not simultaneous in origin, but he did not see that this nonsimultaneity is a law in philosophy of history. The railway station is masked as a knight's castle—but its truth is the mask. Not until the objective world serves domination directly is it in a position to throw off such masks. In the horror of the totalitarian state it is equal to itself" (p. 99).

181. Adorno proposes a purely economic explanation for the extravagance of *Gründerzeit* architecture in all its pomposity: "Such a form of representation is obviously born of the necessity to present oneself as creditworthy. This necessity may be an indication of the shortage of capital during phases of expansion" (*Prismen*, p. 88). The question as to whether these economic explanations can be applied to the Venetian villas of the Late Renaissance must be left open at this juncture.

182. L. B. Alberti, Grayson edition, pp. 194ff.; A. Palladio (1570), Book II, Ch. 12, p. 45.

183. In some regions, such architectural forms with ideological content have survived to the present day. An example is southern Germany, where small and middle-sized enterprises were located in the country in the course of deconcentration of metropolitan organisms. The large farmowners who became small industrialists in this economic restructuring process often still live on the factory premises. In the petty bourgeois villas of these ex–vegetable farmers, joiners and smiths now produce canned foods, furniture, or machine parts and live up to the same standards as the haute bourgeois "magnate villas" of the sixteenth and nineteenth centuries through their rudimentary gardens, "noble" portal designs in wrought iron, colored glass and imitation marble, and their isolated "dominating" location within the industrial *latifundia*.

184. In Chapter 6 of *Frau Jenny Treibel*, Fontane mentions the earliest Mycenean archaeological expedition of Heinrich Schliemann. See Chapter 6 of *Frau Jenny Treibel*, Berlin (1968 reprinting), pp. 58, 60.

185. "*Junkers* are agrarian, professors are of the national party of the center, and

industrialists are progressive. Factories in general tend toward the civil crown." T. Fontane, *Frau Jenny Treibel*, Ch. 3, 1968 edition, pp. 28–29. All further quotations are from the 1968 Ullstein paperback edition, No. 515.

186. "The Treibel villa was situated on a large plot of land . . . that extended down to the River Spree. In the past, . . . only factory buildings had stood here. . . . But when the billions began to flow into the country after the wars of the 1870s and the views of the industrialists began to hold sway, Treibel, the councillor of commerce, found his house in the Alte Jakobstrasse no longer appropriate to the times or his position and built a new fashionable villa on the premises of his factory, with a small front garden and a rear parklike garden. This villa had a raised ground floor above a basement, with a superimposed first floor. The latter, however, created with its low windows the impression more of a mezzanine than a drawing-room floor. Treibel had been living here for sixteen years and could not comprehend how he had been able to last it out for such a long time in the Alte Jakobstrasse, undistinguished as it was and depriving one of any fresh air. . . . The proximity of the factory, if the wind was unfavorable, bore all manner of unpleasantries in its retinue; the north wind, which drove the smoke toward the house, was a notoriously rare occurrence, however. . . . In addition, Treibel had the height of the factory chimneys increased each year" (Fontane, 1968 edition, p. 14).

187. "Jetzt marschiert jeden Küchenjunge durch den Vorgarten, gerade auf unser Haus zu, wie wenn er mitgeladen wäre. Das sieht lächerlich aus und auch anspruchsvoll, als ob die ganze . . . Straße wissen sollte: Treibels geben heut ein Diner. Außerdem ist es unklug, dem Neid der Menschen und dem sozialdemokratischen Gefühl so ganz nutzlos neue Nahrung zu geben [Any kitchen boy can now march through the front garden straight up to our house as if he were also among the invited. That looks ridiculous and pretentious, as if the whole street should know that the Treibels are giving a dinner party this evening. Furthermore, it is unwise to nurture people's envy and socialdemocratic sentiments so needlessly]" (Fontane, 1968 edition, p. 15).

188. Vitruvius, *De Arch.*, Book VI, Ch. 3, Fensterbusch edition (1964), pp. 278–279.

189. B. Rupprecht (1966), p. 250.

190. This was the subtitle for Adorno's *Jargon der Eigentlichkeit*, Frankfurt (1964).

191. B. Rupprecht (1966), p. 249.

192. See, for example, the review of James Ackerman's *Palladio's Villas*, New York, 1967, in the *Bulletin of the Centro Internazionale di Studi d'Architettura "Andrea Palladio,"* Vol. 10 (1968), p. 353. The criticisms made in this review can be refuted with only a superficial reading of the contemporary literature on the villa. To take but one example, Alberti, Marcolini, or Doni all distinguished the types of rural architecture in relation to the social position of the landlord while also making use of aesthetic categories. The same is true of Palladio, who not only discussed the economic function of the villa but also showed how art both ennobled and masked this function, as in the way it integrated the *habitazione* and *fattoria*. Thus, the unification of luxury and the economic function *sotto un tetto* into the villa *Gesamtkunstwerk* was a central artistic problem for Palladio as it had been for Alberti and others in the Quattrocento. As our research has shown, the sociological and economic dimensions were central to the creation of the villa as a whole

193. See Wolfgang Haug, "Wären-Aesthetik und Angst," in *Das Argument. Berliner Hefte für Probleme der Gesellschaft* 28, No. 6 (1964), p. 20.

194. Martin Heidegger, *Über den Humanismus*, Frankfurt (1949), p. 29.
195. Martin Heidegger, *Aus der Erfahrung des Denkens*, Pfullingen (1954), p. 13.
196. Guido Schneeberger, *Nachlese zu Heidegger. Dokumente aus seinem Leben und Denken*, Bern (1962), p. 216.
197. Martin Heidegger, *Der Waldweg*, Frankfurt (1956), p. 4.
198. G. Schneeberger (1962), p. 217.
199. T. W. Adorno, *Jargon der Eigentlichkeit*, 1967, p. 52.
200. Ibid., pp. 49, 50.
201. The quotations by Adenauer, Krupp, et al. are taken from Jürgen Petermann, "Wohnungsbau in Deutschland," in *Der Spiegel* 32, No. 6 (Feb. 1969), p. 30.
202. Marc Augier, *Götterdämmerung. Wende und Ende einer grossen Zeit*, Buenos Aires (1950), p. 52.
203. See *Gartenstadt* 8, No. 3 (March 1914), p. 57. Cited by F. Bollerey and K. Hartmann, *Gartenstadt-Trabantenstadt*, lecture at Twelfth German Art Historian's Meeting, 1970, p. 9.
204. Le Corbusier later disassociated himself from this position.
205. Alexander Mitscherlich, *Die Unwirtlichkeit unserer Städte. Anstiftung zum Unfrieden*, Frankfurt (1968), pp. 52ff.
206. Warehouse architecture is ruining the areas of the old marketplaces and defining the centers in relation to large cities. The escalating prices of real estate in the city center have pushed market life to the side streets in favor of neon-lighted department stores.
207. H. Berndt (1968), p. 77.
208. F. Bollerey and K. Hartmann (1970), pp. 15ff.
209. A. Mitscherlich (1968), p. 52.
210. Ibid.
211. M. Horkheimer and T. W. Adorno (1947), p. 177.
212. With respect to villa suburbs and private housing ideology, see also Mitscherlich (1968), pp. 11–13.
213. F. Bollerey and K. Hartmann (1970), pp. 14ff. The quotation by W. Pehnt is from the *Deutsche Bauzeitung* 104, Vol. 1, No. 2, 1970, p. 106.
214. Max Horkheimer, "Art and Mass Culture," in *Studies in Philosophy and Social Science* 9, No. 2, New York (1941), p. 290.
215. There are avant-garde devices—such as the terraced house, the "conehouse," or the Habitat model in Montreal—that link the penthouse with the necessity of a large apartment block and that are not extremely expensive.
216. A. Mitscherlich (1968), p. 19.
217. T. W. Adorno (1955, 1969), p. 88.
218. Ibid., p. 97.
219. Only when ecologically sound recreational areas have been incorporated into low-income apartments will a rupture with the present situation be possible.
220. H. Sedlmayr (1959), p. 209.
221. K. Marx (1953 edition), p. 31.
222. T. W. Adorno (1970), p. 400.
223. T. W. Adorno, *Versuch über Wagner*, Berlin (1952), p. 104.
224. O. K. Werckmeister, "Das Kunstwerk als Negation. Zur Kunsttheorie T. W. Adorno," *Rundschau* 73, No. 1 (1962), pp. 112ff.
225. Peter Gorsen (1970), p. 59.
226. Henri Lefebvre, *Der dialektische Materialismus*, Frankfurt (1966), pp. 36ff.
227. Ibid.

228. Max Raphael, "Zur Kunsttheorie des dialektischen Materialismus," *Philosophische Hefte* 3, No. 3/4 (1932), pp. 125–129, 150.
229. T. W. Adorno (1970), p. 433.
230. Ibid., p. 430.
231. Ibid., p. 437.
232. Rodolfo Banfi (1967), p. 134.
233. H. Lefebvre (1967), p. 153.
234. Ibid., p. 139.
235. Jürgen Habermas, *Zur Logik der Sozialwissenschaften*, Frankfurt (1971), p. 91.
236. Bertolt Brecht, *Schriften zur Literatur und Kunst*, Frankfurt (1967), p. 210.
237. H. Marcuse (1971), p. 50.
238. T. W. Adorno (1970), p. 473.

Selected Bibliography

Ackerman, James. *Palladio*. Series on the Architect and Society. Edited by John Fleming and Hugh Honour. Baltimore (1966).
———. *Palladio's Villas*. New York (1967).
———. *The Villa: Form and Ideology of Country Houses*. London (1990).
Adorno, Theodor W. *Versuch über Wagner*. Berlin/Frankfurt (1952).
———. "Spengler nach dem Untergang." In *Prismen: Kulturkritik und Gesellschaft*. Frankfurt (1955, 1969): 51–81.
———. *Jargon der Eigentlichkeit: Zur deutschen Ideologie*. Frankfurt (1964, 1967).
———. *Ästhetische Theorie*. Frankfurt (1970).
Alberti, Leone Battista. *Opere volgari*, Vol. 1, *I Libri della famiglia*. Edited by Cecil Grayson. *Scrittori d'Italia*. No. 218, Vol. 3, *Cena Familiaris. Villa*. Bari (1960).
———. *De re aedificatoria*. Latin/Italian edition. Edited by Orlandi-Portoghesi Milan (1966).
Banfi, Rodolfo. "Probleme und Scheinprobleme bei Marx und im Marxismus." In *Folgen einer Theorie: Essays über 'Das Kapital' von Marx*. Frankfurt (1967): 155–177.
Battilotti, Donata. *Le ville di Palladio*. Milan (1990).
Bauer, Fritz. "Kunstzensur." In *Streit-Zeit Schrift* 7, No. 1, Frankfurt (1969): 42–47.
Bauer, Hermann. "Kunst und Utopie. Studien über das Kunst und Staatsdenken der Renaissance." In *Probleme der Kunstwissenschaft*, Vol. 2 of *Wandlungen des Paradiesischen und Utopischen: Studien zum Bild eines Ideals*. Berlin (1966).
Benjamin, Walter. *Illuminationen: Ausgewählte Schriften*. Frankfurt (1961).
Berndt, Heide. *Gesellschaftsbild bei Stadtplanern*. Stuttgart (1968).
Berndt, Heide, et al. *Architektur als Ideologie*. Frankfurt (1968): 9–50.
Bloch, Ernst. *Tübinger Einleitung in die Philosophie*, Vol. 1. Frankfurt (1964).
Bodefield, G., and Berthold Hinz. *Die Villen im Veneto*. Cologne (1987).
Bollerey, Franziska, and Kristiana Hartmann. *Gartenstadt—Trabentenstadt*. Talk given on July 4, 1970, at the Twelfth German Art Historians' Convention in Cologne in the Kunst 1871–1918 Section.
Borchardt, Rudolf. *Villa und andere Prosa*. Frankfurt (1952).
Brecht, Bertolt. *Schriften zur Literatur und Kunst*, Vol. 3. Frankfurt (1967).
Buddensieg, Tilman, ed. *Villa Hügel. Das Wohnhaus Krupp in Essen*. Berlin (1984).
Burckhardt, Jacob. *Die Kultur der Renaissance in Italien*. Edited by Walter Goetz. Leipzig (1928).
Burger, Fritz. *Die Villen des Andrea Palladio*. Leipzig (1909).
Burns, H. *Andrea Pallado: 1508–1580*. London (1975).
Cartari, Vincenzo. *Imagini delli Dei degli Antichi*. Venice (1647).
Carter, John, and Percy Muir. *Bücher, die die Welt verändern*. Edited by Kurt Busse. Darmstadt (1967).
Ceredi, Giuseppe *Tre discorsi sopra il modo di alzare le acque da luoghi bassi*. Parma (1567).
Cicero, Marcus Tullius. *Über das Greisenalter (De senectute)*. Edited by Karl Atzert. Paderborn (1959).

Coffin, D. R. *The Villa in the Life of Renaissance Rome.* Princeton (1979).

Cornaro, Alvise (Luigi). *Discorsi intorno alla Vita Sobria.* Translated by W. F. Butler. Milwaukee (1913).

Falcone, Giuseppe. *La Nuova vaga et dilettevole Villa.* Brescia (1559).

Fiocco, Giuseppe. "Alvise Cornaro: Il suo tempo e le sue opere." In *Saggi e studi di Storia dell' Arte 8.* Venice (1965).

Fontane, Theodor. *Vor dem Sturm. Roman aus dem Winter 1812 auf 13.* Berlin (1944).

———. *Frau Jenny Treibel.* Ullstein (1968).

Forssman, E. *Visible Harmony, Palladio's Villa Foscari at Malcontenta.* Stockholm (1973).

Fromm, Erich. *Psychoanalysis and Religion.* New Haven (1950).

Gallo, Agostino. *Le Deci Giornate della vera agricoltura e piaceri della villa.* Brescia (1550) and revised edition of 1567: *Vinti Giornate dell'agricoltura et de'piaceri della villa.*

Gobbi, Grazia. *La villa fiorentina.* Florence (1980).

Goethe, Johann Wolfgang von. *Italienische Reise. Erster und zweiter Teil* (1786/87). Vol. 25 of *Gesamtausgabe.* Munich (1926).

Gorsen, Peter. "Marxismus und Kunstanalyse in der Gegenwart." *Zeitschrift Aesthetik und Kommunication. Beitrage zur politischen Erziehung* 2, No. 1, Dec. 1970.

Habermas, Jürgen. *Zur Logik der Sozialwissenschaften.* Frankfurt (1971).

Haug, W. F. "Waren-Aesthetik und Angst." *Das Argument. Berliner Heft für Probleme der Gesellschaft* 28, No. 6 (1964).

Hauser, Arnold. *Philosophie der Kunstgeschichte.* Munich (1958).

Heidegger, Martin. *Über den Humanismus.* Frankfurt (1949).

———. *Aus der Erfahrung des Denkens.* Pfullingen (1954).

———. *Der Waldweg.* Frankfurt (1956).

Horkheimer, Max. *Die Anfange der bürgerlichen Geschichts-philosophie.* Vol. 1, *Machiavelli und die psychologische Geschichtauffassung.* Vol. 3, *Die Utopie. Gesammelte Studien.* Frankfurt (1930).

———. "Art and Mass Culture." *Zeitschrift für Sozialforschung* 9, No. 2, New York (1941).

Horkheimer, Max, and T. W. Adorno. *Dialektik der Aufklärung.* Amsterdam (1947).

Kubelik, N. *Die Villa im Veneto.* Munich (1977).

Lefebvre, Henri. *Der dialektische Materialismus.* Frankfurt (1966).

———. "Soziologie der Erkenntis and Ideologie." In *Folgen einer Theorie. Essays über 'Das Kapital' von Karl Marx.* Frankfurt (1967).

Marcuse, Herbert. *Triebstruktur und Gesellschaft.* Frankfurt (1968).

———. *Reflexion zu Theodor W. Adorno. Theodor W. Adorno zum Gedächtnis.* Frankfurt (1971).

Marx, Karl. *Grundrisse der Kritik der politischen Ökonomie.* Berlin (1953).

Mazzotti, Giuseppe. *Le Ville Venete. Catalogo.* Treviso (1952).

———. *Le Ville Venete—Venetian Villas.* Bilingual Edition. Rome (1957).

Mitscherlich, Alexander. *Die Unwirtlichkeit unserer Städte.* Frankfurt (1968).

Mumford, Lewis. *The City in History.* New York (1961).

Muraro, Michelangelo. "Civiltà delle Ville Venete." In *Arte in Europa. Scritti di Storia dell'Arte in onore di E. Arslan.* Milan (1966):533–543.

——— . "Feudo e ville venete." *Bollettino del C.I.S.A.* 20 (1978):203–223.

———. *Civiltà delle Ville Venete.* Udine (1986).

Palladio, Andrea. *I Quattro Libri dell' Architettura.* Venice (1570).

Petermann, Jürgen. *Wohnungsbau in Deutschland.* Special Issue. *Der Spiegel* 23 (Feb. 1969):38–63.

Petrarch, Francesco. "De Vita Solitaria." In *Petrarch: Prosa.* Edited by G. Martellotti, et al. Milan and Naples (1955).

Plinius the Younger. *Epistulae—Gaius Plinius Caecilius Secundus des Jüngeren Werke.* Translated by C. F. Schott. Vol 1, *Briefe.* Stuttgart (1827).

Prinz, Wolfgang, R. Bentmann, M. Müller, et al. *Studien zu den Anfangen des oberitalienischen Villenbaues. Kunst in Hessen und am Mittelrhein.* Vol. 13 (1973):7–45.

Pullan, B., ed. *Crisis and Change in the Venetian Economy in the Sixteenth and Seventeenth Centuries.* London (1973).

Puppi, L. *Andrea Palladio.* Milan (1973).

Raphael, Max. "Zur Kunsttheorie des dialektischen Materialismus." *Philosophische Hefte* 3, No. 3/4 (1932):125–150.

Reutti, Fridolin, ed. *Die römanische Villa.* Darmstadt (1990).

Richter, Wolfgang, and Jürgen Zänker. *Der Burgertraum von Adelschloß.* Reinbek bei Hamburg (1988).

Rupprecht, Bernhard. "Die Villa Garzoni des Jacopo Sansavino." *Mitteilungen des Kunsthistorisches Institut Florenz* 9, No. 1 (1965):1–32.

———. "Villa Zur Geschichte eines Ideals." In *Probleme der Kunstwissenschaft,* Vol. 2. of *Wandlungen des Paradiesischen und Utopischen.* Berlin (1966):210–250.

Saminiato, Giovanni di Vencenzo. *Trattato d'Agricoltura.* Manuscript in the State Archive of Lucca (1580). Published by Isa Belli Barsali, in *La Villa a Lucca dal XV al XIX Secolo.* Rome (1964):233–260.

Sansovino, Francesco. *Venezia Città nobilissima e singalore descritta in XIV Libri.* Venice (1581).

Sanudo, Marino. *Vite de' Duchi di Venezia. Muratori XXII.*

Scamozzi, Vincenzo. *Idea dell'Architettura Universale.* Venice (1615).

Schneeberger, Guido. *Nachlese zu Heidegger. Dokumente aus seinem Leben und Denken.* Bern (1962).

Sedlmayr, Hans. "Zur Revision der Renaissance." In *Gesammelten Schriften zur Kunstgeschichte,* Vol. 1. Vienna/Munich (1959).

Sorte, Cristoforo. *Trattato dell'origine de'Fiumi.* Manuscript in Marciana Library, Venice. Published by C. Frati and A. Segarizzi, *Catalogo dei Codici Marciani Italiani,* Vol. 2. Modena (1911).

Spengler, Oswald. *Der Untergang des Abendlandes,* Vol. 2. of *Welt historisches Perspektiven.* Munich (1922).

Sturm, Hermann. *Fabrikarchitetur, Villa, Arbeitersiedlung.* Munich (1977).

Temanza, Tommaso. *Vite dei più celebri architetti e scultori veneziani che fiorirono nel secolo decimosesto.* Venice and Palese (1778).

Tönnies, F. *Gemeinschaft und Gesellschaft.* Leipzig (1887).

Turner, A. R. *The Vision of Landscape in Renaissance Italy.* Princeton (1966).

Ventura, Angelo. *Nobiltà e popolo nella societa veneta del '400 e '500.* Bari (1964).

———. "Aspetti storico-economico della villa veneta." *Bollettino del C.I.S.A.* 11 (1969):65–77.

Vitruvius. *De architectura libri decem—Zehn Bücher über Architektur.* Bilingual edition by Curt Fensterbusch. Darmstadt (1964).

Warnke, Martin, ed. *Das Kunstwerk zwischen Wissenschaft und Weltanschauung.* Gutersloh (1970).

Werckmeister, O. K. "Das Kunstwerk als Negation. Zur Kunst-theorie T. W.

Adornos." *Die Neue Rundschau* 73, No. 1 (1962).

Wittkower, Rudolf. *Architectural Principles in the Age of Humanism*. London (1952).

Zänker, Jürgen. "Non Amor, sed 'Labor Omnia Vincit'—Crespi d'Adda, eine Industriensiedlung des 19. Jahrhunderts in Oberitalien." *Archithese*, No. 8 (1973).

Index of Names